The Modern Spanish Canon
Visibility, Cultural Capital and the Academy

LEGENDA

LEGENDA is the Modern Humanities Research Association's book imprint for new research in the Humanities. Founded in 1995 by Malcolm Bowie and others within the University of Oxford, Legenda has always been a collaborative publishing enterprise, directly governed by scholars. The Modern Humanities Research Association (MHRA) joined this collaboration in 1998, became half-owner in 2004, in partnership with Maney Publishing and then Routledge, and has since 2016 been sole owner. Titles range from medieval texts to contemporary cinema and form a widely comparative view of the modern humanities, including works on Arabic, Catalan, English, French, German, Greek, Italian, Portuguese, Russian, Spanish, and Yiddish literature. Editorial boards and committees of more than 60 leading academic specialists work in collaboration with bodies such as the Society for French Studies, the British Comparative Literature Association and the Association of Hispanists of Great Britain & Ireland.

The MHRA encourages and promotes advanced study and research in the field of the modern humanities, especially modern European languages and literature, including English, and also cinema. It aims to break down the barriers between scholars working in different disciplines and to maintain the unity of humanistic scholarship. The Association fulfils this purpose through the publication of journals, bibliographies, monographs, critical editions, and the MHRA Style Guide, and by making grants in support of research. Membership is open to all who work in the Humanities, whether independent or in a University post, and the participation of younger colleagues entering the field is especially welcomed.

ALSO PUBLISHED BY THE ASSOCIATION

Critical Texts
Tudor and Stuart Translations • New Translations • European Translations
MHRA Library of Medieval Welsh Literature

MHRA Bibliographies
Publications of the Modern Humanities Research Association

The Annual Bibliography of English Language & Literature
Austrian Studies
Modern Language Review
Portuguese Studies
The Slavonic and East European Review
Working Papers in the Humanities
The Yearbook of English Studies

www.mhra.org.uk
www.legendabooks.com

STUDIES IN HISPANIC AND LUSOPHONE CULTURES

Studies in Hispanic and Lusophone Cultures are selected and edited by the Association of Hispanists of Great Britain & Ireland. The series seeks to publish the best new research in all areas of the literature, thought, history, culture, film, and languages of Spain, Spanish America, and the Portuguese-speaking world.

The Association of Hispanists of Great Britain & Ireland is a professional association which represents a very diverse discipline, in terms of both geographical coverage and objects of study. Its website showcases new work by members, and publicises jobs, conferences and grants in the field.

Editorial Committee
Chair: Professor Trevor Dadson (Queen Mary, University of London)
Professor Catherine Davies (University of Nottingham)
Professor Sally Faulkner (University of Exeter)
Professor Andrew Ginger (University of Bristol)
Professor James Mandrell (Brandeis University, USA)
Professor Hilary Owen (University of Manchester)
Professor Christopher Perriam (University of Manchester)
Professor Philip Swanson (University of Sheffield)

Managing Editor
Dr Graham Nelson
41 Wellington Square, Oxford OX1 2JF, UK

www.legendabooks.com/series/shlc

STUDIES IN HISPANIC AND LUSOPHONE CULTURES

1. *Unamuno's Theory of the Novel*, by C. A. Longhurst
2. *Pessoa's Geometry of the Abyss: Modernity and the* Book of Disquiet, by Paulo de Medeiros
3. *Artifice and Invention in the Spanish Golden Age*, edited by Stephen Boyd and Terence O'Reilly
4. *The Latin American Short Story at its Limits: Fragmentation, Hybridity and Intermediality*, by Lucy Bell
5. *Spanish New York Narratives 1898–1936: Modernisation, Otherness and Nation*, by David Miranda-Barreiro
6. *The Art of Ana Clavel: Ghosts, Urinals, Dolls, Shadows and Outlaw Desires*, by Jane Elizabeth Lavery
7. *Alejo Carpentier and the Musical Text*, by Katia Chornik
8. *Britain, Spain and the Treaty of Utrecht 1713-2013*, edited by Trevor J. Dadson and J. H. Elliott
9. *Books and Periodicals in Brazil 1768-1930: A Transatlantic Perspective*, edited by Ana Cláudia Suriani da Silva and Sandra Guardini Vasconcelos
10. *Lisbon Revisited: Urban Masculinities in Twentieth-Century Portuguese Fiction*, by Rhian Atkin
11. *Urban Space, Identity and Postmodernity in 1980s Spain: Rethinking the Movida*, by Maite Usoz de la Fuente
12. *Santería, Vodou and Resistance in Caribbean Literature: Daughters of the Spirits*, by Paul Humphrey
13. *Reprojecting the City: Urban Space and Dissident Sexualities in Recent Latin American Cinema*, by Benedict Hoff
14. *Rethinking Juan Rulfo's Creative World: Prose, Photography, Film*, edited by Dylan Brennan and Nuala Finnegan
15. *The Last Days of Humanism: A Reappraisal of Quevedo's Thought*, by Alfonso Rey
16. *Catalan Narrative 1875-2015*, edited by Jordi Larios and Montserrat Lunati
17. *Islamic Culture in Spain to 1614: Essays and Studies*, by L. P. Harvey
18. *Film Festivals: Cinema and Cultural Exchange*, by Mar Diestro-Dópido
19. *St Teresa of Avila: Her Writings and Life*, edited by Terence O'Reilly, Colin Thompson and Lesley Twomey
20. *(Un)veiling Bodies: A Trajectory of Chilean Post-Dictatorship Documentary*, by Elizabeth Ramírez Soto

The Modern Spanish Canon

Visibility, Cultural Capital and the Academy

Edited by
Stuart Davis and Maite Usoz de la Fuente

Studies in Hispanic and Lusophone Cultures 28
Modern Humanities Research Association
2018

Published by Legenda
an imprint of the Modern Humanities Research Association
Salisbury House, Station Road, Cambridge CB1 2LA

ISBN 978-1-78188-529-1 *(HB)*
ISBN 978-1-78188-530-7 *(PB)*

First published 2018

All rights reserved. No part of this publication may be reproduced or disseminated or transmitted in any form or by any means, electronic, mechanical, photocopying, recording or otherwise, or stored in any retrieval system, or otherwise used in any manner whatsoever without written permission of the copyright owner, except in accordance with the provisions of the Copyright, Designs and Patents Act 1988, or under the terms of a licence permitting restricted copying issued in the UK by the Copyright Licensing Agency Ltd, Saffron House, 6–10 Kirby Street, London EC1N 8TS, *England, or in the USA by the Copyright Clearance Center, 222 Rosewood Drive, Danvers MA 01923. Application for the written permission of the copyright owner to reproduce any part of this publication must be made by email to legenda@mhra.org.uk.*

Disclaimer: Statements of fact and opinion contained in this book are those of the author and not of the editors or the Modern Humanities Research Association. The publisher makes no representation, express or implied, in respect of the accuracy of the material in this book and cannot accept any legal responsibility or liability for any errors or omissions that may be made.

Trademark notice: Product or corporate names may be trademarks or registered trademarks, and are used only for identification and explanation without intent to infringe.

© *Modern Humanities Research Association 2018*

Copy-Editor: Susan Wharton

CONTENTS

Acknowledgements		ix
Notes on the Contributors		x
Introduction: Visibility, Cultural Capital and the Academy STUART DAVIS AND MAITE USOZ DE LA FUENTE		1

PART I. RETHINKING THE CONTOURS OF PENINSULAR HISPANIC STUDIES

1. New Cartographies of Hispanism: From Spanish to Iberian Literary History? — 12
SANTIAGO PÉREZ ISASI

2. Mare Memoriae: Kirmen Uribe's Memorial Seascapes — 25
DANIELA OMLOR

3. Becoming Undone: Colour, Matter and Line in the Artwork of Marcel·lí Antúnez — 37
EVA BRU-DOMÍNGUEZ

PART II. GOING AGAINST THE GRAIN: GENDER AS CHALLENGE

4. Out of Time: Julia de Asensi and the Historical Legend — 58
ROCÍO RØDTJER

5. Undermining the Discourse of the Spanish Transition: Literary Approaches to Forgetting, Consensus and 'the New Spain' — 72
LETICIA BLANCO

6. Fascinated by Observation: Amalia Domingo Soler and Vicente Manterola's Debates on Spiritism in Late Nineteenth-Century Spain — 92
MARTA FERRER

PART III. NEW FORMS OF CULTURAL CAPITAL

7. *Facha* if you do, coward if you don't? The Problematic Canonicity of Francoist Authors in Post-Franco Spain — 107
DAVID JIMÉNEZ TORRES

8. The Unfortunate Case of Heritage Screen Media: Dismissal, Denial and Definition — 121
LAURA J. LEE KEMP

9. The Gypsies According to NO-DO. The Image of Spanish Roma from Dictatorship to Democracy — 136
LIDIA MERÁS

10 Constructing a Feminist Room of Her Own: The Marketing and
    Reception of María Xosé Queizán   148
    JENNIFER RODRÍGUEZ

    Index   158

ACKNOWLEDGEMENTS

Maite and Stuart would like to thank all the contributors for their patience and support as the volume took shape and became a reality. Thank you also to Susan Wharton for her diligent proof-reading eyes and Graham Nelson for all his advice. We are also grateful to Bárbara Allende for granting permission for the use of her work on the cover of this volume and Girton College's Publications Fund for the funds to support this.

S.D., M.F., Cambridge and London, April 2018

NOTES ON THE CONTRIBUTORS

Leticia Blanco is completing her PhD, entitled 'Revisiting the literary canon: the relevance of the women writers' response to the discourse of the Spanish Transition and their sentimental counter-education' at King's College London, where she also teaches. She also works as a freelance proofreader and translator. She holds a BA in Comparative Literature and Literary Theory, a BA in Spanish Language and Literature, and an MA in Spanish and Latin American Culture. Her research and teaching interests are twentieth and twenty-first century Spain, critical discourse analysis, and global feminisms.

Eva Bru-Dominguez is a Lecturer in Catalan and Hispanic Studies at the Department of Modern Languages and Cultures, Bangor University (United Kingdom). Her main research interests are in the representation of the body and sexuality in Catalan visual culture, performance art and literature. She is the author of *Beyond Containment. Corporeality in Mercè Rodoreda's Literature* (Peter Lang, 2013), which was awarded the prestigious Premi Fundació Mercè Rodoreda by the Institut d'Estudis Catalans. She has published on Catalan cinema and is currently working on the ways in which notions of identity, society and culture specific to the Catalan context are conveyed in contemporary visual culture.

Marta Ferrer is a doctoral candidate and teaching fellow at Columbia University, New York. Her interests include nineteenth-century discourses and practices of science and religion in both Spain and Europe. Her PhD dissertation analyses the popular sciences and their relationship with orthodox medicine, Catholic culture, and the flourishing of the print and literary market during the reign of Isabel II and in the years thereafter. Before working at Columbia, she studied in Salamanca, Edinburgh, and Cambridge.

David Jiménez Torres received his PhD from the University of Cambridge and was Lecturer in Contemporary Spanish Cultural Studies at the University of Manchester. He is currently Associate Professor at Universidad Camilo José Cela (Madrid). His research has focused on Spanish twentieth-century cultural and intellectual history, and more specifically on Spanish-English cultural contacts during the first decades of the century. His first monograph, *Ramiro de Maeztu and England: Imaginaries, Realities and Repercussions of a Cultural Encounter* (Tamesis Books), was published in 2016.

Laura Lee Kemp completed her PhD, 'Negative Affect, Cultural Trauma, Women and Perpetrators: Representations of the Spanish Civil War and Francoist Repression in Contemporary Spanish Screen Media', at the University of Cambridge in 2016.

Her research interests include the analysis of cinematic form as a prominent critical approach, cultural trauma, feminist film theory and how these concerns combine within the field of Spanish 'heritage' cinema. Her publications include 'The reconstrual of *la costurera:* a feminist re-interpretation of the role of the seamstress in *El tiempo entre costuras (The Time Between the Seams)*', *Studies in Spanish and Latin American Cinema,* Vol. 13, No. 2 (2016) and 'The middlebrow Spanish Civil War film: a popular medium of social discourse', in *Belphégor: Popular literatures and media culture* (Middlebrow Edition), Vol. 15, No.1 (2017).

Lidia Merás is a film historian based in London. Among her various contributions to film journals, she serves as the member of the editorial staff of *Secuencias*, a peer-reviewed film journal published by the Universidad Autónoma of Madrid. From 2012 to 2014 she was a post-doctoral researcher at Royal Holloway (University of London) and previously taught at the Universitat Pompeu Fabra (Barcelona), Universidad Autonóma of Madrid and Universidad Carlos III (Madrid). A substantial portion of her work has involved researching Spanish film, often in connection with contemporary arts and politics. A recent interest is Iranian documentary. Her latest publications on this field are a book chapter on *Female Authorship and the Documentary Image* for Edinburgh University Press, edited by Boel Ulfsdotter and Anna Backman Rogers (2017), and two entries in Parviz Jahed (ed.) *Directory of World Cinema Iran, vol 2* (Intellect, 2017). She is currently a member of the research project 'Large Exhibition: Spanish Contemporary Art for Mainstream Audiences' based at the Universidad Autónoma de Madrid.

Daniela Omlor is Associate Professor in Spanish at the University of Oxford, a Fellow of Lincoln College and lecturer at Jesus College. Prior to that, she held the Queen Sofía Junior Research Fellowship at Exeter College, University of Oxford. She received her PhD in 2011 from the University of St Andrews. Her most recent publication, together with Xon de Ros, is an edited volume entitled *The Cultural Legacy of María Zambrano* (Legenda, 2017). Her first monograph *Jorge Semprún: Memory's Long Voyage* was published in 2014 by Peter Lang. Broadly speaking, her research interests lie within the field of contemporary peninsular Spanish literature with a particular emphasis on exile and the recovery of traumatic memories in fiction, in particular that of the Spanish Civil War.

Santiago Pérez Isasi received his BA and PhD from the University of Deusto (Spain) and is currently a researcher at the Centro de Estudos Comparatistas of the University of Lisbon, where he is a member of the DIIA research group (Diálogos Ibéricos e Ibero-Americanos). His research interests include nineteenth-century literary history, national identity, Iberian Studies and Digital Humanities. His most relevant publications are the co-edited volumes *Looking at Iberia. A Comparative European Perspective* (Peter Lang, 2013) and *Los límites del Hispanismo. Nuevos métodos, nuevas fronteras, nuevos géneros* (Peter Lang, 2017).

Rocío Rødtjer is a research associate at King's College London, from which she recently received her PhD. Awarded the AHGBI-Spanish Embassy Doctoral

Publication Prize for 2016, her thesis, 'Women and Nationhood in Restoration Spain 1874–1931: The State as Family' will be published by Legenda. Her main area of interest is fin-de-siècle Spain, and she has published on the Gothic incursions into the Spanish literary landscape of this period, as well as the relationship between scientific discourse and Catholicism. She also holds an MA in Translation and Linguistics and has worked as a translator and editor.

Jennifer Rodríguez completed her PhD entitled 'The Marketing and Reception of Women Writers in the Twenty-First Century Spanish Nation-State' at the University of Liverpool. Her interests include Galician studies and the reception of women writers from Galicia, Catalonia and the Basque Country. During her doctoral studies she assisted with the digitization of the Galician feminist journal *Festa da Palabra Silenciada* at the University of Barcelona.

INTRODUCTION

❖

Visibility, Cultural Capital and the Academy

Stuart Davis and Maite Usoz de la Fuente

Although not at first apparent, Ouka Leele's iconic *Rappelle-toi Barbara* (1987), reproduced on the cover of this volume, illustrates some of the challenges, contradictions and tensions faced by academics, particularly in the arts and humanities, as early career researchers in a disciplinary field variously known as Peninsular Hispanic Studies, Iberian Studies, or Hispanic/Spanish Studies *tout court*. In the image, we see two figures — one female, one male — in what appear to be dancing poses, immediately below the famous statue/fountain of the Greek goddess Cybele in Madrid's Cibeles square. These two figures, representing the heroine Atalanta and her suitor Hippomenes, appear surrounded by strewn bodies (according to the myth, Atalanta's unsuccessful suitors would face immediate death), as well as several other figures, including two satyrs on their right, with two women (one probably representing the goddess Aphrodite) and two children on the left. The image, like the myth it references, combines a sense of ecstatic joyfulness in the two central figures, pitted against the violence and chaos surrounding them, and is located in a monumental setting — *Rappelle-toi Barbara* may be a fitting metaphor for the predicament of the early career scholar, on one hand ecstatic with passion for his/her work, competing to be granted entry into their disciplinary 'temple of knowledge', but painfully aware of the danger of perishing in the process of attempting to attain the seemingly unattainable. Ironically, the fate of Atalanta and Hippomenes is to be turned into tamed lions by Cybele; our playful reading here suggests that successful entry to the monumental hallowed ground of the academy runs the risk of being eternally 'yoked' to the heavy chariot of administrative-bureaucratic duties.

Despite its allusions to Classical mythology, this image is also a work of its time, both in terms of the photographic elements coincidentally captured in the image — the vehicles that can be seen clogging the street, the 'street furniture' (lamp posts, traffic lights, signs) — and also in terms of the visual language deployed, namely the pop-infused use of anti-mimetic colours (pink, blue, gold) which, together with the mythological figures, contrast with and complement the image's naturalistic qualities. As a cultural product *Rappelle-toi Barbara* is revealing of attitudes to cultural change and heritage. Indeed, Ouka Leele is generally presented as one of the most iconic artists from the post-Franco urban youth movement known as *la movida*, a classification that is somewhat limiting given her evolving career as an artist spanning several decades, but that can be in part explained by her dominant visual style explored here. Given Ouka Leele's association with *la movida*, and considering the image was produced in 1987 — at the tail end of the phenomenon — Jonathan Snyder has suggested that the work can be read as both a reflection of 'the temporality of *la Movida* as a mythological present that wishes itself eternal' (2013: 322) and a critique of that very same temporality, as an illustration that the mythological present of *movida* participants is, in fact, 'grafted within an inescapable site of history and memory' (2013: 322), despite the received wisdom that the movement constituted an ephemeral phenomenon with no past and no future. The artist herself has stated that the original intention of her work was to remind *madrileños* of the myth behind one of Madrid's best-known monuments, *la Cibeles* (Gallero 1991: 382). Memory (or, more specifically, remembrance) is explicitly invoked in the title of the work, borrowed from a line by the French poet Jacques Prévert, which can be read as a command from the artist to herself (Ouka Leele's given name is Bárbara) to remember her cultural heritage, a heritage that is both rooted in the city of Madrid and connected to a wider Western cultural tradition, as exemplified by the artist's mobilisation of myth and the use of French in the title.

Ouka Leele thus succeeds in creating an original, visually compelling work which remains very much of its time, while building on a rich cultural heritage that is both broadly Western in its mythical dimension and specifically Spanish in its localisation in a particular corner of Madrid. Read in this way, *Rappelle-toi Barbara* may provide some inspiration to us, as scholars, in terms of the strategies that may allow us to negotiate the often conflicting demands we face currently, such as the imperative to broaden the accessibility and appeal of our outputs while retaining academic rigour; the increasing possibility and desirability of working collaboratively and across disciplines while wanting to preserve a sense of disciplinary and/or methodological grounding; and the drive to discover, review, challenge, and innovate, while respecting and preserving our disciplinary tradition. Ouka Leele's work does not provide an answer to such questions, of course, but it exemplifies how either/or dichotomies can be overcome by viewing them from a more nuanced and dialogic perspective; a work can be both absolutely contemporary and rooted in history;[2] profoundly local(ised), yet with a universal dimension; complex and multi-layered as well as with undoubted popular appeal. While the process of creating a work of art is markedly different from the process of producing academic work, both are creative endeavours, and if we, as academics, may derive some lessons from *Rappelle-toi Barbara*, these might include the importance of collaborative work, including with institutions beyond our immediate sphere of action or comfort zone.[3] In addition, we all need a healthy balance of self-belief and originality on the one hand (exemplified here by the artist's fearlessness in taking on a project on such a scale, which involved cutting traffic in one of Madrid's busiest roads and the use of a large crane), and self-awareness, on the other (as demonstrated, in this instance, through the self-referential title).

While the challenges outlined above affect our discipline as a whole, they are felt particularly acutely by early career researchers (ECRs) who often operate at the margins of academia as hourly-paid lecturers or as teaching fellows on rolling contracts. The desire to be intellectually original and ambitious is often tempered (when not thwarted) by logistical and pragmatic concerns around funding, accessibility of materials, time scale, or lack of institutional support, among others. As Joan Ramon Resina (2005: 181) notes: 'the maverick scholar, who breaks with the routines of symbolic production, is likely to experience a blockage of ordinary channels of diffusion and a freezing vacuum around her work. [...] Although a premium is placed on individual initiative and field renovation, the overall consensus is ensured through highly personalized hiring practices, manipulation of student interest, and diffuse censorship linked to the politics of publishing.' Resina writes here with a concern for the innovative work of scholars established in the field, not those seeking affiliation to the discipline where the classic requirement at PhD level of 'making an original contribution to a specific field of knowledge' is fraught with incognita: how original is original enough, and how original is *too* original? Put differently: while it seems obvious that a doctoral thesis needs to do more than describe a state of affairs or summarise what others have already said, some graduate students face strong resistance if they dare deviate from certain parameters, if, for instance, they choose to write in a less formal language register or not to comply with other established academic conventions, resisting the cultural capital implicit in the acquisition of a doctorate. It is axiomatic of the disciplinary regulations of academia that acceptance and inclusivity are key, as noted by Armin Krishnan (2009: 8): 'It follows that the academic discipline can be seen as a form of specific and rigorous scientific training that will turn out practitioners who have been "disciplined by their discipline" for their own good. In addition, "discipline" also means policing certain behaviours or ways of thinking. Individuals who have deviated from their "discipline" can be brought back in line or excluded.'

A key challenge for ECRs resides in the expectation that their work, in its originality, should play a central role in the re-shaping of the discipline, undermined by the simultaneous awareness by the individuals concerned that they (as yet) lack the visibility and capital (economic, cultural and symbolic) within their field, in order to do so effectively. The ECR often finds his or her status fraught with contradiction: for instance, in the UK, where the editors of this volume work, Spanish has seen an enormous growth in popularity within the education sector, from schools to universities, yet has relatively little cultural or economic capital when compared to the prestige and size of French or German Studies departments; the non-canonical choice of subject for a PhD thesis, while eliciting interest and positive feedback at conferences, seems a disadvantage in a crowded job market where undergraduate university syllabuses are more traditionally focused on canonical textual cultures. It is in part the aim of this volume to provide a voice and find a place for young scholars caught in this kind of double-bind, to showcase their work and reflect on their place in the discipline and their potential to shape it.

Indeed, the very nature of that discipline is itself under question as a variety of methodological and practical concerns coalesce, as we shall discuss shortly. While established scholars assume an explicit role in debating and shaping curriculum content, names of departments, funding projects and approving PhDs, ECRs often find themselves with the feeling of wading through quicksand, as the disciplinary ground in which they operate appears to be constantly shifting under their feet. In the UK academy this involves the unknown consequences — at the time of writing — of the UK's withdrawal from the European Union ('Brexit'), alongside policy changes that suggest progressive privatisation of the higher education sector and the decline in Modern Foreign Languages as subject choices for schoolchildren, alongside a wider need to re-think the role and scope of modern languages amid shifting values and expectations. Each essay in *The Modern Spanish Canon* contributes to that reconsideration of the discipline.

Each section of this volume draws together disparate material and approaches that collectively address a wider concern for the discipline. As alluded to already in this Introduction, the very name of a university department that delivers tuition in language and culture from the Iberian peninsula is an object of debate. Pre-university, many of our students study, or are aware of, a subject called simply 'Spanish', which at its most fundamental level is communicative language tuition, and by Key Stage 5 (age 16–18) increasingly incorporates introductory knowledge of Spanish language, literature, film and historical moments from both the peninsula and Spanish-speaking Latin America. In a university context, as noted by John Macklin (2013: 46), a department of 'Hispanic Studies' or 'Spanish' almost always obscures a wide range of geographical and linguistic variety, caught under an arguably ill-fitting umbrella. That variety not only draws in other languages of the Spanish state, namely Catalan, Galician, Basque — and beyond, with the occasional teaching of Quechua — but also a broader transnational dimension through the inclusion of Portuguese language tuition and the teaching of Spanish and Lusophone cultures from around the world, predominantly Latin American but also occasionally African and Asian. That Spain is only one country amongst many that offer rich cultural material for study is often problematically overlooked in institutions that continue to be enthralled by long-held divisions based on language, themselves frequently rooted in a system that privileges Eurocentric culture, in the process prolonging a legacy that views Spain, in the UK academy at least, as geographically and culturally more accessible, with a longer literary tradition deemed worthy of study. Indeed, Mabel Moraña (2005: xii) notes in the introduction to *Ideologies of Hispanism* that:

> The construction of knowledge in the specific field of Hispanism had its point of departure in the universalistic and ahistorical concept of *Hispania* as a spacial [sic] and temporal extension of what once was Spain's imperial dominion. The suppression of diversity and particularism, and the repression of all references to the colonial origins of the concept, has promoted Hispanism as a program of cultural and linguistic dissemination in modern times.

Attempting to step beyond the all-encompassing nature of 'Spanish', for Pérez Isasi and Fernandes (2013: 7) the rationale for Iberian Studies is one which offers 'the constitution of a new way of looking at the Iberian complex, based on comparative methodologies, and thus aimed at overcoming binary structures as well as any sort of established frontiers.' As such, the discipline may move beyond what Randolph Pope (2010: 100) identified as an unease about the conventions of the discipline and its institutional configuration, when he observes that they are overly specialised, 'seldom recognizing that the contemporary world is more fluid, interpenetrated, and dialogical than the strict and austere disciplines' and that 'our institutions isolate their members by assigning to each of them a larger or smaller pigeonhole, seldom shared, and often competitive'. However, for Joseba Gabilondo (2014: 26) it is what Moraña identified as the *Hispania* legacy that undermines any attempt to reconstitute the discipline as Iberian Studies or Spanish Cultural Studies, since it is always already in service to Spain's 'nationalist excess'; for Gabilondo the Spanish state remains always at large and fundamental to any reconfiguration of the discipline or any attempt to dismantle the hegemonic core. Indeed, much critical ink has been spilt considering the position of Spain within academic practices — both research and teaching — and the potential power of 'Iberian Studies'.[4] It is not the intention of this Introduction, nor indeed this volume, to explore all these important publications, nor even to extend any project by formulating a new position vis-à-vis their approaches to the discipline; *The Modern Spanish Canon* does not go beyond Spanish Studies to dismantle it from without, but seeks to interrogate and probe from within. Although never entirely divorced from its political and cultural heft, 'Spain' in this volume is a geographical context from which, and about which, our contributors explore and question.[5]

The first section 'Rethinking the contours of Peninsular Hispanic Studies' addresses movement, agency and the places and spaces in which peninsular Spanish culture is encountered. The first essay is a contribution from **Santiago Pérez Isasi**, whose published work elsewhere has already asked important questions of common conceptions of the creation and place of cultural heritage.[6] Pérez Isasi's chapter considers the potential of Resina's notion of Iberian Studies as an alternative to traditional literary histories which take the nation-state as their basis, insisting on the importance of transforming approaches and methodologies if we are to produce something which is more than a mere addition to or expansion of the traditional national literary history model. In this context, Even-Zohar's notion of polysystem is seen as a potentially fruitful means of developing the emerging field of Iberian Studies. Also in this section, **Daniela Omlor** explores two novels by Kirmen Uribe, the Basque writer whose works have been translated widely and whose first novel *Bilbao-New York-Bilbao* was awarded the Premio Nacional de Literatura in 2009. Uribe's works have been celebrated for their transnational qualities, which Omlor explores in their intersection with temporal concerns of memory. Specifically, Omlor discusses how Uribe's novels present readers with an 'alternative map of memories' based not on national or regional borders, but on the Atlantic Ocean as a site through which distinct individual and cultural memories traverse and interconnect. According to Omlor, Uribe's innovative approach is underpinned by a transnational approach to memory which sets him apart from the current and on-going 'memory wars' taking place in Spain (a topic explored later on in the volume by David Jiménez Torres), as it enables the author to creatively engage with Rothberg's concept of 'multidirectional memory', a framework that seeks to move beyond exclusive and/or competing versions of cultural memory. The final essay in this section, by **Eva Bru-Domínguez** opens up visual culture and its intersection with new technologies, with a focus on Catalan artist Marcel·lí Antúnez Roca. Bru-Domínguez's chapter explores Antúnez's trajectory from the 1980s to the present and considers the influence of both European and Catalan avant-garde movements and artists on his work. Moreover, Bru-Domínguez mobilises a range of theoretical approaches — from Elizabeth's Grosz's definition of the 'post-human' to Julia Kristeva's 'abject' — to shed light on some of the recurring motifs and preoccupations in Antúnez's work.

That these questions of the contours of the discipline respond to wider political and cultural changes is nothing new in itself, indeed some volumes of essays that showcase new approaches within the discipline indicate precisely the changing politics and culture of post-dictatorship Spain as instructive in shaping research, in part as a product of more permissive research environments but also as academics observe and analyse cultural responses to those changes. As far back as 1994 Paul Julian Smith and Mark Millington's *New Hispanisms: Literature, Culture, Theory* acted as a vehicle for a variety of essays celebrating 'the new found self-confidence of a theoretically informed discipline' (1994: 13). Shortly after, the appearance of Jo Labanyi and Helen Graham's seminal *Spanish Cultural Studies: An Introduction* (1995) set the scene for a widening field of exploration in research, a legacy continued by Barry Jordan and Rikki Morgan-Tamosunas's *Contemporary Spanish Cultural Studies* which gave greater prominence to non-literary objects of cultural production, noting how 'the notion of culture has expanded to include the 'cultures' of hitherto neglected groups, including various movements in feminism and multiculturalism' (2000: 2). More recently Luis Martín-Estudillo and Nicholas Spadaccini's *New Spain, New Literatures* (2010) claims not only that the Spanish state has been transformed in recent decades, post-transition to democracy, becoming plurinational and multicultural (2010: ix) but that this multiplicity within is in tension with Spain's position in the European Union and the wider, global picture (xi). The nature of Spanish Studies must necessarily respond and contribute to these ongoing pressures and concerns.

The three essays in the second section, 'Going against the grain: gender as a challenge', each have at their core questions of women's place in the cultural field. As suggested by Jordan and Morgan-Tamosunas, gender has become a commonplace concern for many researchers, emerging and established; our contributors in this section question, extend and place their interrogations of gender in new contexts. For **Rocío Rødtjer**, the dualities of conservative and progressive political attitudes, so often invoked in the context of late nineteenth-century and early twentieth-century Spain, are inadequate tools to understand a female writer considered canonically peripheral. Her essay focuses on the nineteenth-century writer Julia de Asensi and, specifically, on her legend *El encubierto* (1883), a text which, according to Rødtjer, clearly if indirectly engages with the author's contemporary political reality. That the political dimension of the text has been so often overlooked seems undoubtedly related to its author's gender; but Rødtjer's aim is not simply to highlight how Asensi's gender has conditioned readings of her work, but also to challenge clear-cut binaries such as conservative/progressive, active/passive or traditional/subversive. While Asensi is generally portrayed as a conservative figure and a defender of the status quo, the picture that emerges from Rødtjer's close re-reading of her work is far more complex than such received wisdom suggests. **Leticia Blanco** addresses the role of women writers in a more recent historical context, the post-1975 transition to democracy, which has itself undergone scrutiny in recent years, exposing its mythology. Blanco demonstrates how women's voices were caught up in and worked against the discursive creation of the 'pacto de silencio'. Bringing together analysis of the literary works of Esther Tusquets, Montserrat Roig, Rosa Montero, Lourdes Ortiz and Carme Riera published between 1975 and 1982, Blanco demonstrates how these authors problematized the hegemonic discourse of that period, marked by optimism and by a favouring of consensus over difference and a tendency towards looking to the future rather than engaging with the recent past. Blanco argues that recuperating the work of these authors (some of which have remained peripheral within the contemporary canon) is relevant both in terms of doing their work literary justice, and in terms of gaining a better, more nuanced understanding of the period of the Spanish transition. Finally, in this section, **Marta Ferrer** explores the role of the nineteenth-century writer Amalia Domingo Soler, a dominant voice in Spiritism. Domingo Soler's heated and public debates with the Catholic priest Vicente Manterola bear witness to the struggle for legitimacy in which both Spiritism and Catholicism were engaged at a time of great scientific and technological advances. Domingo Soler's active role in such polemics challenges our perception of gender roles in late nineteenth-century Spain, while her mobilisation of scientific ideas to support her views (echoed in Manterola's work, if with opposite aim) points to the frequent overlap in this period between scientific, pseudo-scientific and religious discourses. This section's essays thus intersect gender with politics and philosophical thought and context to shed new light on recently established themes, such as a more complex and nuanced understanding of political agency and/or engagement by women, how the revision of work by previously marginal (or marginalised) voices can lead to the reassessment of specific historical periods or existing historiography, or the ways in which disciplinary boundaries and discourses evolve over time.

The promotion of new objects of study and the recuperation of non-canonical voices, not only those of women, has done much to revitalise the discipline, as noted by Cornejo Parriego and Villamandos: 'cuando se habla de la crisis del hispanismo, se puede llegar a olvidar la vitalidad que muestra en la actualidad' (2011: 16) [the discussion of the crisis of Hispanism can lead us to forget the vitality of the field at present], yet the sense of crisis evoked is in part due to the continued fragmentation of the higher education institution that, as Pope noted, effectively pigeonholes academics and, as has been noted here already, encourages originality whilst expecting affiliation to a supposed canonical core. Yet that sense of a core is under question, in the UK academy at least, where changes in focus of research, responding to many impulses mentioned in this introduction already, are arguably responsible for changes in the choices of texts and material for study by undergraduates in those departments of Spanish/Hispanic Studies/Modern Languages etc. Survey studies of UK university Spanish degrees, capturing a snapshot of everything taught within an academic year, show that from 1998 to 2016 there has been a significant reduction in the consensus as to which authors should be taught.[7] For literature from Spain, a sense of a canonical core continues, comprising Golden Age writing and theatre, early twentieth-century narrative and theatre and some contemporary writers (and filmmakers), but this is increasingly shrinking and becoming diluted as the number of different authors and texts expands. More challenging texts of longer length and greater linguistic difficulty are becoming scarcer, whilst film, visual arts and shorter texts take greater precedence, in response to student demand for more diverse cultural forms and the recognition of the challenges of transposing a culture to non-native speakers who lack cultural capital. These changes suggest a balancing act between canonical material, that all undergraduates — potential researchers of the future — should read, and research-led material previously marginalised or invisible in the hallowed halls of academe, a balance that is tipping towards the latter.

The four essays in the final section of this volume, titled 'New forms of cultural capital' do not deal exclusively with material that has been identified as gaining a foothold in the undergraduate experience, but indicate new material and approaches that question that canonical core. **David Jiménez Torres** examines the impact of the recent 'memory wars' on contemporary readings of right-wing writers of the past, evaluated more for their message than for their aesthetics. Jiménez Torres argues that the canonicity of Francoist writers in Spain is problematic on two accounts: firstly, a considerable number of critics consider not only these authors, but also anyone with an interest in their work, as ideologically suspect, complicit with Francoist or fascist ideas by association. Secondly, even when the work of Francoist writers such as Agustín Foxá is vindicated, as Andrés Trapiello has done in recent years, the focus tends to be on linguistic innovation and/or literary experimentation, so that authors whose prose is less bombastic — as is the case with Ramiro de Maeztu, on whom Jiménez has recently published a monograph — remain neglected.[8] **Laura Lee Kemp** assesses the impact that concepts of heritage, middlebrow and melodrama have had on film culture in Spain since 2000, with particular reference to re-evaluations of the Spanish Civil War and its legacy for twenty-first century Spain. Kemp traces how these theoretical concepts, originally formulated within the Anglo-Saxon critical tradition, have been adapted to and applied to Spanish cultural products. While the author critiques the (negative) quality assumptions linked to these terms, she nevertheless argues that such conceptual frameworks, particularly the notion of heritage and its derivatives of counter-heritage and post-heritage, can offer a productive means through which to consider an enduringly popular but critically neglected cinematic genre. The contribution from **Lidia Merás** also examines visual culture, in this case of the Francoist period through to post-transition Spain, with reference to the representation of gypsy culture, long mythologised and unauthentically characterised. Merás analyses thirteen NO-DO episodes portraying gypsies and released between 1945 and 1978, using this audio-visual archive to reflect on changing attitudes towards this community within Spain. The early clips (1945–1964), while portraying some distinctively Romani cultural traditions, draw on the (Catholic) religious devotion of the community as a cohesive element that can facilitate its assimilation. By contrast, later NO-DO episodes (roughly from 1970 onwards), offer an increasingly prejudiced and negative view of this ethnic group which was, however, somewhat counter-balanced by the diversification of discourses and cultural and media products about the Roma community in Spain, occurring in the aftermath of Spain's transition to democracy. Our final contribution, from **Jennifer Rodríguez**, presents a case study in the cultural representation and reception of the Galician writer María Xosé Queizán. Rodríguez demonstrates how Queizán's feminist activism and her subversion of certain traditions linked to the Galician literary field have affected the reception of her work, making her an increasingly recognised, yet still not entirely canonical figure within Galician literature, as illustrated by her failed bid to become a member of the Real Academia Galega (RAG). In all four cases, the contributors demonstrate a concern with the legitimization of their objects of study as worthy of academic consideration, as a response to their circulation in other, typically populist, spheres.

In sum, *The Modern Spanish Canon* addresses a rich kaleidoscopic variety of cultural products, approaches and understandings of local cultures within the Spanish state that compete and interact with larger visions of nationhood and state-hood, themselves changing dependent on historical context. Political and cultural dominant forms and expressions within Hispanism continue to be ripe for exploration. The essays exemplify how new academics can no longer simply add more readings of canonical works as contributions to a discipline, but, quite rightly, produce cutting-edge research that engages with the nature of the field itself, that through a spotlight on individual parts allows for the illumination of a whole and, in so doing, the revelation of the porous unexpected interactions going on between them. In a world dominated by the economics of student provision, research grant income and output metrics, such high quality, self-reflexive research stakes a claim for a discipline's continual relevance and importance.

Bibliography

BUFFERY, HELENA, STUART DAVIS and KIRSTY HOOPER (eds). 2007. *Reading Iberia: Theory. History. Identity.* (Oxford: Peter Lang)

CORNEJO PARRIEGO, ROSALÍA and ALBERTO VILLAMANDOS. 2011. 'Introducción. Un hispanismo en clave del diálogo', in *Un hispanismo para el siglo XXI. Ensayos de crítica cultural*, ed. by Rosalía Cornejo Parriego and Alberto Villamandos (Madrid: Biblioteca Nueva), pp. 11–22

DAVIS, STUART. 2001. 'Is there a Peninsular Spanish Canon in Hispanic Studies?', *Donaire*, 16: 5–11

——2010. 'Close Encounters of the Cultural Kind: The Peninsular Spanish Canon in a Pedagogical Context', *Tesserae: Journal of Iberian and Latin American Studies*, 16: 107–26

—— 2018. 'The state of the discipline: Hispanic literature and film in UK Spanish degrees', *Journal of Romance Studies*, 2018, vol. 18, no 1, p. 25-44.
EPPS, BRAD and LUIS FERNÁNDEZ CIFUENTES (eds.). 2005. *Spain beyond Spain. Modernity, Literary History and National Identity* (Lewisburg: Bucknell University Press)
GABILONDO, JOSEBA. 2014. 'Spanish Nationalist Excess: A Decolonial and Postnational critique of Iberian Studies', *Prosopopeya*, 8: 23–60
GALLERO, JOSÉ LUIS. 1991. *Sólo se vive una vez. Esplendor y ruina de la movida madrileña* (Madrid: Ardora)
GRAHAM, HELEN and JO LABANYI (eds). 1995. *Spanish Cultural Studies. An Introduction* (Oxford: Oxford University Press)
JIMÉNEZ TORRES, DAVID. 2016. *Ramiro de Maeztu and England: Imaginaries, Realities and Repercussions of a Cultural Encounter* (London: Tamesis)
JORDAN, BARRY and RIKKI MORGAN-TAMOSUNAS (eds.). 2000. *Contemporary Spanish Cultural Studies* (London: Arnold)
KRISHNAN, ARMIN, 2009. *What are Academic Disciplines? Some Observations on the Disciplinary vs Interdisciplinary Debate* (n.p.: ESRC National Centre for Research Methods)
MACKLIN, JOHN. 2013. 'Modernism and Modernity: Iberian Perspectives' in *Looking at Iberia. A Comparative European Perspective*, ed. by Santiago Pérez Isasi and Ângela Fernandes (Oxford: Peter Lang), pp. 43–58
MARTÍN-ESTUDILLO, LUIS and NICHOLAS SPADACCINI (eds). 2010. *New Spain, New Literatures* (Nashville: Vanderbilt University Press)
MILLINGTON, MARK I. and PAUL JULIAN SMITH. 1994. 'Introduction', *New Hispanisms: Literature, Culture, Theory*, ed. by Mark Millington and Paul Julian Smith (Ottawa: Dovehouse), pp. 7–13
MORAÑA, MABEL. 2005. 'Introduction: Mapping Hispanism' in *Ideologies of Hispanism*, ed. by Mabel Moraña (Nashville: Vanderbilt University Press), pp. ix-xxi
PÉREZ ISASI, SANTIAGO. 2013. 'The Limits of "Spanishness" in Nineteenth-century Spanish Literary History', *Bulletin of Hispanic Studies*, 90: 167–87.
PÉREZ ISASI, SANTIAGO and ÂNGELA FERNANDES. 2013. 'Looking at Iberia in/from Europe' in *Looking at Iberia. A Comparative European Perspective*, ed. by Santiago Pérez Isasi and Ângela Fernandes (Oxford: Peter Lang), pp. 1–8
POPE, RANDOLPH D. 2010. 'A Hispanist's View of Changing Institutions, or about Insects and Whales' in *New Spain, New Literatures*, ed. by Luis Martín-Estudillo and Nicholas Spadaccini (Nashville: Vanderbilt University Press), pp. 99–115
RESINA, JOAN RAMON. 2005. 'Whose Hispanism? Cultural Trauma, Disciplined Memory, and Symbolic Dominance' in *Ideologies of Hispanism* ed. by Mabel Moraña (Nashville: Vanderbilt University Press), pp. 160–86
RESINA, JOAN RAMON. 2009. *Del hispanismo a los estudios ibéricos. Una propuesta federativa para el ámbito cultural* (Madrid: Biblioteca Nueva)
—— (ed.). 2013. *Iberian Modalities. A Relational Approach to the Study of Culture in the Iberian Peninsula* (Liverpool: Liverpool University Press)
SNYDER, JONATHAN. 2013. 'Ghostly Subjectivities: Photography, Spectral Identities, and the Temporality of *la Movida*' in *Toward a Cultural Archive of 'la Movida'. Back to the Future*, ed. by William J. Nichols and H. Rosi Song (Madison: Fairleigh Dickinson University Press), pp. 307–30

Notes to the Introduction

1. The title of the work is sometimes given as *Rappelle-toi Bárbara* (introducing the Spanish version of the name, which is Ouka Leele's given name) and, more intriguingly, *Rappelle-toi Barbará*.
2. Snyder suggests that if the picture is read as an apology for or homage to *la movida*, then the dead

figures could be read as representing *movida* participants who died prematurely (2013: 321–22), and, in fact, the arrows piercing their flesh are suggestive of heroin needles.
3. Ouka Leele explained the crucial role played by collaborators in the coming-to-being of the image, as well as how she required municipal cooperation to make the project possible. See Gallero 1991 for further details.
4. See, for example, Joan Ramon Resina (2009 and 2013). Volumes of self-reflexive essays on Hispanism not referenced elsewhere in this Introduction include Epps and Fernández Cifuentes (2005) and Buffery, Davis and Hooper (2007).
5. It is our sincere hope that similar volumes can be created that tackle Lusophone and non-peninsular Spanish speaking cultures and, indeed, the intersections of those with questions raised in *The Modern Spanish Canon*.
6. As well as his edited volume with Fernandes, see also Pérez Isasi (2013) which addresses the limits of 'Spanishness' in early literary histories of Spain.
7. The three data collections were taken in the academic years 1998–99, 2006–07 and 2015–16. The first collection was only peninsular literature, later collections also included film and non-peninsular literature. See Davis (2001, 2010 and 2018).
8. See Jiménez Torres 2016.

CHAPTER 1

❖

New Cartographies of Hispanism: From Spanish to Iberian Literary History?[1]

Santiago Pérez Isasi

Literary history, national identity, canon

The idea of 'revising the canon' also necessarily means revising the way in which it was created diachronically, through a succession of operations that, although ideological in nature, were presented as objective or aesthetically driven. It is well known by now, to the point of being almost a commonplace, that literary history and national identity were derived from the deep reconfiguration of European mentalities brought by Central-European Romanticism.[2] Not only was literary history born simultaneously with nationalist ideology, as its creative twin: it was born attached to it, to the point that many scholars think that separation could be fatal (in other words, that literary history is inseparable from nationalistic ideology).

It is not my intention to imagine a parallel universe in which literary history and national identity were not so strongly intertwined from the beginning; we should not forget that this impulse to promote the knowledge of national literatures paved the way for the rediscovery of literary productions which were forgotten or underrated by previous classical standards. What I would like to show in the following pages is, firstly, that this national model of literary history relies on an implicit conception of the linguistic and cultural territory that promotes and celebrates homogeneity and erases difference; that in doing so it forgets and underrates other literary phenomena which do not respond well to the homogeneous conception of the nation; and in the last section, I will propose an alternative model for national literary history, which still has not had the development it probably merits: a non-national, non-teleological version of Iberian literary history, based on the idea of 'cultural polysystems', following the most recent publications in the field of Iberian Studies.

Of course, Romantic literary history had predecessors: the interest in literary productions and the need to give exhaustive accounts of their history had models from the eighteenth century and earlier, although the differences between such models and what was to become established nineteenth-century literary history are multiple. During the eighteenth century, literary histories (or rather, proto-histories) accentuated the cosmopolitan distribution of literature; they did not strictly differentiate literature in its modern sense from all other written works (scientific books, for instance); and they were less interested in constructing a narrative, than in gathering all possible evidence regarding their object. In fact, they varied greatly in genre and disposition, from the bibliographical catalogue (for instance, both *Bibliothecas* by Nicolás Antonio), to the *apologia* or defence of Spanish literature (such as the one included in the history of Spanish literature written by the Mohedano brothers, 1766–1791), with some early examples of a narrative chronological history, such as the *Orígenes de la poesía castellana* (1754) by Velázquez.

In contrast, nineteenth-century literary history soon adopted a narrative, chronological and teleological model, placing a people and its literature at the centre of the narrative focus, and limiting the scope of texts to those genres considered as 'literature' in a more restricted sense (epic and lyric poetry, theatre, fiction and history, only the latter having since lost its canonical status). As for the geographical, cultural or linguistic scope, although works as *Über dramatische Kunst und Literatur* (1809–11) or *Geschichte der alten und neueren Literatur* (1815) by August Wilhelm and Friedrich Schlegel respectively, maintained a global approach to literary history, the tendency towards the identification of nation and literature had already started; in fact, the classification of nations into Classical and Romantic, or into Catholic and Protestant (in works by the Schlegels), or even into Latin, Anglo-Saxon and Slavic (in Mme de Stäel's *De l'Allemagne*), was the first step towards a hierarchical division of literatures, the bottom layer of which would be the national space.

This new Romantic configuration of national literary history was applied, of course, to Spain and its literary production as well as to the rest of European –and non-European- nations and literatures; in fact, Spanish literature was a cornerstone of the Romantic critical paradigm because, together with England (and Shakespearean theatre in particular), it epitomized the idea of a nation that had reached the summit of Western literature by following its own spirit (and Catholic orthodoxy) and discarding classical rules. With this starting point, the histories written by Friedrich Bouterwek, J. C. L. Simonde de Sismondi or George Ticknor developed not only a canon, but also a fixed set of criteria with which to classify and assess Spanish literary productions, the first of which was their identification (not exclusive, but preferential) with the Spanish language, the Catholic religion and with popular production over high culture.[3] And while some of the ideas that guided the German and Anglo-Saxon readings of Spanish literature were rejected by Spanish critics and historians (mainly in what concerns its relation with Eastern cultures and Arabic literature), the basic principles at the heart of modern literary history were adopted fairly quickly.[4]

A partial and anachronic cartography

Until very recently, geography played a limited, almost non-existent role in literary history: none of the literary histories from the nineteenth century and the first third of the twentieth century include maps as a mnemotechnic or visual aid (although some of them include schematic summaries or tables of content, thus showing their pedagogical objective). There are, of course, geographical references in literary histories, but they are for the most part limited to the writers' birthplaces and places of residence, or to the place of publication of the literary works; geography is rarely a determining factor in the organization of the history. Literary works are presented chronologically (in some cases, like Cejador y Frauca's history, in strict chronological order) or classified according to their genre and style, or in the case of Catalan or Galician literature (whenever included in Spanish literary history) by language. Literature, it seems, is produced in a common geographical pool, a cartographic and semantic vacuum that encompasses the whole Spanish space and in which all points seem to be equal.

This does not mean, however, that no geographical (or, better still, meta-geographical) conceptions are implied, or that they do not condition the way in which 'Spanish' literature is configured. The opening line of Bouterwek's *Historia de la literatura española* (which can, in a way, be considered as the opening line of modern Spanish literary historiography)[5] is paradigmatic in this sense. According to Bouterwek: 'Aunque el verdadero origen de la poesía castellana se pierde en las tinieblas de la Edad Media, no puede dudarse que los primeros acentos poéticos que resonaron en el Norte de la España fueron romances y canciones populares.' (Bouterwek 1829: 1) [Although the origins of Castilian poetry are lost in the mists of the Middle Ages, there is no doubt that the first poetic accent that resounded in the North of Spain were *romances* and popular songs].[6]

This sentence, in its simplicity, operates as a programmatic declaration that conditions most of the literary history that follows — not only the one by Bouterwek, but also most of those produced after him. Firstly, it equates Spanish literature with that written in Spanish (or 'castellano'), without any further explanation, as if no explanation was in fact needed; then, it locates its focus in the North of Spain (i.e., the Christian kingdoms), thus showing both the ambiguity of the term 'Spain' (which can be used to refer to the territory, to the State or to the nation that inhabits it) and an obvious ideological bias in the definition of Spanish identity; and it also shows the Romantic preference for some genres (popular productions in this case) over others in the creation of the canon. The external limits of Spanish literature, as (implicitly) defined here are not geographical, not even political, but linguistic, cultural and religious ones; however, the use of the generic term 'Spanish' in an anachronistic and partial way, serves to create an illusion of continuity between some (but only some) of the literary productions of the Middle Ages and the Golden Age, and the present-day (nineteenth-century, that is) Spanish nation-state: the *romances*, Golden Age Literature or *Don Quixote* were not just the oldest precursors of Romantic poetry, drama and novel, but also the models which would guide and inspire the new creators in order to regain the greatness of Spanish literature.[7] Spain, in this sense, is an abstract concept, a meta-geography, that is not linked to space as much as it is to the concept of 'people' or *Volksgeist*, and which therefore could live (hypothetically) without even a physical link to the territory it inhabits.

Let us examine another example, in this case from Amador de los Ríos. Amador de los Ríos's history, although incomplete (he only wrote the volumes devoted to the Middle Ages and to the period of Carlos I), is the most comprehensive literary history in terms of linguistic, cultural and geographical diversity, with chapters devoted to Latin, Hebrew and Arabic literatures, and to the literatures written in all the Peninsular kingdoms. In this case, Castile, or 'central Spain', does not have the monopoly of linguistic and cultural identity, but it is granted prevalence as the leading pole of literary development:

> ...aunque semejante desarrollo, que hemos procurado caracterizar en todas sus relaciones, se ha operado principalmente en la España Central y teniendo por intérprete la lengua castellana hablada en tan diversas comarcas, no es lícito olvidar la correspondencia legítima que halla en las regiones de Oriente y Occidente, donde hemos visto formarse dos diferentes dialectos, aspirando al par a constituir dos distintas literaturas. (Amador de los Ríos 1861–65, IV: 102)

> [This development, which we have tried to characterize in all its relations, has been operated mainly in Central Spain and with the Castilian language, which is spoken in so many regions, as its vehicle; however, it is not licit to forget the legitimate correspondance it finds in Eastern and Western regions, where different dialects were formed, aspiring to constitute two differeng literatures]

Not only are Galician and Catalan languages downgraded to 'dialects [...] aspiring to constitute different literatures', but, as Amador de los Ríos states more clearly later, it was central Spain that best expressed the otherwise multiple Spanish culture: 'Cabe a la España Central, que había adoptado por término de expresión la lengua castellana, la gloria de reflejar más poderosamente y con un fin más general aquella múltiple cultura.' (1861–65, IV: 151) [Central Spain, which had adopted Spanish as means of expression, was also worthy of the glory of reflecting, more powerfully and with a more general purpose, that multiple culture]. Ticknor expresses a very similar vision of Iberian multiplicity: Castile progressively adopted a cultural homogeneity that did not, in his view, stem from the changes in the political configuration of Spain and its different kingdoms, but from an alleged inherent linguistic and cultural superiority of Castile (and Castilian) over the other kingdoms (and languages):

> ...desde este momento la superior autoridad del castellano quedó finalmente asegurada y reconocida. El cambio no fue por cierto ni injusto ni inoportuno: la lengua del Norte era en aquel tiempo más llena, robusta y rica en idiotismos, y bajo todos los conceptos más apta y adecuada que los dialectos del sur, para ser la lengua nacional. (Ticknor 1851–56: I, 362)

> [From that moment, the superiority of the Castilian language was finally established and recognized. This change was not in any way unfair or inappropriate: the language of the North was at that time fuller, more robust and richer in idiomatic expressions, and by all means more apt and adequate than the Southern dialects to become the national language.]

Needless to say, these arguments are nothing but an *a posteriori* justification of the conception of Spain as a unified and monolingual nation: Castilian dominance of the Peninsula is teleologically defined as the desired final destination of literary history, and the inclusion of all literary phenomena that do not agree with this conception are nothing but obstacles that need to be explained, justified and progressively pushed to the periphery of the canon or to oblivion, as we will see in the next section. The key lies, I think, precisely in the different meanings attributed to the words 'Spain' and 'Spanish', whether in reference to the literature produced in the Spanish territory, or to the Spanish language, or to Spaniards in any language. This multiplicity of meanings leads to the confusion between Spanish (which could mean the whole territory) and Castilian (which is clearly limited) literature, which we have already seen in Bouterwek and again in Ticknor: 'Muy difícil es, por no decir imposible, designar con precisión la época en que nació la poesía española, o hablando con más propiedad, castellana' (Ticknor 1851–56: I, 15) [It is very difficult, if not impossible, to designate precisely the moment in which Spanish, or better said, Castilian poetry was born]. The narrative of Spanish literature, then, appears as the progressive correction of an undesirable situation: the polymorphic, plurinational and heterogenic medieval Spain was over the centuries transformed into one state, with one language and one common spirit — or so literary history would have us believe.

The myth of homogenous nations (and literatures)

Of course, this geographical, cultural or linguistic reduction, which promotes the idea of a progressive and valuable homogeneity, is not the only distortion that Spanish literary history produces on the materials with which it works. In fact, it could be argued that Spanish literary history, as it was understood during the nineteenth and twentieth centuries, failed in its objective to represent the reality of a cultural landscape that was, for the most part, multilingual, heterogeneous, mixed and complex. By focusing on literature written in Spanish, and by offering a homogeneous and compartmented image of the other literatures written in the Peninsula (if they were included at all), literary history hid or misrepresented the systemic relations that occurred through history between these different literary and cultural systems, and also between them and other European systems.

However, literary historians were aware that this homogenising image of Spanish (or Iberian) literatures did not coincide with the reality of the phenomena they were trying to describe; that historical and cultural reality was much more complex than what the dominant paradigm suggested. And so, they had two options: to apply strictly the one nation — one language — one literature paradigm, or to negotiate the inclusion of other linguistic realities within Spanish literature under certain, restricted conditions. The cultural capital of some literary productions, it seems, was too high for them to be just left out of the canon. This is obviously the case of the Galician *cantigas*, which not only connected Iberian literatures to other prestigious European traditions, but were (supposedly) written by a Castilian king himself.

> Tales *Cantigas*, en número de cuatrocientas veinte, poco más o menos, no pertenecen a la literatura castellana, puesto que están escritas en gallego, lengua que han empleado bastantes autores castellanos; pero no podemos dejar

enteramente a un lado un monumento de semejante importancia. (Fitzmaurice-Kelly 1901: 40)

[Those *Cantigas*, more or less four hundred and twenty in total, do not belong to Castilian literature, because they are written in Galician, a language used by many Castilian authors; but we cannot leave such an important monument completely aside.]

The same can be said about the productions written in Catalan during the Middle Ages and the Early Modern age: they are included in literary history because of their aesthetic value, but they are clearly subordinated to the nuclear identity configured from the geographical centre; they are located in a secondary position regardless of their literary value, because they do not conform to the prototypical 'national' canon.[8] When Galician and Catalan literatures start their decline and almost disappear from the literary map by the end of the 16th century, historians note it almost with relief, since this means that the unification of Spanish literature under one common language is almost complete, and this is considered to be a precondition of the literary Golden Age that would follow unification:

> ...a pesar de la vitalidad que todavía entrañaba la nacionalidad catalana, y verdes aún los brillantes lauros ganados por sus más celebrados poetas, comienza a recibirse en aquellas regiones, y dentro de su propio parnaso, la influencia de la lengua y del arte, que florecen en la España Central, augurando ya claramente, conforme dejamos advertido, la grande unidad literaria, cuya realización no estaba en verdad muy lejana. (Amador de los Ríos 1861–65: VI, 487)

> [...despite the vitality still latent in Catalan nationality, and when the laurel leaves granted to their most important poets were still green, the influence of the language and art of Central Spain was felt in those regions and in their Parnassus, thus anouncing very clearly, as stated before, the great literary unity which was really not very distant.]

However, the most obvious conflict between the national model of literary history and the Iberian cultural reality case is the intense and complex relation between Spanish and Portuguese literature, which over the centuries has passed through stages of both close interdependency and mutual ignorance: from reading Spanish literary histories, it would be difficult to imagine how closely intertwined Spanish and Portuguese literary systems were in diverse periods of time, especially during the 'Dual Monarchy' (1580–1640). During those sixty years in which both Spain and Portugal were governed by the same kings, but also in years prior and subsequent to those, there was a strong relation between both literary systems, to the point that it could be argued that they both merged into one: Portuguese authors wrote in Spanish; Spanish authors wrote with a Portuguese audience in mind; texts and genres circulated in both directions, and bilingualism was a general trait not only of many authors, but also of the texts they produced.

If we read Spanish literary histories, this complex reality does not become apparent, because it does not fit the national-monolinguistic configuration of literary history: to include the Portuguese writers who wrote in Spanish would violate self-imposed geographical limits, and therefore negate the principles that sustain modern literary history: the correlation between one nation (with its *Volksgeist*), one language and one literature. Therefore, when one author's work must be included because of its significance and its relevance in the Spanish literary system, it becomes an anomaly that needs to be explained and justified. About Gil Vicente's works, for example, Ticknor states that 'lo primero que llama la atención en [sus] composiciones [...] es su forma enteramente española, y el estar la mayor parte escritas en idioma castellano' (Ticknor I: 297) [...the first thing noticeable in his compositions is their entirely Spanish form, and the fact that they were mostly written in Spanish], and about Jorge de Montemayor he says that 'tanto en las composiciones que intercaló en aquella pastoral [la *Diana*], en prosa, como en un tomo de rimas que más tarde dio a luz, se encuentran a menudo composiciones castellanas y de lo mejor que salió de su pluma, pertenecientes a la escuela nacional' (III, 189) [both the compositions he included in his pastoral work in prose [the *Diana*], and in the volume of rhymes that he published later, Castilian compositions are often found which are among the best he ever wrote, and which belong to the national school], and later that his *Diana* 'está escrita en castellano muy castizo' (III, 276) [(The *Diana*) is written in a very proper Spanish]. The fact that he is Portuguese is not hidden, but it is compensated with an extra dose of 'Spanishness', both in the type of compositions he chose, in the style he used and in the language he adopted.

On the other side of the border, in Portuguese literary histories, the conflict between historiographical models and reality is even more acute. It is difficult for Portuguese historians to justify why their writers chose not only literary styles that differed from the 'national' ones (whatever that means), but even chose to write in a different language and subject themselves to a different literary rule. The solution was to erase those authors from literary history, to consider them traitors to the national order, and to gloss over that whole period by labelling it 'decadent'. The most extreme manifestation of this rejection of Spanish influence or dominance over Portuguese literary history, is simply to ignore the authors and works who adhered to it, and even complete periods of time which embody this idea of decadence and submission to a foreign rule:

> ...prescindi n'este Ensaio de mencionar os Poetas, que só escreveram em latin, e em hespanhol, bem que entre estes haja muitos de grande merecimento, e cujas obras possuo, ou tenho visto: mas fallando em rigor, esta falta não deve tornar-se mui sensivel, porque Poetas, que só escreveram em verso Latino, ou Castelhano, posto que nacessem em Portugal, não sam Poetas Portuguezes. (Silva 1850–55: I, 5–6)

> [...I left out of this Essay the poets which only wrote in Latin or Spanish, even if among them there are some which would deserve it, and whose works I possess or have seen: but strictly speaking, this absence should not have great impact, because poets who wrote in Latin or Castilian verse, even if they were born in Portugal, are not Portuguese.]

> Tenho, senhores, de passar em silencio, como improficuo para as boas lettras, todo reinado de D. João V [1707–1750], no qual o máo gosto em Portugal tocou o ultimo gráo da degradação nas poesias de soror Violante do Céo, Francisco de Vasconcellos, Frei Jeronymo Vahia e outros, sem que haja nesse longo periodo

um só escriptor de nome, poeta, ou prosador, que mereça ser analysado. (Sotero dos Reis 1866: III, 248)

[I have, gentlemen, to pass in silence, as not beneficial to fine letters, the whole reign of D. João V [1707–1750], in which bad taste reached in Portugal the utmost degradation in the poetry of Sister Violante do Céo, Francisco de Vasconcellos, Frey Jeronymo Vahia and many others, not being in that long period one single writer of poetry or prose worth analysing.]

Of course, this is an extreme example of a common trend. It shows how, even when a specific geographical territory is selected, and a specific set of literary phenomena is given priority over all the others, the modern literary historiography still has problems justifying itself, and accounting for a reality in which multilingualism, mixture and internal and external interrelations are the rule and not the exception. The ideal of linguistically and culturally homogeneous societies, to which both literary history and the nationalist ideology it embodies seem to aspire, never truly exists in reality; to achieve it, a distortion is needed, either of the reality itself, or of the narrative that explains it, and often, in both cases, with catastrophic consequences for difference and heterogeneity. In fact, this process has (or tends to have) a homogenizing effect in two ways: in relation to the past, because it favours some literary products over others, it creates the illusion of a progressive and desirable monolingualism in Spain; and to the future, especially since the development of the educative system in Spain, because it offers reductive models of literary creation and, if uncontested, limits the prestige and visibility of minor literatures in the Iberian context. The limitations of this national and monolinguistic model, however, altogether with the evolution of literary criticism, suggest that new approaches to literary history should be considered and put into practice; in the case of Spanish literature (or rather, of the literatures in Spain), Iberian Studies is one of the most promising alternatives.

Is it time for an Iberian literary history?

Despite all its shortcomings and inadequacies (some of which have been exposed in the preceding pages), and despite its continuous state of crisis, the national paradigm of literary history has maintained its almost undisputed hegemony for nearly two centuries, as both a scientific and a pedagogical tool. The continued publication of national literary histories (although with different approaches, for instance with a collective authorship or a wider conception of the canon, in recent years) has proved it to be resistant to the questions posed to its methodological and theoretical basis: the narrative and teleological structure, the creation of a hegemonic discourse, the selection of certain genres, authors and works over others, and so on. The limitation of literary history to national boundaries is also, of course, under scrutiny, and several proposals have arisen that favour a supranational approach to literary productions, from Comparative Literature to World Literature, including Area Studies, which offer a more cultural and interdisciplinary perspective.

In the case of Spanish and Portuguese literatures, this questioning of the national model of literary history has adopted the form of a new field, which still stands on dubious epistemological and academic grounds, but which has seen an impressive growth, both in the US and in Europe, in the last ten to fifteen years. The starting point of this new field is the adoption of a supranational object of study, with a geographical basis: the Iberian Peninsula.[9] Iberian Studies (at least, in their literary manifestation) focus on the Iberian interliterary system (in the terms of Dionýz Ďurišin), or the Iberian cultural polysystem (in the terms of Itamar Even-Zohar): the complex net of historical, cultural, political, and literary interrelations developed over centuries, with different degrees of intensity, and expressed in different languages.

It is not enough, of course, to substitute 'Spain' with 'Iberian Peninsula' to solve all the problems of national literary history; firstly, because Iberian Studies should not be a mere juxtaposition of Spanish, Portuguese, Catalan, Galician or Basque literary histories; the objective is not merely to expand the canon to include a few tokens from each literary and cultural space, but to expose the interactions between the different cultural areas; to understand the Iberian Peninsula not as the sum of monolinguistic and homogeneous entities, but as complex societies in which languages and literatures play shifting roles and relate with each other, and with various forms of power, in complex and not static ways.

We already have one such history of Iberian literatures: the *Comparative History of Literatures in the Iberian Peninsula*, published in two volumes in 2010 and 2016 by the International Comparative Literature Association. This history adopts the theoretical and methodological principles of Iberian Studies (most notably, the consideration of the Iberian Peninsula as a single but complex interliterary polysystem), and also the most recent configuration of literary history (collective authorship, opposition to chronology and teleology, plurality of methods, objects and perspectives...). This *magnus opus* has greatly contributed to consolidating the scope and prestige of Iberian Studies at an academic level.

I think, however, that yet another history of the Iberian literary system is possible: one that confronts the problems that afflicted national literary history as seen in the first sections of this text, which avoids teleology and essentialism, but which offers a chronological account of the evolution of the Iberian literary polysystem with a comparative and multicentred (rhizomatic, if you prefer) approach. This new literary history would not, let us emphasize once more, supersede all problems and limitations of national literary history, but it would solve some of the issues mentioned in the previous sections. Firstly, it would not extrapolate the contemporary concept of Spain (or Portugal) to times in which its political, linguistic and cultural configuration was very different; secondly, it would not impose an image of cultural homogeneity on the Iberian Peninsula as a whole, nor on any of the subareas it encompasses (which is so often the case when monolinguistic sub-canons are created in response to the monolinguistic, centralized and centralizing canon); it also would not impose an aprioristic centrality of Castilian literature over other manifestations, and it would have no trouble dealing with multilingual societies, writers or texts.

Itamar Even-Zohar's concept of polysystem could form the basis of a new Iberian literary history which better reflects the cultural realities of the Iberian Peninsula, in its long and complex evolution (what Joan Ramon Resina calls 'la dialéctica entre las naciones', 2009: 91 [the dialectic of nations]): if Iberian Studies are to be productive in the way of a new, more comprehensive and integrated literary history, they must be able to show how the Iberian interliterary community — or literary polysystem — is something other, richer than the mere sum of other smaller literary histories. It would also need to include phenomena that were eluded or excluded in the national literary histories, in particular multilingual or transculturated writers (what Ďurišin calls 'multi-domicile writers', 1988: 130), and it would also give a central role to the means of exchange between cultures, translation in particular. Cultural and literary relations between cultural centres and peripheries do not always take the form of peaceful cooperation, but can be shaped by tense negotiation with episodes of explicit aggression (see Ribera Llopis 2014 or Lourido 2014).[10]

It would also be useful to remember that these systemic relations are in themselves a construction, and not an essential and a-historical reality. Iberia as an object is itself the result of cultural and ideological negotiations, which cannot be understood without the concepts of South and East (see César Domínguez 2006 or Vecchi 2013). Iberia is an idea, a meta-geography, constructed both from outside and from inside, for example by those literary historians quoted in the first sections of this chapter (Bouterwek, Sismondi, Ticknor et al.) and then by the Spanish historians who adopted it. A history of the Iberian literary system as the one we are proposing should also include the history of the (self-)definition of Iberia, from the point of view of literary studies.

This reconfiguration of the field of Iberian Studies and of Spanish and Portuguese literary history is of course an ideological enterprise (although not in the same sense of nineteenth-century Iberianism, of course). This history of the multiple and dynamic relations historically established between the nations and cultures of the Iberian Peninsula is also a history of the struggle to gain and maintain visibility and centrality, to impose and reject certain linguistic, cultural, political and identitarian hegemonies in certain areas and periods. We should never forget, however, that these tensions and struggles are reproduced fractally, in each of the possible levels of study; the idea of cultural homogeneity is as false and as distorting whether we apply it to Spanish literature, to Iberian literature, or to any of the literatures that form it. The idea of complex heterogeneity, as proposed by Itamar Even-Zohar, must be the guiding principle of our job as historians of Iberian literatures: the moment we betray this idea, and we begin to impose an homogenising and teleological narrative, or to extrapolate to historical periods the cultural or political configurations of the present, we will be repeating the same patterns as the national literary history, regardless of our amplification of the canon or of the encompassed geographical area.

Bibliography

AMADOR DE LOS RÍOS, JOSÉ. 1861–65. *Historia Crítica de la literatura española* (Madrid: Imprenta de José Rodríguez)
BEHLER, ERNST. 1993. *German Romantic Literary Theory* (Cambridge: Cambridge University Press)
BIRKERTS, SVEN. 1993, *Literature: The Evolving Canon* (Boston, MA: Allyn and Bacon)
BLOOM, HAROLD. 1994. *The Western Canon: The Books and School of the Ages.* (New York: Harcourt Brace)
BOUTERWEK, FRIEDRICH. 1829. *Historia de la literatura española* (Madrid: Verbum, 2002)
CABO ASEGUINOLAZA, FERNANDO, ANXO ABUÍN and CÉSAR DOMÍNGUEZ. 2010. *A Comparative History of Literatures in the Iberian Peninsula* (Amsterdam: Benjamins)
CARNERO, GUILLERMO. 1978. *Los orígenes del romanticismo reaccionario español. El matrimonio Bohl de Faber* (Valencia: Universidad de Valencia)
DAVIS, STUART. 2012. *Writing and Heritage in Contemporary Spain. The Imaginary Museum of Literature.* (Woodbridge: Tamesis)
DOMÍNGUEZ, CÉSAR. 2006. 'The South European Orient: A Comparative Reflection on Space in Literary History', *Modern Language Quarterly* 67: 419–49
— . 2007. 'The Horizons of Interliterary Theory in the Iberian Peninsula: Reception and Testing Ground', in *The Horizons of Contemporary Slavic Comparative Literature Studies*, ed. by Halina Janaszek-Ivaničková (Warsaw: Elipsa): 70–83
DIONÝZ ĎURIŠIN. 1988. *Theory of Interliterary Process* (Bratislava: Veda, Slovak Academy of Sciences)
ITAMAR EVEN-ZOHAR. 1979: 'Polysystem Theory', *Poetics Today*, 1: 287–310
FITZMAURICE-KELLY, JAMES. 1901. *Historia de la literatura española*, 2nd edn (Madrid: Librería general de Victoriano Suárez, 1914)
FLITTER, DEREK. 1992. *Spanish Romantic Literary Theory and Criticism* (Cambridge: Cambridge University Press)
GABILONDO, JOSEBA. 2013. 'Spanish Nationalist Excess: A Decolonial and Postnational Critique of Iberian Studies' *Prosopopeya. Revista de crítica contemporánea*, 8: 23–60.
GORAK, JAN. 1991. *The Making of the Modern Canon.* (London: Athlone Press)
LEERSEN, JOEP. 2006. *National Thought in Europe. A Cultural History* (Amsterdam: Amsterdam University Press)
LOURIDO, ISAAC. 2014. *História literária e conflito cultural. Bases para umha história sistémica da literatura na Galiza* (Santiago de Compostela: Laiovento)
PITOLLET, CAMILLE. 1909. *La Querelle caldéronienne de Johan Nikolas Böhl von Faber et José Joaquín de Mora, reconstituée d'apres les documents originaux.* (Paris: Alcan)
POZUELO YVANCOS, JOSÉ MARÍA. 1995. *El canon en la teoría literaria contemporánea.* (Valencia: Episteme)
RESINA, JOAN RAMON. 2009. *Del hispanismo a los estudios ibéricos. Una propuesta federativa para el ámbito cultural* (Madrid: Biblioteca Nueva)
RIBERA LLOPIS, JUAN MIGUEL. 2014. 'Las letras catalanas y el entramado peninsular contemporáneo: modos y tópicos interliterariamente conectores' en *1616: Anuario de la Sociedad Española de Literatura General y Comparada*, 4 (special issue on 'Relaciones culturales ibéricas'), 59–76
SILVA, JOSÉ MARÍA DA COSTA E. 1850–55. *Ensaio biographico-critico sobre os melhores poetas portuguezes* (Lisbon: Imprensa Silviana)
SIMONDE DE SISMONDI, JEAN CHARLES LEONARD. 1841–42. *Historia de la literatura española* (Seville: Imprenta de Álvarez y Compañía)
SOTERO DOS REIS, FRANCISCO. 1866–73. *Curso de literatura Portugueza e Brazileira* (Maranhão: Tipografia de B. de Matos)

TICKNOR, GEORGE. 1851–56. *Historia de la literatura española* (Madrid: Imprenta de la Publicidad)
VECCHI, ROBERTO. 2013. 'Thinking from Europe of an Iberian 'South': Portugal as a Case Study', in *Looking at Iberia. A Comparative European Perspective,* ed. by Santiago Pérez Isasi and Ângela Fernandes (Oxford: Peter Lang), pp. 69–86

Notes to Chapter 1

1. This work is a result of my ongoing research contract, funded by the Fundação para a Ciência e a Tecnologia (ref IF/00838/2014), at the Centre for Comparative Studies at the Faculty of Letters, University of Lisbon, to develop the project 'Nationalism and Literary Regenerations in the Iberian Peninsula (1868–1936)'
2. J. Leersen explains the birth of nationalism in these terms: 'nationalism emerges in the nineteenth century from eighteenth-century roots: Herder's belief in the individuality of nations, Rousseau's belief in the sovereignty of the nation, a general discourse of national peculiarities and 'characters'. What changes from the eighteenth century to the nineteenth is this: 1.- an unprecedented imperial campaign mounted by Napoleon and fiercely resented outside France; this turns the eighteenth-century notions of tyranny and liberty from a power imbalance within the state (between rulers and governed) into one of power imbalance between states (between occupier and occupied); 2.- the rise of Romantic idealism which sees national character as a spiritual principle, a 'soul', rather than as a set of peculiarities; 3.- the Romantic belief that a nation's culture, and in particular its language, are the manifestation of its soul and essence; 4.- the historicist belief that all culture must be seen as an organic tradition linking generations across centuries' (2006: 125–26). Some of these traits (the idea of 'national spirit', the identification between nation and language or the historical approach to cultural phenomena, for instance) also condition the configuration of literary history from its birth. On the birth of (Spanish) literary history, see Behler (1993) or Flitter (1992).
3. Much might be said on how canons are created, maintained and dismantled, and the question of their validity, their ideological foundations and their use as tools for the creation of collective identities. Since the publication of Bloom's *The Western Canon* (1994), which sparked much debate and received fierce attacks and equally fierce defences, much bibliography has been published on the subject. In Spain, Pozuelo Yvancos analysed Bloom's arguments and confronted them with different theoretical approaches, specially with (poly)systemic theories. Other publications, such as Gorak (1991) or Birkets (1993) accentuate the construction and evolution of the canon, thereby questioning its stable and monumental nature, while Davis (2012: 53–56) shows the polysemy of the word and concept of canon, which could be at the origin of many of the debates and misunderstandings it provokes. For the purpose of this work, we adopt a constructive approach to the concept of canon, since, as we will try to show, it is an ideological object that depends on political and identitarian considerations as much as (if not more than) on aesthetic or critical criteria.
4. The transition between the old and the new critical paradigm was however not made without a fight; its most prominent and best known episode was the 'polémica calderoniana' [Calderonian controversy] between Böhl de Faber and José Joaquín de Mora, regarding the assessment of Calderón de la Barca's works. See Pitollet (1909) and Carnero (1978) for a detailed reconstruction of the controversy.
5. Bouterwek's *Historia de la literatura española* (1829) was a translation of the section on Spanish Literature included in his *Geschichte der Poesie und Beredsamkeit seit dem Ende des Dreizehnten Jahrhunderts* (Göttingen, 12 vols., 1801–1819). It was not only the first *History of Spanish Literature* published in the nineteenth century, but also the first one to apply the emerging German Romantic Literary Theory.
6. All translations of Spanish quotations are my own.
7. Not all writers and literary works were equally valid as models or as creators of a tradition: Juan de Mena, Góngora or even Garcilaso were considered, for most of the nineteenth century, as

heterodox writers who had abandoned the national trend of poetry.
8. This is also the case of some Castilian authors who, even if they write in Spanish, are not 'Spanish enough'; as the cases of Juan de Mena or Góngora suggest, being a good poet or writer is enough to be mentioned in most literary histories, but it does not grant a high position in the canon, nor the condition of 'model worth of imitation'.
9. César Domínguez has already advised against 'el peligro de transformar los espacios en entidades naturales, es decir, desideologizarlos' (Domínguez 2007: 78) [...the danger of transforming spaces into natural, de-ideologized entities]. It is necessary, as Enric Bou proposes, to consider the Iberian space as an ideological but not essentialist construct.
10. Of course, Iberian Studies do not exclude other possible configurations of literary and cultural space, nor do they aspire to solve all theoretical and methodological problems without contradiction. Joseba Gabilondo has pointed out, for instance, the problem of excluding coloniality from Iberian Studies (2013); other phenomena such as insularity, diaspora or the inclusion/exclusion of non-national minorities (from Asturian or Aragonese speakers to gypsies) also question the limits and limitations of Iberian Studies.

CHAPTER 2

❖

Mare Memoriae: Kirmen Uribe's Memorial Seascapes

Daniela Omlor

Kirmen Uribe's two novels *Bilbao-New York-Bilbao* (2008) and *Lo que mueve el mundo* (2012), originally written and published in Basque, mark a departure from the so-called *boom de la memoria histórica* in part due to Uribe's innovative style.[1] Unlike bestselling authors such as Almudena Grandes, who produce Realist fiction that is emblematic of the success of this boom, Uribe deliberately chooses to write in a hybrid genre that does not fall clearly into the category of the novel. His experimentalism goes beyond Javier Cercas's postmodern *relatos reales*[2] and could be considered more akin to the style of the *Nocilla* generation — in line with his date of birth — which is characterized by 'non-linear and symbolic structures; an emphasis on spatial rather than temporal organization; opaque language that calls attention to itself rather than acting as a mere vehicle for story. They also embrace technology and mass media as an integral part of personal consciousness and contemporary culture' (Barker 2011: 237).[3] While not all these descriptions are applicable to Uribe's fiction, he is certainly attuned to technological advances. Thus *Bilbao-New York-Bilbao* features illustrations of the plane's on-board computer detailing the distance to destination as well as extracts from Wikipedia. These direct references to technology are not present in the later novel, although a photograph of the protagonist is included, yet we must also take into account that Uribe's openness to experimentation transcends the realm of the written page. The performances of his texts, including his novels, both as video animations on the internet and as theatrical productions are testament to this attitude.[4] The intrusion or inclusion of technology, other media and the internet is important since they form a space which is normally considered to be that of non-fiction.[5] Uribe's stylistic choices are therefore not purely formal but are indicative of a shifting conceptualization of the realm of literature. As Alex Saum-Pascual observes:

> Así, la reconfiguración de géneros como la novela histórica, la crónica o la autobiografía, tradicionalmente encargados a rastrear las andanzas del explorador o el camino vital del sujeto, se enfrentan hoy en España al pasado de la historia oficial desde el presente de nuestra 'sociedad de información', permitiéndonos

repensar metodologías clásicas de narratividad así como reflexionar acerca del cambio en la manera contemporánea de experimentar y navegar el espacio y la memoria expandidas del entorno virtual. (2014: 118)

[Thus, the reconfigurations of genres like the historical novel, chronicles and autobiography, which traditionally had the task of following the adventures of the explorer or tracing the life path of an individual, nowadays in Spain confront the past of official history with the present of our 'information society', allowing us to rethink conventional methodologies of narrativity as well as to reflect on the change in the contemporary way of experiencing and navigating the expanded space and memory of the virtual environment.]

In addition, Uribe's works represent a change in perspective thanks to the new memory sites that his literature uncovers by looking towards the sea as a geographical connector between different (hi)stories, expanding precisely on the space and the memory that Saum-Pascual mentions.[6] In so doing, the author links the experience of the Civil War in the Basque Country to that of traumatic historical events in other countries bordering the Atlantic, drawing up an alternative map of memories. The author thus no longer views the evacuation of Basque children or the commissioning of Picasso's *Guernica* as solely relevant to the context of the Spanish Civil War. Instead, these episodes become integrated into a transnational history which is not clearly delimited by geographical borders.

In this chapter I propose to investigate to what extent the two novels represent an imaginative exploration of *multidirectional memory* (Rothberg 2009), as well as the importance of the sea as the backdrop for alternative narratives of the past. In his seminal work, Michael Rothberg urges us to move away from competitive memories, which are akin to 'a zero-sum struggle over scarce resources' (2009: 3). Instead the memory of the Holocaust should enable us to articulate 'other histories of victimization' (2009: 6), revealing 'collective memory as partially disengaged from exclusive versions of cultural identity and acknowledg[ing] how remembrance both cuts across and binds together diverse spatial, temporal, and cultural sites' (2009: 11). Furthermore, Uribe's shifting view of the past will be traced from nostalgia for a lost time in *Bilbao-New York-Bilbao*, which is associated with the stereotypically male intergenerational relationship between father and son, to a more forward-looking stance in *Lo que mueve el mundo* which demonstrates that literature can transcend the realm of the past and preserve what is worthwhile for future generations.[7]

Although Pierre Nora's influential *Les Lieux de mémoire* (1996) takes French history as its focal point, his observations can serve as a valid springboard for the analysis of Uribe's works. Nora opens his seminal work as follows:

Our curiosity about the places in which memory is crystallized, in which it finds refuge, is associated with this specific moment in French history, a turning point in which a sense of rupture with the past is inextricably bound up with a sense that a rift has occurred in memory. But that rift has stirred memory sufficiently to revise the question of its embodiment: there are sites, *lieux de mémoire*, in which a residual sense of continuity remains. *Lieux de mémoire* exist because there are no longer *milieux de mémoire*, settings in which memory is a real part of everyday experience. (1996–1998: 1)

Nora thus very clearly underlines that sites of memory are necessary once memory culture as such is no longer alive. Uribe's work *Bilbao-New York-Bilbao* is conscious of this step as it gathers in writing the formerly orally transmitted family history of the first-person narrator. The framework of the journey from Bilbao to New York then is not purely spatial, given that, while the narrator's memory is triggered by the locations that appear on the in-flight screen en route, he simultaneously travels through time both towards the future that awaits him at the end of the novel and the past which he captures within his narrative. Thus, he follows in his father's footsteps: 'A mi padre no le gustaba hablar del pasado. Como buen marino, prefería mirar al futuro' [My father did not like to talk about the past. As a good mariner, he preferred to look to the future] (2011: 17).[8] Notwithstanding the father's dislike of the past, Uribe's novel intends to make up for the lacunae derived from the paternal refusal to communicate the past, complementing thereby the maternal family's tradition of orality, at the same time as looking forward.

The desire to recover the father's hitherto unexplored past is intimately intertwined with the experience of loss. Indeed, the novel opens with a poetic comparison of the rings that delineate the lived years of trees and the winters experienced by a fish, stating that, 'Lo que para los peces es el invierno, para las personas es la pérdida. Las pérdidas delimitan nuestro tiempo; el final de una relación, la muerte de un ser querido' [What the winter is for fish, for people is loss. Losses demarcate our time, the end of a relationship, the death of a loved one.] (2011: 12). The narrator further elaborates: 'Cada pérdida es un anillo oscuro en nuestro interior' [Every loss is a dark ring on our inside] (2011: 12). Memory is thus literally an absence left behind by the dead and its mastery through narrative is a way of coming to terms with the loss suffered. Like his mother who, ever since her husband's death, keeps a diary to continue the dialogue with her deceased spouse, Uribe writes the novel also as a creative response to the death of his father (2011: 165). Having chosen not to continue in the family's seafaring tradition, Uribe decides nonetheless to map the sites of his memory onto a nautical chart of the Atlantic.

By structuring the narrative axis around the plane journey, Uribe might initially seem to select a no place (a utopos?) for the setting of his plot. However, when taking a closer look, it becomes evident that this is not the case. In the final instance, Uribe's narrative follows the Atlantic Ocean, the only exception being Frankfurt, whose airport represents a transit zone or hub on the journey to New York. Far from being uncharted territory, the Atlantic is both liminal and central to the world map. As Paul Gilroy has shown in *The Black Atlantic*, to consider 'the shape of the Atlantic as a system of cultural exchanges' (1993: 14), particularly given the triangular geography of the slave trade, is to shed new light on our understanding of the interconnectivities of black experience. Gilroy explains: 'I want to develop the suggestion that cultural historians could take the Atlantic as one single, complex unit of analysis in their discussions of the modern world and use it to produce an explicitly transnational and intercultural perspective' (1993: 15). The desire that Gilroy expresses to question 'the unthinking assumption that cultures always flow into patterns congruent with the borders of essentially homogenous nation states' (1993: 5) is one clearly shared by Uribe, who picks maritime rather than land borders to map the history of his Basque family. Of course, Uribe's subject-matter is completely different from Gilroy's, and applying some of the ideas developed by Gilroy to Uribe's fiction does not aim to relativize or belittle slavery; instead, creative application of some of Gilroy's theoretical framework may serve as a contrasting background against which to explore Uribe's writing.[9] Uribe draws on connections made by Gilroy in order to reconfigure the cartography of Basque history. Rather than representing a border, the sea comes to represent a web of alternative routes and connections that put Basque history into dialogue not just with the national history of Spain, for which it has to look inland, but that of other overseas territories which are not divided along the separation lines of nation states.[10] In the case of Galician literature, Kirsty Hooper mentions that 'texts and materials, crossed and recrossed the ocean between Coruña, Vigo, Habana and Buenos Aires' (2011: 19). Again, Galician history as profoundly marked by the trauma of emigration differs from Basque experience, even if Uribe includes the story of the *indiano* Berriozabalgoitia and the later one of Karmentxu Pascual's emigration to New York (2011: 49–50 and 182).[11] Nonetheless, for Uribe, the Atlantic also 'provides a means to re-examine the problems of nationality, location, identity and historical memory' (Gilroy 1993: 16).

Indeed, the narrator of *Bilbao-New York-Bilbao* describes the point of departure for the book as follows: 'Sentía que tras ese *Dos amigos* había una novela, una novela sobre ese mundo del mar a punto de desaparecer. Pero ese no fue más que el proyecto inicial. El trabajo de recopilación de datos para la novela me ha llevado por otros derroteros y, de paso, me he encontrado con muchas sorpresas' [I felt that behind this *Two Friends* there was a novel, a novel about the world of the sea which was about to disappear. But that was only the initial project. Working on compiling information for the novel took me into other directions and, en route, I made many surprise discoveries.](2011: 19). *Dos amigos* is the name of the small trawler owned by the narrator's grandfather, whose second named friend is unknown to him. The ship as another trigger for the narrative is relevant because, when focusing on the Atlantic, Gilroy considers it a chronotope (1993: 17) and much the same could be said of the aeroplane onboard which the narrative is conceived.[12] Many different stories are crystallized in this chronotope,[13] as such time and space are once more completely interwoven. The evocative name of the vessel alludes to the story of two different friends: Ricardo de Bastida and Aurelio Arteta, whose friendship forms another narrative arc which carries the novel forward. Coincidentally, Bastida's son's diary as a young boy recounts the same journey that the narrator is undertaking to New York, but onboard a ship in 1926.

The superposition of different temporal planes onto the same geography draws out their differences and similarities. However, one period that is of particular importance and which represents an anchor for many of the embedded stories is that of the Spanish Civil War. Thus, the engineer who worked for the narrator's father on his vessel *Toki-Argia*, Miguel Gallastegi, arrived in the narrator's hometown of Ondarroa after the war. Although he had been born in Madrid, Miguel's father was originally Basque and provided him with the addresses of trustworthy people shortly before being executed in the post-war period. Ondarroa appears as an idyll that provides refuge and remains untouched by the cruelties of the war. The only direct reference to violence is related to the behaviour of Italian soldiers, who clearly represent the foreign invader (2011: 89). This impression is heightened by the tale of the grandparents' lodgers, who came from opposite ends of the political spectrum as Communists and Falangists respectively but treated each other with courtesy (2011: 143). The rescue of Indalecio Prieto by Basque fishermen, who help him cross to France, constitutes another such instance (2011: 90).[14] Most importantly, Arteta is revealed as the artist who declined the commission for what was to become Picasso's *Guernica* (2011: 126). Instead of turning his art into testimony, Arteta prefers to focus on his family's safety in exile. It is not clear whether his rejection is to be interpreted as a missed opportunity. After all, Arteta dies in the supposed safety of his Mexican existence. Arteta's significance goes beyond that of a global symbol, since his murals for the BBVA building in Madrid were inspired by his summer holidays in Ondarroa, and a fold-out reproduction of *En la romería I* [On a pilgrimage I], now in the Museo de Bellas Artes of Bilbao, is included in the novel. It is also in front of these murals that the narrator learns of the peace treaty with ETA in 2006 (2011: 175). Most importantly, however, the mural in Bilbao is supposed to include a depiction of the narrator's grandmother Ana (2011: 198). The mural thus becomes another site of overlapping memories.

In the end, the anticipated mystery of the second friend mentioned on the trawler is discovered to be devoid of any significance, since the boat was named by its previous owners (2011: 187) — an ironic *clin d'œil* that plays on the reader's literary expectations. Yet another shameful revelation is made in the novel, namely that Liborio, the narrator's grandfather, sided with the Francoists during the war. This fact, which the narrator is unable to comprehend, motivates the book's 'confession': '[...] sentía la necesidad de contar la historia del abuelo Liborio, de no seguir obviando una realidad tantas veces silenciada. La guerra civil también fue una guerra entre vascos [...]. Debía verbalizarlo, exteriorizar que uno de mis abuelos optó por el bando incorrecto. Aunque me pesara mucho.' [[...] I felt the need to tell the story of grandfather Liborio, the need not to continue to omit a reality which had been silenced many times. The Civil War was also a war between Basques [...]. I had to verbalize, externalize that one of my grandfathers had opted for the wrong side. Even if I felt bad about it.] (2011: 142).[15] Even though the division runs right through the family, given that the maternal grandfather is a Basque nationalist, it does not cause a rift. When Liborio lies on his deathbed, the Basque-nationalist aunt Amparo keeps him company by reading Francoist press to him, all the while criticizing the lies it propagates (2011: 176). Moreover, the readers are also told about Liborio's imprisonment on account of his allegiance, which seems to counterbalance his dubious convictions. In spite of this awareness of the grandfather's wrong decision, then, the paternal lineage seems unproblematic. Women, who in one poem are compared to water (the water on which the fishermen travel?) (2011: 101), are rather more marginal for the narrator's creation of a space of belonging. While the narrator starts out declaring that 'El reto consistía en hablar de tres generaciones distintas de una familia, sin volver a la novela del siglo XIX' [The challenge consisted of talking about three different generations of one family without returning to the nineteenth-century novel] (2011: 136), the purpose seems to be much more that of creating a paternal genealogy for the narrator. The challenge is brought about by the death of the father, but also the acquisition of a son: 'La paternidad, por ejemplo. Hasta ahora ése ha sido un continente que ha estado completamente a oscuras para mí' [Fatherhood, for example. Until now it had been a completely unknown territory for me] (2011: 124). Paternity is an unmapped territory, particularly as the son comes to the narrator already as a fully formed human being, because his partner Nerea had Unai when she was very young. On the map of the Atlantic onboard the aeroplane are also traced the crossing paths of Unai and the narrator, for example, the first time Unai replied to one of his text messages, the first time they go together to the cinema and their discussions of football (2011: 139, 151, 165). The latter is indicative of their growing rapprochement and love: Unai, who only ever chooses Chelsea as his team on the Playstation, finally seems to pay heed to fatherly advice when he picks Athletic Bilbao. This incident constitutes a humorous, mutual acceptance, as it turns out that the Bilbao team now includes Drogba, Messi and other top players. On a more serious note, despite Uribe not becoming a mariner, he still gives ample space to his paternal family's connection with the sea, thereby unifying the maternal tradition of story-telling with the paternal one of nautical navigation, building his place in the paternal genealogy. Uribe's addition of a copy of a *Boletín Oficial del Estado* detailing all the trawlers registered in Ondarroa in 1982 further highlights this achievement. Moreover, we know that, when he started out as a writer, the first-person narrator longed for his father's approval, and can assume that the present narrative would obtain it. Initially, the father responded with an allegory about two village priests, one who preached in a comprehensible way and one who gave a twisted discourse which was only directed at the rich men of the village (2011: 46). That danger of not reaching the right audience for his story has been circumvented for good by the narrator.

Filiation and parentage are brought together in what could be deemed his inheritance, Unai. Thus, the novel ends with a poem dedicated to Unai with the following lines: 'Naciste a mis ojos con trece años./ Así, de repente' [When you were thirteen I saw you being born./ Just like that, suddenly] and towards the end: 'Hay que aprender a compartir/ a aquellas personas que amamos./Y yo soy otro más, el último en aparecer a la fila' [We have to learn to share/ those people we love./ And I am just another one, the last one to join the queue] (2011: 203). In his own role of the son, the narrator has transformed himself into the keeper of family (hi)stories. Reluctantly, his father traces the carefully-guarded fishing route to Rockall for him onto the pages of an atlas, where they will remain after the father's demise as physical proof of his existence (2011: 43). This is an extended image which reflects the continued presence of the grandfather, when after his death '[e]l motor del *Dos amigos* volvió a sonar dentro de la casa de Liborio, como un viejo corazón' [the engine of the *Two Friends* started to make a sound again inside Liborio's house, like an old heart] (2011: 198). Beyond the immediate family, the message of hope and love also continues. This idea is first expressed through aunt Maritxu's gesture of '*maite-maite*' and her assessment of the divisions of the war that 'Una cosa son las ideas y otra el corazón' [Ideas are one thing but the heart is an altogether different matter] (2011: 175). The potential for peace is illustrated by the aircraft cabin, which unites people of all different origins and backgrounds in peaceful sleep (2011: 136), more concretely, it is distilled into the idyllic image of two girls playing in Ondarroa, 'una blanca y la otra negra. Jugaban a cazar mariposas...' [one white and one black. They played chasing butterflies], most importantly: 'Hablaban euskera' [They were speaking in Basque] (2011: 199). This comes close to creating Borges's perfect map, the world (2011: 156), in which the Basque language is not marginalised.[16] The question arises whether the narrative manages to cut through the circularity of loss or whether it simply puts forward a vision of restorative nostalgia.[17] After all, there seems to be a generalized shying away from politics as a useful tool for human interaction, instead it is shown as arbitrary and brutal, a value which is to be replaced with an apolitical love for which ideologies do not matter.

Lo que mueve el mundo [What Keeps The World Moving] is still a personal novel; even if it does not take the author's family history as its starting point, it immediately presents the reader with the larger picture by describing the evacuation of Basque children as a result of the bombing of Gernika (2014: 13). From the very beginning it maps itself again on to the Atlantic by mentioning the steamer *Habana* and its usual route Bilbao-Havana-Mexico-New York. Only after the history of the ship is provided does the narrative zoom in on Karmentxu Cundín Gil, who is on board. Karmentxu is evacuated to Ghent in Belgium in 1937 as one of thousands of Basque children sent abroad. She is hosted by Robert Mussche, whose name constitutes the original Basque title of the novel. There is no connection to fishing or seafaring in this novel, but the Atlantic still features prominently. The narrator first hears the story of Karmentxu and Mussche while attending a literary festival in Medellín, which although not on the sea, lies within a country that does have an Atlantic coast (2014: 212). Furthermore, one of the evacuated children, Graciano del Río, later crosses the Atlantic to live in exile in Mexico (2014: 57) and Robert and his best friend Herman spend summers in England in their youth. It is on the return ferry from England to Belgium that Robert reads an underlined passage by Matthew Arnold on the importance of poetry for human existence (2014: 53).[18] In many ways, Belgium is thus also portrayed as open to the Atlantic in the same way as the Basque country.[19] Other connections emerge, for example the book *El dolor de Euskadi* [The Pain of the Basque Country] edited by Pedro Basaldúa, which the narrator finds in the library of Mussche's daughter in Ghent. Published as propaganda material for the Basque government in 1937, it also contains a poem in *euskera* whose author was shot in Vitoria during the Civil War (2014: 60). Mussche has first-hand experience of the Spanish Civil War, as he was sent to the Catalan front as a reporter in 1938. Yet both World Wars are also experienced by him indirectly and directly. In fact, Mussche meets his future wife Vic Opdebeeck when he is convalescing from injuries inflicted by the Germans in 1940 (2014: 96) and when their daughter is born they call her Carmen in memory of Karmentxu who returned to Euskadi after the Francoist victory, something that the Mussches always regretted (2014: 121 and 93). When Robert, a Resistance fighter, goes underground in Antwerp to evade capture by the Nazis , 'se acordaba continuamente de sus dos Cármenes' [he continually remembered the two Carmens] (2014: 133), whose fates are united in his mind and through Uribe's narrative.

In Uribe's later novel the Atlantic thus firmly connects the history of the Basque country with world history outside of a framework made up of nation states (significantly, this occurs via Flanders, another region striving for linguistic and national independence). This time it is Carmen Mussche who sets out to decipher her past (2014: 126), given that she was only a baby when her father was betrayed to the Nazis by a friend.[20] Like the narrator's mother in *Bilbao-New York-Bilbao* Mussche's wife Vic also keeps a sort of epistolary diary recording her feelings for Robert. Some of the letters were written without her knowing whether Robert was dead or alive and continue beyond his death. This effect is heightened through their intercalation in the narrative before the reader is aware of Mussche's fate. It is only towards the end that Mussche's deportation to the German concentration camp of Neuengamme and his enforced evacuation from there towards the end of the war are related. The Nazis brought thousands of inmates to the Bay of Lübeck on the Baltic Sea, where they were newly imprisoned on several ships, the most prominent being the former ocean liner *Cap Arcona* which had travelled between Hamburg and Buenos Aires via Rio de Janeiro before the war. As the prison ships were not marked as such, the RAF decided to bomb them one day before Germany's unconditional surrender, on 3 May 1945, causing the death of more than four thousand prisoners overall. Robert's body was never identified. This final 'naufragio' [shipwreck] (2014: 205) completes Uribe's map of the Atlantic in a painful climax.[21] Notwithstanding the traumatic denouement, the redemptive function of literature is ultimately once more underlined, since Carmen 'siente la carencia de la tumba de Robert, un lugar al que acudir cuando se siente triste y derrotada, o cuando le quiere dar una buena noticia' [mourns the lack of a grave for Robert, a place to which to turn when she feels sad and depressed, or when she wants to give him good news] (2014: 197). This acute lack of a grave is counteracted by the novel at hand, as is stated: 'Que este libro sea además una pequeña sepultura de papel para Robert. Esa tumba que Carmen nunca ha podido visitar' [May this book also be a small paper tomb for Robert. The grave that Carmen has never been able to visit.] (2014: 213). Within the context of the Holocaust this has become somewhat of a trope, even though a powerful one, starting perhaps with Paul Celan's 'Todesfuge' [Death fugue]. In addition, the last chapter reports Carmen's meeting with Karmentxu's brother and discloses that Herman named his daughter after his best friend Robert so that his memory may live on (2014: 225).

On a personal level, the second novel also represents the coming to terms with a loss, this time not that of the father but of the friend Aitzol Aramaio. However, it also relates to the birth of a child: 'Aquella pérdida coincidió con la llegada a casa de nuestra hija pequeña' (2014: 212). Thus, the memory of Robert and Herman's friendship mirrors the silent memory of another male friendship and the birth of the daughter has a certain echo in Carmen Mussche's birth. '[E]l hundimiento de un mundo y el comienzo de otro' [the sinking of one world and the beginning of another] (2014: 213). Other similarities between the two novels can be found in the importance of love as a guiding principle for life. Love constitutes the answer to the question that makes up the Spanish title and is the conclusion that Robert comes to in discussions with Herman: '¡Lo que nos hace vivir es el amor! Esa fuerza profunda es el amor' [What makes us live is love! That deep force is love] (2014: 36). Hence love triumphs over Nietzsche's will to power and Marx's emphasis on economy. This triumph is later embodied by Carmen's friendship with the son of the doctor who attended her mother during her birth, who was executed as a collaborator of the Nazis after the war (2014: 221). In effect, this bears resemblance to the overcoming of the divisions of the Civil War in Ondarroa. Nonetheless, there are some subtle differences between the two novels. Firstly, when the narrator reveals that he was suffering from a creative crisis after the death of his friend, writing no longer seems an uncomplicated therapeutic outlet (2014: 212). Secondly, although the narrator eventually follows Aramaio's advice to write about heroes by focusing on Mussche, it is with the awareness that '[e]n la Guerra quizá murieran los mejores, los de buen corazón. Pero ser un héroe tiene también su cara oculta, su reverso' [maybe those who died during the War were the best, those with a good heart. But being a hero also has a dark side, a flip side] (2014: 217). The negative side effects of being a hero are the impact of the decision on the family, as exemplified by Carmen's fatherless upbringing. This recognition is supplemented by the insight that '[c]uando tienes un hijo, los miedos aparecen al momento' [once you have children, fears appear immediately] (2014: 133). Political activism is thus not relativized but depicted in a less idealized way, and, unlike in *Bilbao-New York-Bilbao,* it now appears a risk worth taking.

By way of conclusion, it remains beyond doubt that Uribe underlines the importance of remembrance in both his novels. This is made particularly evident through his repeated refrain in *Lo que mueve el mundo*: 'Hay cosas que nunca se olvidan' [There are things which are never forgotten] (2014: 14). Even Alzheimer's cannot wipe out those most crucial moments of one's (hi)story as one witness testifies (2014: 15). In the latter novel Basque history is associated with WWII and the Holocaust through the evocation of Mussche, and Uribe thus cuts across national histories in the way that Rothberg intended.[22] Nonetheless, we cannot be certain that the collective memory of Basqueness remains entirely outside the realm of a commemorative national past. In fact, narrative multidirectionality might be perceived as aiding the endeavour of creating a past which is not only defined through its links with Spanish history. Therefore Uribe's use of the Atlantic seascape is not completely focused on 'routes' versus 'roots' as Gilroy would have it (1993: 20). Svetlana Boym states that restorative and reflective nostalgia 'are not absolute types' (2001: 41); it might then be that Uribe is only slowly moving from one to the other, aiming for 'reflective nostalgia' as 'a form of deep mourning that performs the labour of grief both through pondering pain and through play that points to the future' (2001: 55).

Bibliography

BARKER, JESSE. 2011. 'The Nocilla Effect: What is New in the New Wave of Spanish Narrative', *Journal of Spanish Cultural Studies*, 12: 237–48
BOYM, SVETLANA. 2001. *The Future of Nostalgia* (New York: Basic Books).
CELAN, PAUL. 1995. 'Todesfuge' in *Nachkrieg und Unfrieden: Gedichte als Index 1945–1995*, ed. by Hilde Domin and Clemens Greve (Frankfurt am Main: Fischer), pp. 17–18.
CERCAS, JAVIER. 2009. *Soldados de Salamina* (Barcelona: Tusquets).
CRUZ, JUAN. 2010. 'Kirmen Uribe: "El medio audiovisual está muy presente en la novela"' [interview], *El País* 22 April 2010, http://cultura.elpais.com/cultura/2010/04/22/actualidad/1271887204_850215.html [accessed 29 February 2016].
GILROY, PAUL. 1993. 'The Black Atlantic as a Counterculture of Modernity', in *The Black Atlantic* (London: Verso), pp. 1–40.
HOOPER, KIRSTY. 2011. 'Introduction', in *Writing Galicia into the World: New Cartographies, New Poetics* (Liverpool: Liverpool University Press), pp. 1–9.
—— 2011. NEW CARTOGRAPHIES? TOWARDS A GEOPOETICS OF GALICIAN CULTURAL HISTORY' IN *Writing Galicia into the World: New Cartographies, New Poetics* (Liverpool: Liverpool University Press), pp. 10–38.
LABANYI, JO. 2007. 'The Difficulty of Coming to Terms with the Spanish Civil War', *Poetics Today*, 28: 89–116.
—— 2010. *Spanish Literature: A Very Short Introduction* (Oxford: Oxford University Press).
NAFRÍA FERNÁNDEZ, MARÍA JÉSUS. 2014. 'Bilbao-New York-Bilbao: Un viaje por el universo literario de Kirmen Uribe', *Revista de lenguas y literaturas catalana, gallega y vasca*: 267–87.
NORA, PIERRE. 1996–1998. *Realms of Memory: Rethinking the French Past*, trans. Lawrence D. Kritzman (New York: Columbia University Press).
RODRÍGUEZ FISCHER, ANA. 2010. 'Dos mundos juntos' [review], *El País* 27 March 2010, http://elpais.com/diario/2010/03/27/babelia/1269652345_850215.html [accessed 29 February 2016].
ROTHBERG, MICHAEL. 2009. *Multidirectional Memory: Remembering the Holocaust in the Age of Decolonization* (Stanford: Stanford University Press).
SAUM-PASCUAL, ALEXANDRA. 2012. *Mutatis Mutandi: Spanish Literature of the New 21st Century* [unpublished doctoral thesis] UC Riverside: Spanish. <http://escholarship.org/uc/item/7sp5h42q> [accessed 30 May 2016].
—— 2014. 'Literatura española post-web: al borde de lo virtual, lo material y la historia. El caso de Jordi Carrión', *Arizona Journal of Hispanic Cultural Studies*, 18: 115–33.
URIBE, KIRMEN. 2011. *Bilbao-New York-Bilbao* (Barcelona: Seix Barral).
—— 2014. *Lo que mueve el mundo* (Barcelona: Seix Barral).

Notes to Chapter 2

1. While Jo Labanyi claims that '[t]he memory boom remains unabated, with practically all Spanish novelists having produced their Civil War novel' (2010: 73), elsewhere she also states that it 'has not translated into an increased interest in the workings of memory but into an assumption that the past can be unproblematically recovered' (2007: 106).
2. In the immensely successful *Soldados de Salamina* [*Soldiers of Salamis*] (2001) Cercas takes the 'true story' of the Falangist Rafael Sánchez Mazas as the point of departure for his narrative and includes the reproduction of a page of the diary that Sánchez Mazas kept while hiding in the woods after his failed execution in the book.
3. Of course, generalizations in terms of generation are problematic, but the limited scope of this essay does not allow for a detailed discussion of this issue here. References to the *Nocilla* generation are merely employed for the purposes of comparison.

4. See for example <http://ccaa.elpais.com/ccaa/2014/03/24/paisvasco/1395678292_452181.html> and <http://kirmenuribe.eus/en/multimedia/>.
5. Compare Saum-Pascual (2014: 117).
6. It is noteworthy that the verb 'navigate' should refer both to seafaring (its etymological root) and to travels through cyberspace.
7. As a caveat, I should add here that this chapter relies entirely on the Spanish versions of both Uribe novels translated from the Basque by Ana Arregi and Gerardo Markuleta respectively.
8. All translations are my own unless otherwise indicated.
9. Uribe is aware of the connection between slavery and the sea and incorporates the story of the slave ship *Two Friends* as a nested story, which Renata, his African-American seat neighbour, tells the narrator during the flight. In addition, there is an account of a slave arriving in Skagen as a present from the USA (2011: 107 and 170).
10. Interestingly, Nora also employs a maritime metaphor in his description of *lieux de mémoire*. He says that '...moments of history are plucked out of the flow of history, then returned to it — no longer alive but not yet entirely dead, like shells left on the shore when living memory has receded'. (1996: 7). This is also reminiscent of Unamuno's definition of 'intrahistoria'.
11. In the context of a discussion of Rosalía de Castro's *Cantares gallegos* and *Follas novas* Hooper remarks that '[t]he primary markers of Galician identity that remain in force today [are]: language, culture, and territory, the latter often inseparable from emigration, its "dark other"' (2011: 18).
12. Therefore, María Jésus Nafría Fernández's contention that the plane 'no deja de ser un terreno neutro, deprovisto de carga identitaria' [still remains a neutral territory, devoid of an identitary burden] (2014: 279) is questionable.
13. Uribe's statement that he wanted to 'situar la novela en un no-lugar. Pero en un no-lugar en movimiento' [situate the novel in a no-place. But in a no-place in movement] and that he wanted to represent 'el mundo como red de lugares' [the world as a web of places] does not contradict this observation (2011).
14. Indalecio Prieto was the President of the Socialist Party and a Minister in the Republican government.
15. This creates a parallel with the Welshmen fighting on both sides of the Falklands War (2011: 107).
16. As we can see, in the novel the Basque language itself is highly symbolic as a pure space of communication, untainted by evil. This is not only shown in the last scene featuring the two girls but also as a beacon of hope during the dictatorship, when it allows the mother and sister of the narrator to communicate without being understood by Francoist police: 'En aquellos años oscuros, la lengua marginada y clandestina salvó a mi madre y a mi hermana de aquel apuro' [In those dark years the marginalized and secret language saved my mother and my sister in that difficult situation] (2011: 199).
17. Svetlana Boym defines restorative nostalgia as 'at the core of recent national and religious revivals, it knows two main plots — the return to the origins and the conspiracy' (2001: XVIII). Further, '[r]estorative nostalgia puts emphasis on *nostos* and proposes to rebuild the lost home and patch up the memory gaps' (2001: 41).
18. A concrete example of the use of poetry is provided by the singing of 'À la claire fontaine' by one of the inmates of Neuengamme concentration camp to give new hope to the others and encourage them to continue the enforced march (2014: 206).
19. Mussche asks himself at one point why he writes in Flemish, a small language sandwiched between the big languages of German and French and comes up with the following reply, which could also serve as the explanation to Uribe's writing in Basque: 'Porque me coloca en el mundo como persona' [Because it places me within the world as a person] (2014: 139). Both novels under discussion here constitute this putting on the map of Basque history, memory and language by the author. Mussche only discovers euskera when he travels to Spain during the Civil War and a wealth of languages unfolds before his eyes (2014: 80).
20. Interestingly, the friend is not portrayed in Manichean terms, rather her actions are explained by her love for her children whom the Nazis threaten to kill. Prior to the denunciation and

entrapment of Mussche, Aline featured as another soul sympathetic to the Spanish Republican cause who housed another Basque child. Upon giving him up, Aline asks for Robert's forgiveness and is herself detained (2014: 147).
21. The lexical choice indirectly mirrors a shipwreck that affected Uribe's own family in 1908, when boats had gone out fishing from Santander: 'La tragedia fue tan terrible, que al recordarla incluso cambiaron el lugar de la muerte. Lo aproximaron, de Santander a Ondarroa. La memoria acercó la desgracia. [The tragedy was so terrible that when it was remembered the location of death was changed. It was moved closer, from Santander to Ondarroa. Memory brought misfortune closer.] (2011: 48).
22. A Jewish family who lodges Basque children in Belgium also stands for this encounter of different histories: 'La Segunda Guerra Mundial no trajo ningún bien a la familia Eckerman. Tanto el padre como la madre murieron en un campo de exterminio' [WWII did not do the Eckerman family any good. Both father and mother died in a death camp]. (2014: 28).

CHAPTER 3

Becoming Undone: Colour, Matter and Line in the Artwork of Marcel·lí Antúnez

Eva Bru-Domínguez

The human arts are thus as inhuman as the human itself is: both are the transformation, the reworking, the overcoming of our animal prehistory and the beginning of our inhuman trajectory beyond the human (Grosz 2011: 186)

The performance and installation artist Marcel·lí Antúnez has been a key figure in Catalan visual culture since the early 1980s. He is the co-founder of the internationally renowned urban theatre collective, La Fura dels Baus, a company that burst onto Catalonia's artistic arena with the experimental and groundbreaking performance *Accions* (1984), an initial version of which was first presented at the Annual Sitges Theatre Festival in 1983.[1] Informed by the artistic tendencies of the 1960s and the collective's experience in street theatre, the 1983 foundational version of *Accions* was enacted in an underground railway passage crowded with spectators. It was an enclosed setting which forced the public into direct physical contact with the performers. In this occasion, several nude men rushed into the confined space covered in egg, flour, sand and mud (Feldman 2009: 75). Avant-garde music, organic materials and industrial objects (including a car) were used in this seemingly chaotic performance, which 'appeared to be in a constant state of construction or undoing' (75) and which would ultimately propel La Fura onto the international stage. In the course of the 1980s, another two performances following these principles ensued, *Suz/o/Suz* (1985) and *Tier Mon* (1988), before Antúnez left the collective for good. However, the radical character of La Fura's creations alongside its use of live music and incorporation of technology and media would leave an indelible mark on an artist who was about to begin a solo career. It was a critical moment, for La Fura had been commissioned for the opening ceremony of the Barcelona Olympic Games (1992) and their show *Mar Mediterrània* would be under the gaze of the international community. That same year, Antúnez found himself 'abocat a una nova vida' [thrown into a new life] (2014: 88).[2] After a few years with the experimental graffiti, performance, and music group Los Rinos (1985–92), in the early 1990s Antúnez began to forge his own path. He remained true to the spirit and methodologies developed with La Fura, combining live performance, drawing, mechatronics, digital media, video and sound with an interest in the natural world, organic matter and biological processes. From the mid-1990s, the artist began to integrate virtual imagery in his life performances and the screen became the surface where his virtual double re-enacted some of civilization's founding myths and taboos. In his rather humorous and subversive approach to corporeality, the human body is situated at the interface between the spectator and the virtual field where it plays a key function in the visual retelling of narratives of origin and rebirth.

Drawing on Elizabeth Grosz's conceptualisation of 'modes of becoming', this chapter reads narratives of renewal and rebirth in Antúnez's body of work. In line with posthumanist thinking, which contests the privileged status and location granted to humans in relation to other species (animals and plants) and objects (technical and virtual), Grosz revisits Charles Darwin's theory of the evolution of life to explore processes of transformation in natural and manufactured objects. She reads the writings of Bergson and Deleuze through the prism of Darwin to explore how 'becomings undo the stabilities of identity, knowledge, location, and being' (2011: 3). According to the feminist philosopher, it is through these 'processes of destabilisation' (3) that new paths are forged and new identities come into being. For Grosz, this transformative force occurs within the parameters of history and culture. Whilst her approach to Darwinism is clearly intended as the advancement of feminist theory, the emphasis that she places on the unsettling of identity is fitting — to read Antúnez's artistic output, for the (un)doing of the body in his work is driven either by biological change or technical/digital intervention and often contextualised in the realms of myth.

This chapter considers formal, conceptual and aesthetic aspects in Antúnez's artistic output, focusing primarily on his 1994 performance *Epizoo* and his autobiographical documentary of 2005, *El dibuixant* [The Draughtsman]. In *Epizoo*, the artist explores the posthuman condition by situating his body at the interface between the computer and the spectator. Each physical interaction between public and artist is mediated by a computer game that simultaneously generates brightly coloured and distorted images of his body on a large screen. In *El dibuixant*, the artist identifies with the figure of the draughtsman to chronicle his own trajectory and to reflect on questions of methodology and practice. In this visual text, drawing is enacted as a means to review the past 'i després endreçar-ho en la memòria' [and then tidy it up in the memory] (Antúnez 2005). In my analysis I examine three interrelated areas: the use of colour in virtual imagery; the (dis)location of the material, biological and cultural body in virtual environments; and the notion of drawing as a form of thinking. Attentive to national and international art movements, this chapter reflects on the (dis)location of the embodied subject in Catalan postmodern artistic production.

1. Visual and performance art from the 1960s to the early 1980s

In September 2013, while working on a research project funded by the Irish Research Council at University College Cork (Ireland), I invited Antúnez to do a performance/lecture at the conference I had organised about the body in Catalan visual culture. His intervention took place at the Triskel Arts Centre and was followed by the screening of *El dibuixant*. Antúnez's interactive presentation centred on his use of technical devices in dramatic composition, a method he terms *sistematúrgia* [systematurgy]. Wearing his famous dreskeleton (an exoskeletal body interface), Antúnez moved gracefully on the stage, operating and manipulating with his gestures and shrieks a series of pre-recorded sequences that were being projected on the big screen and constructing a narrative that was governed by the movements of his body. More than this, by physically locating himself in the in-between of image and technology, he asserted his status as artistic creator while giving prominence to action and corporeality and celebrating his own artistic heritage. The first sequence that Antúnez activated was a clear allusion to the emergence of an art movement in 1960s Europe that would challenge existing artistic practices and establish the body as the artist's medium. With the images of female bodies covered in paint hustling towards a large wall canvas, Antúnez was citing the work of several international and national figures in the world of art, from Yves Klein's revolutionary *Anthropometries of the Blue Period* shown at the Galerie Internationale d'Art Contemporaine in 1960, to the 1978 performance *Trasa V = BPLWB* by the radical Catalan performance artist Jordi Benito. Moreover, the frenzied and vigorous movements of these women could also be read as the artist's wry sideways glance at his own trajectory. I am referring here to *Accions*, the first large-scale production by La Fura dels Baus in 1984, which featured a large white wall covered with bags of paint against which feeble male figures pressed their exhausted bodies. As Sharon Feldman has noted '[t]he pigments spewed across the canvas in an ironic recollection of the work of Jackson Pollock and Yves Klein' (2009: 76).

In order to unpack the ways in which these artists have informed Antúnez's practice,[3] I shall begin by discussing Klein's *Anthropometries*, for this performance is illustrative of a major shift in twentieth-century art which signals a turn to what Amelia Jones terms the 'postmodern performative' (1998: 86), of which body art is one of its salient expressions. Jones discusses Klein's practice in relation to the modernist masculine artist epitomised in the figure of Jackson Pollock:

> [t]he artist must be embodied as male in order to be considered an artist — placed within a (patri-)lineage as originary and divinely inspired — but his embodiment (his particularlity as a gendered and otherwise vulnerable, immanent subject) must be hidden to ensure his transcendence *as* disembodied and divinely inspired. (1998: 62)

This is a view rooted in the Cartesian privileging of cognition and mind, and as Jones argues, it is the role of the modernist art critic to communicate *his* (the artist's) transcendence as well as to veil *his* body. Jones coins the term 'Pollockian Performative' to explain how the body of the artist is performed in art discourse (61). She studies art historians and critics' popularisation of the photographs of the artist-at-work — where Pollock is seen leaning over the large horizontal canvas energetically flinging paint over it — and argues that these can be read as a form of unveiling the body of the creator as well as his excessive masculinity. Pollock's painting technique — and abstract expressionism in general — became associated with this hyperbolic, virile and phallic masculinity. Paradoxically, Jones notes that it is the indexicality of these images, that is, the traces or imprints of the physical body on the canvas, that conflate artist and his oeuvre and render him disembodied, and therefore transcendent (73). It is for this reason that Jones situates the Pollockian Performative at the threshold of postmodernism, where another type of artist is being configured, one who 'is self-consciously *performed* through new, openly intersubjective contexts (including video or ironicized modes of photographic display) which insist upon the openness of this and all subjects to the other' (67).

Generally acknowledged as a paradigm of the 'changing role of the body in art', and despite its contested use of the female body (O'Reilly 2009: 49), Klein's *Anthropometries* exemplifies Jones's notion of the postmodern performative. Imbued with irony, this performance dismantles the transcendent masculinity of Pollock's working methods: the phallic paintbrushes are replaced by female bodies, his bright palette is replaced by the emblematic IKB, International Klein Blue (developed by the artist himself), and the creative artistic practice no longer takes place in an isolated studio but at a gallery in front of the public (Jones 1998: 87). In so doing, 'Klein's work opens up the processual aspect of making and viewing art (with the engagement of spectatorial desire as part of the experience and meaning of the work)' (87). The emphasis on process and the involvement of the spectator in the performance are key elements in the work of Antúnez, yet these are taken to another level with his use of robotics, digital technology and computing where the body of the artist is placed in the in-between of a complex web of physical and virtual relations. As we shall see, in Antúnez's mesh of visual, digital and physical networks the (Pollockian) paintbrush and its association with masculinity, transcendence and the phallus is replaced by the playful figure of the draughtsman, situating the pencil and the paintbrush in relation to the material, biological and cultural body. Moreover, with his humorous and parodic approach to the act of drawing, the artist dismantles the masculinist attributes traditionally ascribed to the paintbrush.

This subversion of the realm of the masculine can also be recognised in the application of science and engineering to his work, which the artist deploys in either a critical or burlesque manner. Since his early days with La Fura, the incorporation of technology in art has been of concern to Antúnez and he has acknowledged the influence of the Swiss artist, Jean Tinguely, for his design of the musical automata of their *Suz/o/Suz* performance (2014: 86). Renowned for his kinetic art and sculptural machines, Tinguely was also a pioneer in carrying out collaborative projects with technicians. In the 1960s, he worked alongside Billy Klüver — an electrical engineer at Bell Laboratories — and the avant-garde artist Robert Rauschenberg. One of their most emblematic pieces is the machine-sculpture *Homage to New York*, installed in the gardens of the Museum of Modern Art in 1960 to perform an act of self-destruction in front of invited guests (Miller 2014: 37). Knowledge of American and European avant-garde artistic practices began to reach Catalonia in the late 1960s, and Barcelona soon became one of the most active experimental centres in the Iberian Peninsula with the emergence of numerous platforms and collectives exploring the points of contact between artistic disciplines and also literature (Marcer 2016: 264). In this context, video came to be a popular medium; not only was it employed as a technical tool to register ephemeral artworks (actions and happenings) but it was also exploited for its artistic potential (Parcerisas 2007: 512). By the early 1970s, video was being used by artists such as Francesc Abad, Jordi Benito, Robert Llimós and Antoni Muntadas (Parcerisas 2007: 510) and filmmakers like Antoni Padrós (Marcer 2016: 264). The artists of this period were interested in the erosion of borders between disciplines, as articulated by the Fluxus artist and poet Dick Higgins in his 1966 seminal essay 'Intermedia' (269). As an affordable technology, video was well liked among experimental groups and artists, for it opened up new possibilities in multimedia installation and many other art forms (Parcerisas 2007: 511). It was a format associated with the dematerialisation of the art object, a term coined by the American art critic Lucy Lippard in her influential book of 1973 to refer to the concept behind the work of art, be it material (sculpture, painting), ephemeral (actions, happenings) or processual (525–26). In Catalonia, dematerialisation was intimately associated with conceptual art and the highly politicised artistic practices that emerged in the last years of the dictatorship. Collectives of intellectuals and artists, like the Grup de Treball (1973–75), regarded art as a means of social and political struggle. In general, conceptual artists sought to broaden the boundaries of traditional art disciplines, exploring new methods and technologies and rejecting visual representation in favour of sensory stimulation and body art (528). Needless to say, many of these groups had been influenced by Joan Brossa's 1950s innovative *accions espectacles*, but also by the practices developed in the late 1960s by the group Zaj (Ferrando 2004: 232).[4]

Undoubtedly, the art movements and practices outlined above are part of Antúnez's own artistic lineage, yet other influences include the Viennese Actionists, in particular the performances of Günter Brus, Otto Muehl and Herman Nitsch. As the artist has stated, being the son of butchers, he found in Nitsch's slaughtering of animals an echo of his own childhood (2014: 83). Indeed, traces of Nitsch and his Dionysian rites are discernible in many of Antúnez's performances, especially in *Hipermembrana* (2007) but also in La Fura's *Suz/o/Suz* (1985), where the performers are seen eating raw viscera. While all these elements need to be taken into account, attention must also be paid to dramaturgy in order to grasp fully the complexities and nuances of Antúnez's artistic output, particularly, with regards to his work with La Fura. Because of its acknowledged global impact and long-lasting presence in the international stage, La Fura's productions have been studied extensively in the field of theatre studies (Delgado 2012; Feldman 2009; Sánchez 2006; Saumell 2007). For the purpose of this chapter, I shall provide a brief account of this collective's main traits and origins, focusing primarily on the aspects that are relevant to the analysis of Antúnez's solo career.

La Fura dels Baus began as an itinerant theatre company in the summer of

1979, touring the Catalan region with a cart and a mule. Feldman has noted that the experimental character of the collective's performances is rooted in an autochthonous theatre tradition in Catalonia that had been forced to explore alternative modes of expression because of the regime's privileging of theatre in Castilian and exemplified by theatre companies such as Els Joglars and Comediants (2009: 48). Informed by the ideas put forward by Antonin Artaud in his manifesto for a Theatre of Cruelty, La Fura was interested in exploring new methodologies, eager to liberate theatre from the constraints of the text, and to draw the public physically as well as emotionally into the spectacle (Sánchez 2006). The collective abandoned any notion of theatrical tradition and shifted the location of the spectacle to 'alternative, "found" spaces, uncontaminated by theatrical connotations' (Feldman 2009: 85), where the boundaries between spectator and performer were eroded. The performances of La Fura celebrated a return to the primitive and ritualistic man, to carnality, and to the assertion of the male body and his sexuality. Its multidisciplinary creations took place in post-industrial spaces and entailed a synthesis of artistic, performance and audiovisual modes of expression that was in line with the Bauhaus School of Art and many of the art practices previously discussed. The sexual and physical excesses that characterised its early performances were germane to the transgressive and hedonistic art forms that erupted in Barcelona in the years following the death of General Franco and the end of the dictatorship. As Feldman states, La Fura's works in the 1980s 'paint an emblematic portrait of Spain during a time in which unstable identities are in constant motion, competing in an ongoing struggle for legitimacy' (2009: 79).

In 1989, Antúnez left La Fura. His exit from the collective took place at a time when the group was consolidating its presence and status in the global context. It was a sudden — albeit firm — decision, which would plunge him back into the periphery of the art world. In the words of the artist, 'La necesidad de afirmarme como artista sin los privilegios que otorga una marca como La Fura dels Baus, no fue fácil' [the need to affirm myself as an artist without the privileges granted by a brand like La Fura dels Baus was not easy] (Antúnez in Salabert 2009: 283). Antúnez continued working with Los Rinos, a small group of multidisciplinary artists with whom he had been collaborating since 1985. Focusing initially on graffiti, the artistic production of Los Rinos also extended to installation, mural and video performance. Their approach to art was humorous and provocative, but the group mainly operated at a national level and had by no means the international prestige enjoyed by La Fura. In their 1991 performative cabaret, *Rinolacxia*, Antúnez saw 'el declive de una forma de trabajo colectivo, su fase terminal' [the decline of a collective way of working, its terminal phase] (283) and made the decision to develop his own line of artistic methodologies and research (283).

2. Virtual becomings and the (dis)location of the material body in *Epizoo* (1994)

In 1994, Antúnez presented the groundbreaking interactive performance *Epizoo*, a piece that marked yet another turning point in his career and signalled a return to the international market, from which he had been excluded since his work with La Fura (Antúnez 2014: 88). As an early example of human interaction with a machine, *Epizoo* aroused a lot of curiosity in international art circles and to date it has been performed in more than fifty cities in three continents. For the first time the spectator could control the movements of the performer's body by operating a video game. Each one of these interactions was translated into a digital image and projected on a large screen situated behind the artist. Antúnez had already created an interactive machine in 1992, *JoAn, l'home de carn*, a male robot covered with pigskin and cowhide and installed in a glass cabinet at the entrance of the busy Mercat de la Boqueria in Barcelona. The robot moved different parts of its body (shoulder, neck, elbow and penis) in response to a range of sound frequencies, attracting a lot of attention, spontaneous reaction (such as clapping) and much laughter among the people that visited the market. Clearly, *JoAn* not only belongs to the tradition of the automata, which originated in the fifteenth century, but also has its roots in the 1960s sculpture-machines of Tinguely, Rauschenberg and Klüver. However, with this installation there is a biological turn, that is, an attempt to bring together the material with the technological body that would pave the way to the development of the 'cyborg figure' (Giannetti 1998: 17) he becomes in *Epizoo*. Maintaining the playful approach to the body and sexuality already present in *JoAn*, in *Epizoo* the artist was connected to a computer system that allowed the spectator to interact physically with him. In this sense, we may speak of it as a performance that is in dialogue with Yoko Ono's *Cut Piece* (1964) and Marina Abramovic's *Rhythm 0* (1974) where the women artists submit their bodies to the whims of the audience. In contrast to the performances of these influential women artists, in Antúnez's work physical contact is always mediated by the machine and even the pleasuring or punishment of the artist is interpreted in mechanistic terms and expressed in the form of a flame situated at the top of his head that ignites only in response of sexual stimulation or pain. The exoskeleton is connected to a computer system, which allows the public to control his body movements by operating purposely-designed software, causing his buttocks, pectorals, mouth, nose and ears to move. Each interaction with the body of the artist is converted into grotesque and mutating images of his body and projected on a screen.

In his 2005 autobiographical documentary, Antúnez appears to have deliberately staged a type of audience/performer interaction for the purpose of discussing and showcasing *Epizoo* that parodies traditional notions of the male gaze and masculine sexual fantasies. A young, attractive, and wheelchair-bound woman uses a computer to take control over the body of the artist. The use of the wheelchair might be a reference to *Standard*, the feminist action by Fina Miralles in 1976, where the performance artist from Sabadell watches a screen tied to a wheelchair to question consumerist society's depiction of women in publicity (Aliaga 2012: 205).

In Antúnez's *El dibuixant*, the woman is seen to gaze studiously at the artist and purposely activate the electronic devices that simulate erotic spanking. This form of sexual foreplay is translated onto the screen as the hammering of grotesquely large buttocks while the exoskeletal device forces the artist to sway his hips in a manner that mimics humorously a movement that, traditionally, would have been associated with women. Here, long-established gender roles are reversed, the woman is the bearer of the gaze and her power over the object of desire is mediated through technology.

Antúnez had initially designed this performance as a pleasure machine that enabled erotic contact at a distance in order to question the social and psychological consequences of epidemics such as AIDS, but also to challenge enduring social and moral mores (Giannetti 1998: 17). In practice, the experience made the artist acutely aware of his powerlessness, which he equated to standing at the edge of the abyss (2014: 90), and concluded: 'la màquina sexual que imaginava una relació de carícia telemàtica i sense contagi es convertia en un pervers mecanisme de vulnerabilitat' [the sexual machine that imagined a relationship of telematic caress and without contagion turned into a perverse mechanism of vulnerability] (2014: 90). The same view is echoed by Claudia Giannetti, who argues that in *Epizoo* the audience 'is not a simple *voyeur*, but rather is transformed, without realising it, into a kind of instrument of martyrdom' (1998: 17). Giannetti analyses the work of Antúnez in terms of the posthuman subject and contrasts it with Stelarc's artistic production, where the body of the artist is situated in a continuum with the machine (19).

Studies of the posthuman analyse the (dis)location of the material subject in virtual environments and through digital and technical manipulation and the implications of this with regard to traditional humanist thinking (Braidotti 2013; Toffoletti 2007; Hayles 1999). The new relationships that are generated when the material subject comes into direct contact with (digital and virtual) technology, problematises the nature, location and status of the human. It follows that the posthuman subject challenges the basis of humanist thinking that renders the modern subject immutable and situates *him* (and his body) at the centre of history, politics, culture and thinking (Toffoletti 2007: 13). While not all posthuman subjects are by all means disembodied, the posthuman condition disrupts long-standing definitions of subjectivity, identity and the corporeal (13–14). Needless to say, the theoretical positions in the posthuman debate vary widely. In cultural theory, the most positive analyses have originated from the field of feminist studies and account for questions of corporeality, gender and race.[5] Katherine Hayles's (1999) exploration of disembodiment in virtual environments sets out to assert the links between the material body and electronically coded information. Her emphasis on matter and embodiment is particularly relevant to the reading of Antúnez's configuration of the body and (virtual) image as a continuum in *Epizoo*. Kim Tofoletti (2007), explores how the posthuman challenges binary definitions of gender identity and argues that it offers new possibilities, or rather, post-gender alternatives to the formulation of human subjectivity. For Rosi Braidotti (2013), the posthuman is laden with political significance, for it questions the typically racialised, sexualised, colonised, and otherised subject of humanism.

In his performance *Ping Body* (1996), Stelarc connects himself to the Internet allowing it to function as an external network of nerves that 'induces involuntary movements through his body' (127). Despite the fact that both Antúnez and Stelarc use their own bodies as an interface, the differences in their approach to corporeality are striking. In *Ping Body* there is no cultural, social or political agency for the external stimuli that trigger Stelarc's movements, which are disembodied and dematerialised, that is, they consists exclusively of random digitally and electronically coded information. In this case, the body of the artist is incorporated in a digital economy that has no specific origin or end. In this sense, *Ping Body* echoes Katherine Hayles's (1999) concern about the (dis)location of the material body in the posthuman, for while it 'deconstructs the liberal humanist subject, it thus shares with its predecessor an emphasis on cognition rather than embodiment' (5). In Stelarc's performance cultural and biological specificity are eroded, rendering the artist a truly cyborg figure, a mere material extension of the international digital network. In Antúnez's *Epizoo*, on the other hand, there is complicity, as well as (good or bad) intention on the part of the spectator when s/he decides to manipulate the body of the artist. With respect to the merging of corporeality and technology, Toffoleti argues that the body emerges 'as a boundary site — neither entirely natural nor cultural but a configuration that negotiates the limits of corporeal existence within an increasingly technological environment' (125). The fact that in *Epizoo* the audience can willingly inflict pain (or pleasure) on the artist, and the rendering of technology as the innocuous mediator of such relationships, poses ethical, cultural, and political questions about subjectivity, technology and the new systems of (physical, digital and virtual) communication.

The idea and/or possibility of a disembodied subject is one of the recurrent themes in studies of the posthuman. In *Cyborgs and Barbie Dolls*, Toffoletti suggests that the transcendence of the corporeal is in line with masculinist systems of thought that embrace the technological as a means to transcend the boundaries of a natural and biological body that is primarily coded as feminine:

> Rather than technology acting as a threat to humanity, it assists man in his endeavours to transcend bodily limitations and reach a pure state of selfhood. Evidently, this desire is grounded in a fear of the feminine and its associations with the body and abjection that threaten the primary of rational humanism. By becoming like the machine, man may control and contain the body, and accordingly, nature and the feminine (25).

The notion of the transcendent body of the artist brings us back to Jones's concept of the Pollockian Performative, where the indexicality of the image of the artist-at-work causes the symbolic dissolution of his own physicality. Pere Salabert — who has thus far produced the most comprehensive study of Antúnez's body of work — has explained the process of 'becoming an artist' in Freudian terms. The art critic and historian notes the recurrence of the father figure in Antúnez's work and argues that it habitually takes the form of an eye, which he associates with 'el falo allí presente, activo, sin perder su erección' [the phallus, present, active and erect] (2009: 197) [Fig. 3.1].[6] According to Salabert, in many of his performances, the panoptic father acquires mythical proportions and emerges as a sign of 'un

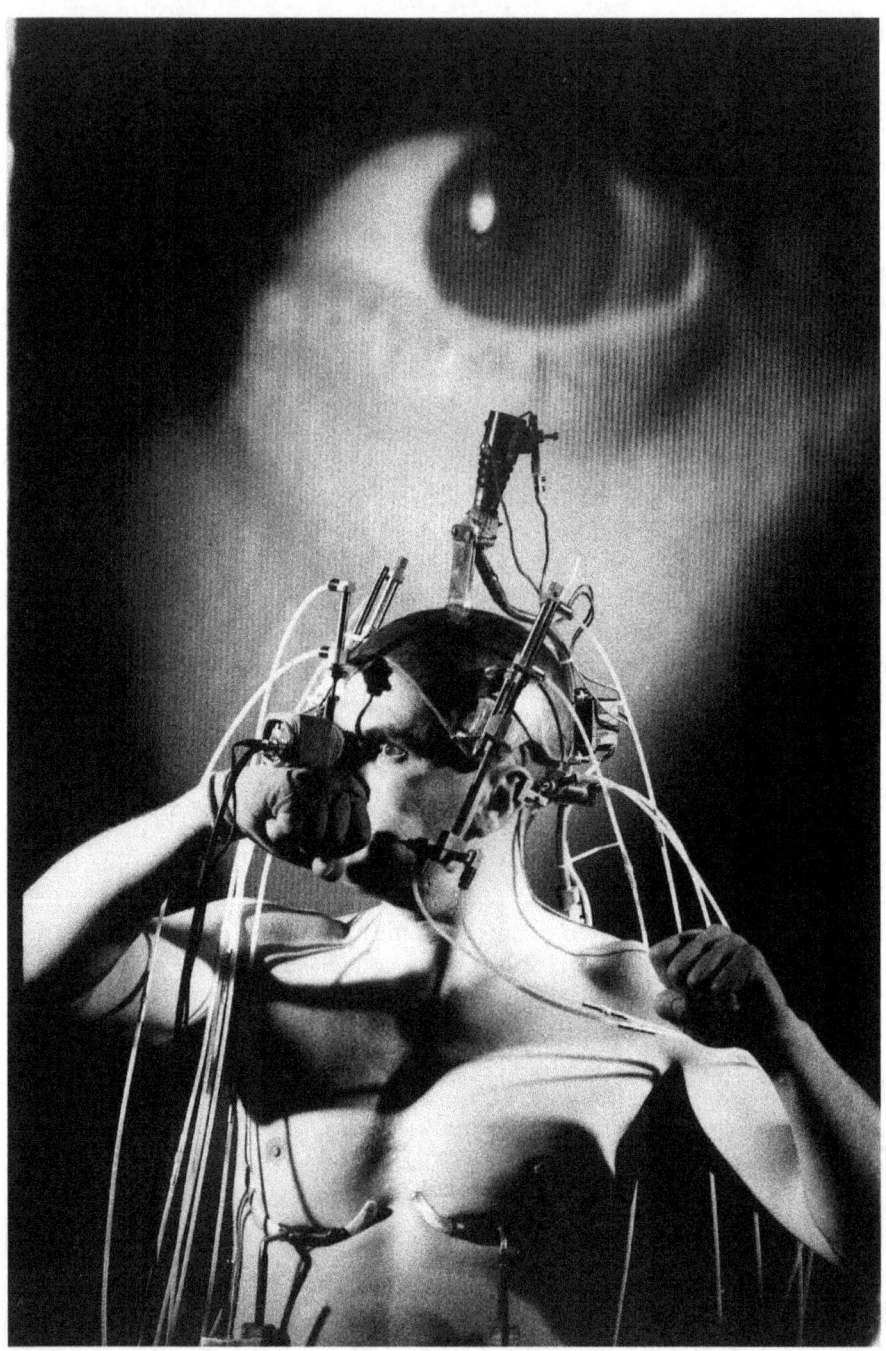

Fig. 3.1. Marcel·lí Antúnez, *Epizoo* (1996) © Núria Andreu

deseo-poder ilimitado que el hijo deberá igualar e incluso superar por la misma vía de la sexualidad, o bien, en su defecto, por la otra vía simbólica de un trabajo creador' [the unlimited desire that the son has to match or exceed either sexually or symbolically, by means of creative work] (198). While Salabert's analysis is grounded on the assertion of masculine sexuality in symbolic processes of identity formation, the art historian has also identified vestiges of the maternal, the semiotic and the abject body in the work of Antúnez. With regards to *Epizoo*, he has defined the imagery that is generated on screen as a 'metáfora visual del parto' [visual metaphor of giving birth] (376). Indeed, the artist's engagement with narratives of birth and the undoing and reconstruction of identity often takes him close to the realm of the feminine, the maternal, the embryonic and pre-linguistic, as well as the sexually undetermined. As I argue in the next section, this aspect of his work is conveyed visually in his symbolic use of colour.

Yet Antúnez's work also needs to be considered in terms of the postmodern subject, understood as one who is self-consciously performed through a variety of media. This is particularly relevant for *Epizoo*, where the artist has designed a variety of ways in which the software causes his body to become undone and reconfigured in the virtual (and visual) field. With respect to this imagery we may speak of a symbolic rebirth that is being enacted time and again, bringing different results in each interaction, but also one that is intimately related to the biological, cultural and historical body. If we are to consider these material specificities, it is useful to read *Epizoo* through Grosz's conceptualisation of 'modes of becoming' for it accounts for the complexities and nuances that each of these modes of (posthuman) existence might entail. In *Becoming Undone* (2011), Grosz asserts the importance of biological process in her readings of Deleuze and Bergson by drawing on Darwin's notion of sexual and natural selection. The feminist philosopher argues that nature acts as an agent of transformation, and as such, rather than being passive matter, it facilitates modes of becoming. Following Grosz's theoretical approach to becoming, in *Epizoo* the computer software functions as the enabling field that makes possible these new forms of emergence, that is to say, this virtual field would be the equivalent of the natural environment in Darwinian terms of life emergence, the Deleuzian plane of immanence, or Bergson's notion of duration, understood as the becoming of difference:

> If Darwin demonstrates man's immersion in and emergence from animal (and ultimately plant) life (or even life before plants and animals separated), it is Bergson, and through him Deleuze, who demonstrates man's immersion in and emergence from the inhuman, the inorganic, or the nonliving. (27)

According to Grosz, each becoming offers the possibility of actualising both the material and the virtual, the past and present, and the cultural, the technological and the biological, in other words, becoming is a means of congealing that which is latent and immanent (35). The art of Antúnez is born out of difference: it emerges out of the tension between technology and matter, biology and culture, reason and (sexual) desire, chaos and system, line and colour, and these are the dynamics that are in play in the structure, narrative and form used in *El dibuixant*.

Fig. 3.2. Marceŀlí Antúnez, *Bacteria Mural* (2005) © Marceŀlí Antúnez

3. Between colour and line: fluidity and system in *Epizoo* (1984) and *El dibuixant* (2005)

In *Chromophobia* (2000), the Scottish artist and writer David Batchelor argues that in the history of Western art, colour has habitually been considered of lesser value than line or form. The book sets out to explore this long-lasting suspicion of colour through the writings of a variety of authors, philosophers, artists and architects, and notes how, since Aristotle's time, colour has been perceived as feminine and dangerous: as the loss of form, identity and the self. The association of colour with the undoing of identity and form is worth considering in relation to Antúnez's artistic output. In his early work with La Fura, the pouring of tins of coloured paint over the performers' bodies was a habitual practice, and this approach to paint has continued in his solo productions, in particular, *DMD Europa* (2007), *Hipermembrana* (2007) and *Metamembrana* (2009). If the slippery and fluid texture of paint has been a feature of his life performances, his computer-generated imagery is filled with contrasting bright and bold colours which tint over the surfaces of the virtual bodies in *Epizoo* (1994), *Afàsia* (1998) and *Pol* (2002) as they are seen to fragment, merge, dissolve and reconstitute on the screen.

On the other hand, while colour and paint have such a central role in virtual figuration and performance, in *El dibuixant* the artist presents himself as a draughtsman [Fig. 3.2], the embodiment of technology, masculinity and control, for the pencil and the paintbrush have traditionally been associated with discipline, precision and, above all, the phallus. In fact, we only need to consider Picasso's engraving, *El pintor y su modelo,* to apprehend the gendering of the paintbrush in the history of Western art. In this engraving, Picasso links the drawing of a line with the penetration of the female body: a body that opens and unfolds under the weight of the artist as a surface or canvas where he inscribes and fulfils his desire (as artist and desiring male subject). As Salabert has noted about this image, 'pintar y penetrar el cuerpo femenino son en ella actos simultaneos, más aun: equivalentes' [to paint and to penetrate the female body are in this image simultaneous acts, more than this, equivalent acts] (2009: 573). The affinity between the paintbrush and penetration has also been ascribed to Pollock's action painting, as Jones asserts, the artist's 'conception of painting as an act of *penetration*, involving the ejaculatory activity of "dripping paint" from sharp, phallic objects onto a "resistant" (but ultimately yielding) surface exposes what is at stake in the particular embodiment of the artist' (1998: 73). Jones's statement, and its implicit reference to the 'Pollockian Performative' and the transcendent male artist, harks back to the excesses of masculinity in display present in La Fura's *Accions* and described by Salabert as an '[e]jaculatory discharge of that which is there — the world' (in Feldman 1998: 448). Surely the art critic's choice of words is by no means fortuitous, for as we have seen with regards to Picasso and many other male artists, the association of creative endeavour with masculine sexuality is a commonplace in visual culture. In this sense, Salabert's reference serves to situate the early work of La Fura in a continuum with the configuration of masculinity and sexuality in modernist art.

Having identified the problematic relationship between the act of painting and the hyperbolic and transcendent masculinity that haloes the modernist male artist, can we speak of Antúnez, the draughtsman, in the same terms? Does his artistic practice conform to this type of masculinity? In order to begin to address these questions, it is useful to return to Jones's definition of the postmodern artist, as seen with Yves Klein's *Anthropometries*, who self-consciously performs his identity through different media. In the course of *El dibuixant*, Antúnez is seen to transform gradually into this symbol: he smears his body in white and paints black cells and other micro-organisms all over it [Fig. 3.3]. In so doing, the material body unfolds as the artist's own canvas, he becomes a parodic embodiment of the paintbrush, as well as an assertion of the biological and physical body. In what follows, I will read Antúnez's identification with the draughtsman in his documentary as an ironic performative device that allows the artist to narrate the becomings and excesses in his work, for the undoing and reconstruction of identity and the body in Antúnez are visually represented by means of colour.

In *El dibuixant*, the documentary genre provides the artist with a platform from where to look back and draw a coherent and detailed picture of his career. The piecing together of all the aspects of his past artistic production is explained and performed through the act of drawing, which Antúnez executes in black paint over a large white wall. Some of these drawings are then animated and used as a means of narration, and each time a mural is completed, it is either covered over with white paint to give way to a new one, or simply redrawn in a manner that reshapes and

Fig. 3.3. Marcel·lí Antúnez, *El dibuixant* (2005) © Marcel·lí Antúnez

resignifies the biological forms and grotesque figures that populate it. Thus, the white wall becomes a palimpsest that bears traces of former images and histories. Sequences of this process, as well as the artist's own gradual transformation into a draughtsman, are woven into the documentary's narrative and create a space for reflection and analysis between the various artworks, performances and installations showcased and discussed. The black and white animations, the monochrome murals, and the sinuous black lines and forms that cover Antúnez's white body contrast with the dizzying toxicity of the colours in the virtual images screened. His bright palette — reminiscent of the artwork of Gilbert and George –is an assault on the sensory apparatus of the spectator, a form of aggression that is intensified by his use of music, electronic sounds, and a constant flow of movement.

Batchelor has noted how the slippery quality of colour renders it difficult to contain and categorise: '[it] is truly fluid: it spills over subjects and seeps between disciplines; and no one area can mop it up and claim a privileged or proprietorial relationship with the subject' (2008: 15). This view is evocative of Wassily Kandinsky's meditations on colour and form, where the Russian painter argued that 'form can stand alone as representing an object (either real or otherwise) or as pure abstract limit to a space or a surface' (1977: 36) whereas colour 'cannot dispense with boundaries of some kind' (36). Batchelor argues that the properties of colour exclude it 'from the higher concerns of the Mind' (2008: 23), for colour signifies irrationality or derangement, femininity, primitivism, ecstasy, kitsch, the oriental and, ultimately, the Other. Colour is also associated with cosmetics and, as such, it is deceptive because it veils, it covers and conceals. The Scottish artist remarks that the nineteenth-century French colour theorist, Charles Blanc, called for 'the need to subordinate colour to 'the "masculine" discipline of drawing' (23), and made use of the biblical image of the Fall to bring the allure of colour under control:

> The union of design and colour is necessary to beget painting just as it is the union of man and woman to beget mankind, but design must maintain its preponderance over colour otherwise painting speeds to its ruin: it will fall through colour just as mankind fell through Eve. (Blanc in Batchelor 2000: 23)

As Batchelor demonstrates in his book, Blanc is not alone in considering colour as that which needs to be regulated and contained. However, what interests me most from Blanc's passage is the way in which he weaves the idea of 'falling through colour' with the biblical narrative of creation. According to the French art theorist, colour is associated with the crossing of boundaries, more specifically with disobedience as well as with guilt and, as such, it is symptomatic of humankind's proclivity for sin.

The feminist philosopher Julia Kristeva has taken the discussion of colour in a different direction by situating it in the domain of psychoanalysis. In her essay 'Giotto's Joy', she explores the vital dimension of colour by associating its energies and rhythms with instinctual drives or pressures (understood in the Freudian sense as forces located between the psyche and the soma). Kristeva notes the impossibility of defining colour in linguistic terms or units and, in line with Kandinsky's writings, she suggests that, contrary to drawing and form, which are tied to the realm of true-likeness and representation, colour is fluid and transgressive for it resists any terms of codification (1980: 220). As such, colour poses a threat to the unity of the self but also offers the possibility of reconstruction: 'the chromatic experience constitutes a menace to the "self", but also, and to the contrary, it cradles the self's attempted reconstitution' (1980: 220). It follows that colour is linked to the pre-Oedipal stage prior to the acquisition of language, or the law of the father. Therefore, in the Kristevan system of thought, colour belongs to the realm of the maternal, the abject and the semiotic.

Kristeva's conception of colour as a powerful regenerative force is particularly useful for the reading of Antúnez's virtual imaginary, where the body is never bounded or complete but in a state of constant flux, and where gender boundaries are eroded and social mores upturned. The artist has a way of understanding and representing corporeality that is close to the concept of the grotesque and carnivalesque body elaborated by Mikhail Bakhtin in his influential *Rabelais and His World*. For the Russian philosopher and literary critic, while the grotesque constituted the threat of corruption of the official and refined by the vulgar and deformed, it was also a form of renewal and rebirth. This last point brings me back to the thesis of colour put forward by Kristeva, who ascribes to colour the properties of the embryonic, pre-Oedipal and sexually undetermined. Saturated images of modes of becoming are a constant in the work of Antúnez, and these are particularly relevant to *Epizoo* [Fig. 3.4]. In this performance, there are instances when the computer depicts the dwarfed body of the artist with grotesquely enlarged buttocks in harsh fluorescent yellow and contoured (and contained) by a thin border of bright ultramarine. Other figurations include manipulated shots of the naked artist depicted in contrasting harsh colours and featuring a disproportionately large head.

Often, Antúnez's on-screen persona appears enclosed in an almond-shape cavity and surrounded with gelatinous fluids. This luminous oval contour is reminiscent of the mandorla, a recurrent motif in medieval Christian art and architecture, which typically frames the figure of Christ in scenes of the Transfiguration and the Ascension, signalling the threshold between the material and the holy and incorporeal world. As Ann E. Pearson notes, this common medieval visual trope also harks back to the Incarnation of Christ 'when the immaterial divine took on form in Mary's womb' (2001: 83) and can therefore be read as 'a somatic sign for entrance into the cosmic cycle of birth-death-rebirth' (83). Needless to say, the references to the female external genitals (vulva) and the maternal body (womb) in this instance are obvious. In *Cyborgs and Barbie Dolls*, Toffoletti reminds us of the way in which technology and the machine is gendered, and inscribed as feminine: '[t]he desire to transcend bodily confines via technology is in keeping with the masculinist fantasy to escape the limitations of a corporeality coded "feminine". This utopian, technological rhetoric envisions the human merging *with* the machine' (2007: 25). According to Toffoletti, technology facilitates man's endeavour to transcend the body and, consequently, to overcome his fear of the abject (female) and material body: 'by becoming like the machine, man may control and contain the body, and accordingly, nature and the feminine' (25). In this sense, *Epizoo* challenges this view

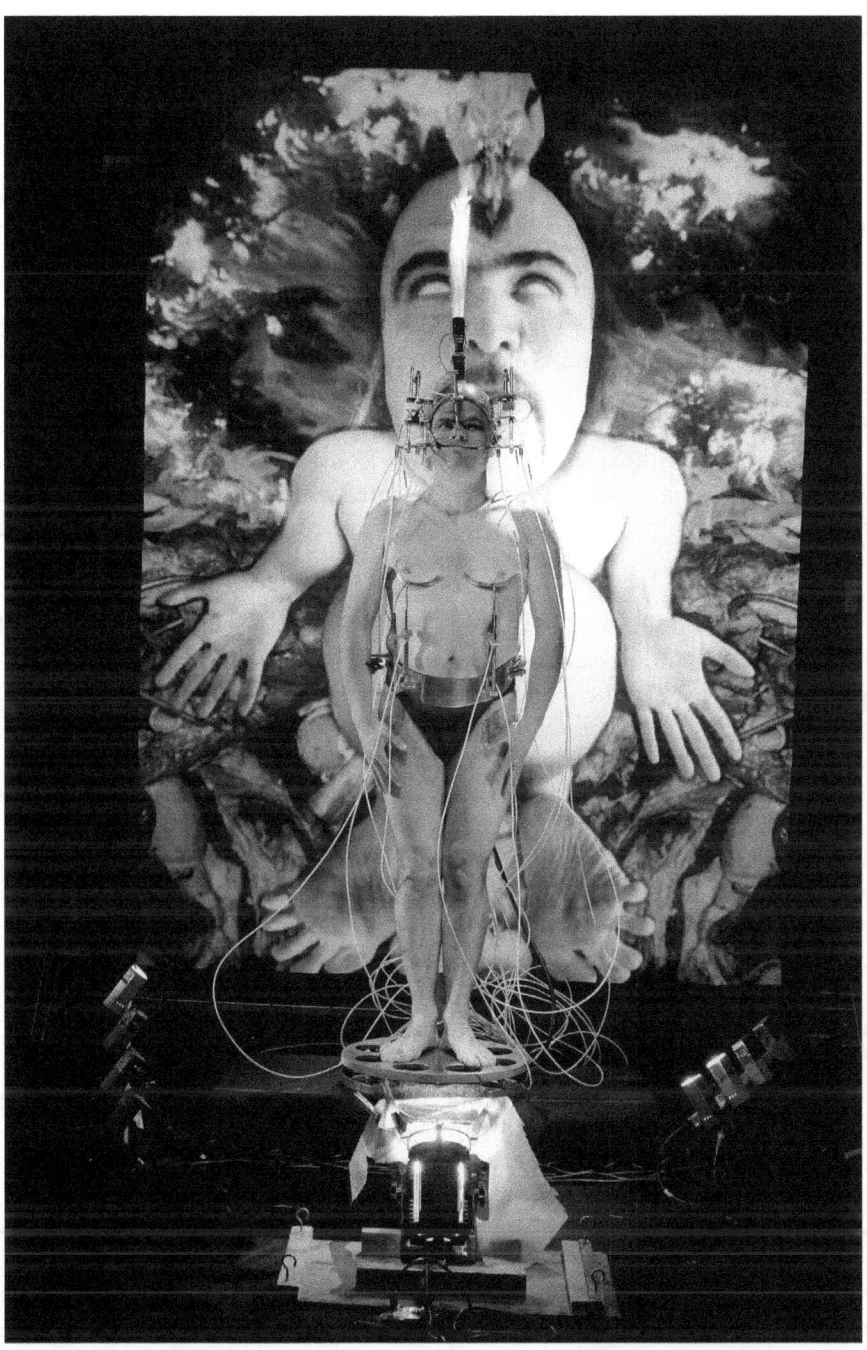

Fig. 3.4. Marcel·lí Antúnez, *Epizoo* (2015) © Carles Rodríguez

of the posthuman subject, for the interactive machine in this performance functions as an umbilical cord that links the biological and culturally specific body of the artist to a virtual maternal womb (the Kristevan pre-linguistic realm), where new forms of emergence are explored and alternative modes of being are represented in biological terms, that is to say, in an ongoing process of transformation.

However, if Antúnez's virtual undoings and reconstructions of the subject's identity are to be considered as a celebration of the mutating and sexually undetermined material body, some thought should also be given to the function of the computer as the 'brain' and generator of the images that are projected during the performance. After all, in *Epizoo*, each of the interactions and images have been thought out, pre-defined and codified in advance by Antúnez and his technical aides. Whereas the association of the computer with the mind — and the domain of the masculine — is inevitable, the more 'intellectual' act of writing a programme and its association with drawing needs to be considered in relation to the artist's views on methodology. In 2001, Antúnez wrote an article in a specialist art journal noting that while art historians and critics had studied his work for its symbolic and/ or aesthetic value, the design of the interactive devices and how these influence the structure of the narrative of his performances had often been overlooked (186–87). Since his early work with La Fura, Antúnez has been concerned with methodology and planning, and, in line with the collaborative projects between technicians and artists advocated by Tinguely and Klüver in 1960s New York, he has defended a work ethos that integrates the technological with the visual and the interactive. This system is especially relevant when preparing performances that require high levels of planning and interaction between virtual, computational and performative spheres: '[t]al com va passar a *Epizoo*, en la producció d'*Afàsia* es va fer necessaria la previsió. El dibuix en fou l'eina. ... Poc imaginava com d'important seria aquesta pràctica en el meu treball futur [Like in *Epizoo*, planning was a necessity in the production of *Afàsia*. Drawing became the tool... Little did I imagine how important this practice would be in the future] (2014: 96). In *El dibuixant*, the artist asserts drawing as a means of storytelling, yet rather than stressing its links with the domain of the mind, masculinity and transcendence, he relocates it to the realm of the bodily, the performative and the parodic. In this documentary, Antúnez defines drawing as a form of 'intuitive thinking', referencing the feminine — perhaps inadvertently — but also the unconscious, the undetermined and all that is associated with colour. In his performances, visual imagery and installations, Antúnez strives to collapse the borders between nature and technology, mind and matter, masculinity and femininity. His artwork is concerned with relocating the subject's identity in a non-binary field of emergence and he effectively combines colour, matter and line to explore new 'modes of becoming'.

In true posthumanist fashion, the performances and artwork of Antúnez articulate both the anxieties and hopes for an embodied existence that is increasingly dependent on and interwoven with simulacra, technology and the machine. Despite his ongoing dialogue with the international avant-garde, this experimental and multidisciplinary Catalan artist has occupied a mostly peripheral position in the arts scene. Until very recently, and with the exception of Salabert's comprehensive study, his oeuvre has been largely overlooked by cultural institutions, art historians and critics alike. Extant studies generally have primarily emerged from within the discipline of Art History in Catalonia and, as noted by the artist, have focused on the aesthetic and formal value of his production. In line with the research methodologies currently being undertaken in the field of Hispanic Studies, this chapter has examined these aspects of his work in relation to a much wider context, which does not only account for artistic heritage and historical context but is also concerned with unveiling the gendered, cultural and political dimensions beneath questions of methodology, aesthetics and form.

In the course of the last two years, Antúnez has begun to gain more recognition and visibility in national and international art circles, with a major retrospective at the Arts Santa Mònica (Barcelona) in 2014,[7] and the inclusion of his sound machine in the exhibition about the legacy of punk in contemporary art held at the Museu d'Art Contemporani de Barcelona in May 2016. Furthermore, in February 2016, Antúnez won the Excellence Award at the Japan Media Arts Festival (Tokyo) for his work *Ultraorbism* (2016), which combined live performance with animation and was held simultaneously in two locations, Barcelona (Spain) and Falmouth (United Kingdom). This increased visibility and process of canonisation will, it is to be hoped, invite further research into his vast body of work.

Bibliography

ALIAGA, JUAN VICENTE. 2012. 'El seient (atrabiliari) del binarisme de gènere' in *Circuits de gènere i violència en l'era tecnològica*, ed. by Mau Monleón Pradas (Valencia: Universitat Politècnica de València), pp. 199–213

ANTÚNEZ, MARCEL·LÍ. <http://marceliantunez.com> [accessed 29 May 2016]

—— 2014. 'Les formes del meu accionisme' in *L'accionisme. En els límits de l'art contemporani*, ed. by Tania Alba, Enric Cuirans and Magda Polo (Barcelona: Universitat de Barcelona)

—— 2013. 'Systematurgy' Performance/lecture [6 September 2013]. (Cork: Triskel Arts Centre)

—— 2001. 'Fenòmens temporals, accions tecnològiques i dramatúrgies interactives'. *Assaig de Teatre. Revista de l'Associació d'Investigació i Experimentació Teatral*, 28: 185–91

—— and MIGUEL RUBIO. 2005. *El dibuixant* (Panspermia, Benecé Produccions and Televisió de Catalunya)

BAKHTIN, MIKHAIL. 1984. *Rabelais and His World*, trans. Hélène Iswolsky (Bloomington: Indiana University Press)

BATCHELOR, DAVID (ed.). 2008. *Colour* (Cambridge, MA: MIT Press)

—— 2000. *Chromophobia* (London: Reaktion Books)

BRAIDOTTI, ROSI. 2013. *The Posthuman* (Cambridge: Polity Press)

DELGADO, MARÍA. 2012. 'Performing Barcelona: Cultural Tourism, Geography and Identity', in *Barcelona: Visual Culture, Space and power*, ed. by Helena Buffery and Carlota Caulfield (Cardiff: University of Wales Press), pp. 173–92

FELDMAN, SHARON. 2009. *In the Eye of the Storm: Contemporary Theatre in Barcelona* (Lewisburg, PA: Bucknell University Press)

—— 1998. 'Scenes from the Contemporary Barcelona Stage: La Fura dels Baus's Aspiration to the Authentic', *Theatre Journal*, 50 (4): 447–72

FERRANDO, BARTOLOMÉ. 2004. 'El arte acción en España entre los últimos veinte años y algunos más', in *Arte Acción 2. 1978–1998*, ed. by Richard Martel (Valencia: Institut Valencià d'Art Modern)

FUKUYAMA, FRANCIS. 2002. *Our Posthuman Future: Consequences of the Biotechnology Revolution* (New York: Farrar, Straus and Giroux)

GIANNETTI, CLAUDIA. 1998. 'Natura (et ars) non facit saltus' in *Marcel·lí Antúnez Roca. Performances, objetos y dibujos*, ed. by Claudia Ginnetti, trans. Matthew Tree (Sabadell: Mèdia Centre d'Art i Disseny)

GROSZ, ELIZABETH. 2011. *Becoming Undone. Darwinian Reflections on Life, Politics and Art* (Durham, NC: Duke University Press)

HAYLES, KATHERINE. 1999. *How We Became Posthuman. Virtual Bodies in Cybernetics, Literature and Informatics* (Chicago and London: University of Chicago Press)

JONES, AMELIA. 1998. *Body Art. Performing the Subject (*Minneapolis: University of Minnesota Press)

KANDINSKY, WASSILY. 1977 [1911]. *Concerning the Spiritual in Art*, trans. Michael T. H. Sadler (New York: Dover Publications Inc)

KRISTEVA, JULIA. 1980. 'Giotto's Joy', in *Desire in Language. A Semiotic Approach to Literature and Art*, ed. by Leon S. Roudiez, trans. Thomas Gora, Alice Jardine and Ledon S. Roudiez (Oxford: Basil Blackwell)

MARCER, ELISENDA. 2016. 'La transmedialitat com a eina de desastabilització a *Ice Cream* d'Antoni Padrós', in *Poètiques liminars: imatge, escena, objecte, transit*,ed. by Margalida Pons and Josep Antoni Reynés (Palma: Publicacions de la Universitat de les Illes Balears), pp. 263–76

MILLER, ARTHUR I. 2014. *Colliding Worlds: How Cutting-edge Science is Redefining Contemporary Art* (New York: W.W. Norton)

O'REILLY, SALLY. 2009. *The Body in Contemporary Art* (London: Thames & Hudson)

PARCERISAS, PILAR. 2007. *Conceptualismo(s) poéticos, politicos y periféricos* (Madrid: Akal)

PEARSON, ANN E. 2001. 'Revealing and Concealing: the Persistence of Vaginal Iconography in Medieval Imagery: the Mandorla, he *vesica piscis*, the Rose, Sheela-na-gigs and the Double-tailed Mermaid', (unpublished doctoral thesis: University of Ottawa)

SALABERT, PERE. 2009. *El cuerpo es el sueño de la razón y la inspiración una serpiente enfurecida. Marcel·lí Antúnez: cara y contracara* (Murcia: Cendeac)

—— 1998. 'Epifanías de lo espeluznante', *Cuadernos El Público* 34: 5–13

SÁNCHEZ, ANTONIO. 2006. 'La Fura dels Baus and the Legacy of Antonin Artaud', *Contemporary Theatre Review* 16: 406–18

SAUMELL, MERCÈ. 2007. 'La Fura dels Baus: Scenes for the Twenty-first Century', *Contemporary Theatre Review*, Special Issue*: Catalan Theatre 1975–2006: Politics, Identity and Performance* 17: 335–45

TOFFOLETTI, KIM. 2007. *Cyborgs and Barbie Dolls. Feminism, Popular Culture and the Posthuman Body* (London: I.B.Tauris)

Notes to Chapter 3

1. La Fura was formed in 1979 and the other founding members were Carles Padrissa, Pere Tantinyà, Teresa Puig and Quico Palomar.
2. Unless otherwise stated, all translations from Catalan and Castilian into English are mine.
3. Antúnez has noted the influence of the second avant-gardes in his work, mostly represented by the Fluxus movement, Yves Klein's Salon des Réalités Nouvelles, Jean Tinguely and the Viennese Actionists (2014: 83).
4. *Accions spectacle* refers to a range of formally and conceptually radical actions written by Brossa between 1946–62 with the objective of undermining the conventions of scenography, structure and text in favour of participative human actions and the everyday.

5. Posthuman studies cover a range of disciplines, including medical science, biotechnology and information technology. Francis Fukuyama (2002) is renowned for envisioning a bleak future where the essence of the human is compromised by biotechnological advancement and warns of both the ethical implications and the potential for the economic exploitation of life. Fukuyama does not make any theoretical contributions to posthumanism, but dwells instead on the dangers of medical enhancement, which in his view, jeopardise the basis of liberal democracy.
6. The artist's father had his face rebuilt and the eye replaced by a glass one after having been wounded in an explosion.
7. The exhibition *Sistematúrgia. Accions, Dispositius i Dibuixos* (Arts Santa Mònica) was complemented by a symposium about the work of the artist.

CHAPTER 4

Out of Time: Julia de Asensi and the Historical Legend

Rocío Rødtjer

Relegated nowadays to a footnote in literary histories — if mentioned at all — Julia de Asensi (1859–1921) is best remembered for her children's stories, redolent of a Victorian sentimentality. Labelled a 'romántica rezagada' ['belated Romantic'] in most recent studies (Díez Ménguez 1999, 2006; Castro Antonio 2010), this depiction reduces a complex legacy and portrays Asensi as a stern sepia-coloured matron policing the borders of morality. Yet stories like *El encubierto* ['The Covert/ Cloaked One'] published in 1883, in which she revisits the myth of the returning king, complicate this narrative despite a conscious effort on her part not to broach the subject of politics. The story has been read as a late ahistorical reworking of the historical figure of the eponymous Encubierto, believed by some to be the long-lost grandchild of the Catholic Monarchs, and therefore true heir to the throne. Historical chronicles record how in sixteenth-century Valencia, El Encubierto, a self-appointed royal, briefly presided over the uprising of craft guilds against the centralist government of Carlos I, in the so-called *Rebelión de las Germanías* [Revolt of the Brotherhoods] between 1521 and 1523. Eventually caught and executed, his claims were most likely false, yet his true identity still remains an enigma (Salle 2002, García Cárcel 1981). The episode provided perfect fodder for writers, revisited and elaborated upon many times, interest peaking during the first half of the nineteenth century for those discontent with the contemporary political set-up and seeking an alternative lineage (Muñoz Sempere 2011: 69). Spain's first serious attempt at constitutional monarchy, embodied by Isabel II, had disappointed both progressives and conservatives. El Encubierto became a key trope when discussing the visibility of the monarch in the nineteenth century, as liberalism gradually replaced the feudal model with more representative state models (García Cárcel 1981: 6). To read Asensi's *El encubierto* as merely a product of a residual Romanticism overlooks this political ancestry. It is a vantage point that reduces the story to a *timeless* sentimentalism rather than considering it a *timely* response, product of a specific socio-economic context. Whether the story itself addresses issues covertly or not, the choice to engage with such a controversial trope is in itself a political gesture. Revisiting overlooked texts like *El encubierto* can throw new light on what a critic has called 'one of the most studied (and yet, I would argue, still least understood) periods of Spanish and cultural history' (Hooper 2010: 196). This analysis aims to lend some visibility to forgotten women like Asensi, and to recover her from a sentimental and ahistorical no-man's land, or rather all-woman's land, since we find so many marooned there for failing to conform to canonical models. *El encubierto* challenges conventional notions of feminism, political agency and modernity, pointing instead towards a veritable spectrum of female lobbying and public involvement.

Although *El encubierto* occupies a mere forty pages, a re-evaluation of such texts has to contend with many foundational narratives before we can reinsert it within a wider network of discourses. This chapter is therefore divided into two main sections. The first part provides an overview of the discursive legacy that has led to the marginalization of women like Asensi, followed by a recontextualization of *El encubierto*, or rather its repoliticization. Such reframing can generate fresh readings of a century that witnessed the consolidation of Spain's constitutional system and of the role played by women in shaping it.

The second part offers a close reading of Asensi's take on the Encubierto legend. It highlights its surprisingly ambiguous ending — the disputed ancestry of El Encubierto remains a mystery. The men who killed the pretender portray him as an opportunistic impostor, whereas the women believe him to be a legitimate descendant of the Catholic Monarchs and the rightful heir. Asensi does not commit herself to any of the versions — the only known author to do so. As we will see in more detail, El Encubierto's true origins would be relentlessly instrumentalized, used to support different visions of Spain. Establishment historians dismissed any claims of legitimacy, whereas those eager to overturn the system validated them. Given Asensi's purported conservative persona, one might expect her to support the official version that depicts El Encubierto as a fraud. Instead, her unresolved ending destabilizes such expectations, and can be read as a commentary on this divided political landscape. It certainly becomes increasingly untenable to regard Julia de Asensi as someone unwilling to engage with her time.

Rethinking the Long Nineteenth Century

As a period, turn-of-the-century Spain has often been overlooked in favour of the Second Republic that succeeded it, when universal female suffrage was finally granted.[1] If anything, the perceived lack of progress when compared to some of its European counterparts was blamed on the weak hold of feminism in Spain — a feminism defined by equal electoral representation. The country has been depicted as trailing behind other European countries when it came to an explicitly political suffrage movement that demanded votes for its female citizens, characterized instead by a more diffuse concern with social improvements for women. Popularized by Geraldine Scanlon's *La polémica feminista en la España contemporánea, 1868–1974* ['The Feminist Debate in Contemporary Spain, 1868–1974'; 1986], this interpretation still colours our view of the period, in the same way that an insufficiently implemented liberalism was held responsible for the Francoist dictatorship. These two narratives of arrested development are in fact intertwined. Historians had traditionally not delved further into the political participation of women in the foundation and dissemination of a constitutional project they already regarded as incomplete and built on feet of clay (Burguera 2012: 18). Instead, initial revisionist efforts were directed towards documenting the years leading up to the Second Republic and its proclamation. This is understandable. Faced with a vacuum after forty years of Francoist regime and with the wish to show the contribution of women to politics, it follows that feminist scholars would initially recover those more in tune with modern sensibilities. These newly assembled genealogies of early advocates of female suffrage and subsequent supporters of the Second Republic helped legitimize the re-entry of Spain into democracy, propping it up with a respectable and progressive pedigree.

However, recent decades have seen a widening in our understanding of political participation as determined not only by the ability to vote, but by a whole series of practices and beliefs that underpin the emergence of constitutionalism and sustain representative democracy. Again, it has benefitted from similar attempts to reframe Spanish liberalism within European political cultures (Paquette 2015), contributing to a re-evaluation of the role played by women in its construction and dissemination. The involvement of women in these so-called political cultures has been addressed by Joyce Tolliver (2011), Ana Yetano Laguna (2013), María Cruz Romeo (2014) and Mónica Burguera (2012) amongst others. In her re-evaluation of female participation in the first half of the nineteenth century, Burguera in turn refers to the influential work of the historian Mary Nash, an early advocate of a more diffuse take, who in 1994 had already highlighted a plurality of feminisms, not all of them aligned with the goal of equal political representation.[2] Instead Nash suggested new models outside the conventional heuristic traditions to better assess the fight for rights in the closing decades of the nineteenth century (Burguera 2012: 18).

With the focus no longer exclusively on female suffrage and other overt signs of political engagement, this analysis suggests a more plural account of the different ways women sought to gain agency or visibility, recovering previously neglected contributions. Asensi's work should be read through this lens. It complicates the private/public dichotomy which early feminist revisions denounced and which led them to ascribe a passive role to the domestic realm. As Anne K. Mellor suggests '[a]t the very least, the conception of a hegemonic "domestic ideology" [...] must be fundamentally revised to include women's active role in the discursive public sphere' (2000:7). The division was in some respects more of a prescriptive, rather than a descriptive one. 'How things should be' rather than 'how they actually were', was shown most visibly by the many working-class women compelled to contribute to the household economy (Haidt 2011). It is true that women were excluded from the liberal project at its foundational stage by reserving suffrage to men and barring them from public office. While men occupied political positions and took part in military campaigns, the field allocated to women was plotted along more domestic lines, bound above all by their maternal role. One cannot deny such marginalization, yet the domestic sphere was not bereft of impact. Given its centrality in nineteenth-century discourses, by making domestic bliss a bourgeois ideal the private sphere became public, and women became national subjects (Cruz-Fernández 2014: 254). In the act of turning women into the moral barometers of the nation, the private was also political, or as María Cruz Romeo puts it, 'the writings on women and the family were political, in spite of the liberal aversion to mixing up these fields' ['[l]os escritos sobre mujer y familia eran políticos, a pesar de la aversión liberal a confundir ambos planos'] (2014: 109).[3]

Like many of her contemporaries, Asensi often shielded herself behind the modesty topos. In a rare candid moment, or perhaps a textbook example of this modesty topos — it could be read as both — Asensi alludes to the predicament that affected many of her female contemporaries:

> Porque mi atrevimiento no comenten
> nunca quise escribir nada profundo,
> mas tu libro es de aquellos que se sienten
> y que puede juzgarlos todo el mundo.
> Gracias te doy por él por vez primera,
> y faltando a una idea en mí arraigada,
> ofrezco mi opinión franca y sincera,
> aunque tal parecer no valga nada.
>
> [So that my audacity would not be commented upon
> I never wanted to write anything of substance,
> yet your book is one of those that are felt
> and that everyone can judge.
> I thank you for it for the first time,
> and disregarding an idea deeply entrenched within me,
> I offer my opinion frank and sincere
> even though such opinion is worthless.] (1890: 209)

Yet this did not prevent Asensi from engaging with the political landscape of the time. As Cruz Romeo writes: 'lo importante no es narrar la ausencia de las mujeres en las instancias institucionales o formales, sino atender otros entornos que, sin ser directa y abiertamente políticos, eran relevantes en el mundo de la política' ['the important thing is not to narrate the absence of women in formal or institutional instances, but to deal with those environments that, without being directly or openly political, were relevant in the world of politics'] (2006: 77). The literary realm is of course one of these key areas of influence. In the case of *El encubierto*, the legend could be read as a response to the so-called Carlist Wars, named after the pretender Don Carlos and his descendants. Brother of the deceased Fernando VII, Don Carlos had opposed the accession of Isabel II to the throne. With no male descendants, Fernando VII had changed the law so that his daughter Isabel could inherit the crown — a move opposed by Don Carlos as the next male in line. Liberals gathered behind Isabel II, Absolutists sided with Carlos, and the clash resulted in the first of three civil conflicts — the Carlist Wars — that would plague Spain during the nineteenth century.[4] Framed superficially as dynastic disputes, it was clear from the start that behind family feuds over lineage legitimacy lay the *political* legitimacy of competing visions of the nation. They would shadow the first footsteps of the constitutional monarchy inaugurated with Isabel's accession and later that of her son Alfonso XII. Asensi echoes this schism in her story, brought by a disagreement over whether the eponymous Encubierto is the true pretender to the throne or just a calculating impostor. Written in the aftermath of the closing conflict, Asensi laments the political tribalism that has led to so much bloodshed. The end of the last Carlist clash (1872–1876) had prompted even Asensi to abandon her nonpartisan position and express her public support for the newly-crowned Alfonso XII, whilst lamenting the human cost of the civil confrontation: '¡Cuatro años de lucha fratricida/cuatro años de tristes privaciones;/Tanta sangre vertida/Y tantos desgarrados corazones! [Four years of fratricidal fights,/ four years of sad shortcomings;/ So much spilled blood/ and so many torn hearts!] (1876: 481).

The poem had been published in the *Gaceta de Madrid* [Madrid Gazette], a previous incarnation of the *Boletín Oficial del Estado* [Official Bulletin of the State], to commemorate the end of the armed conflict. In other words, we find the normally shy Asensi voicing her version of events and asserting the legitimacy of Alfonso in an official organ. It reveals the establishment connections of Asensi, the daughter of a former Secretary of State (Díez Ménguez 2006: 20). Similarly, the publication in which *El encubierto* appeared lends it an added political dimension. The tale opens her book *Leyendas y tradiciones en prosa y verso* ['Legends and Traditions in Prose and Verse', henceforth referred to as *Leyendas*], which had been released as volume VXXXIII of the *Colección de los Mejores Autores Antiguos y Modernos, Nacionales y Extranjeros* ['Collection of the Best Authors Old and Modern, National and Foreign']. Started by Biblioteca Universal ['Universal Library'] in 1872 to capture a growing market of readers, curated collections like these abounded in the second half of the nineteenth century. With them, publishers aimed to make cultural milestones more affordable, driven by a mixture of patriotism and bourgeois capitalism.[5] Above all, the selection process helped shape a canon by deciding which texts represented the nation and were thus worthy to form part of its literary lineage — the notion of a transcendental national culture existing outside the realm of discourse, and merely awaiting discovery. This was reinforced further by the presence of politicians as contributors. Francesc Pi i Margall, former president of the First Republic, inaugurated the Biblioteca Universal collection with a volume on the Middle Ages.

Asensi and Pi i Margall were friends. The cultural cachet this carried is highlighted in an introduction to Asensi, who is described as '(s)olicitada su colaboración por hombres tan eminentes como el Sr. Pi i Margall' ['her collaborations solicited by such eminent men as Mr. Pi i Margall'] (Bastinos 1903: 197). Proof of this connection can be found in the National Library of Spain, which holds a first edition of Asensi's *Leyendas* that belonged to Pi i Margall, expensively bound together with another of her contributions to Biblioteca Universal. Yet despite these connections and her decision to tackle El Encubierto, a figure with such a controversial pedigree, she remains depoliticised. This is partly due to Asensi herself and the oblique fashion in which she pursued any political agenda. With this strategy, she was following the indirect approach suggested by progressive politicians like Pi i Margall. Speaking to a female audience in 1869, he warned women to abstain from 'mezclarse en nuestras sangrientas luchas civiles' [getting involved in our bloody civil fights] advising them instead that 'influir en la política, sin separarse del hogar doméstico' [influence politics without separating themselves from the domestic home] (quoted in Espigado Tocino 2010: 160).

Asensi's decision to write legends can also be interpreted in an ambiguous light that pre-emptively excuses any possible transgression, but transgresses nevertheless. In other words, Asensi downplays her intervention, and yet by picking El Encubierto, she is wading straight into ongoing debates on the limits of sovereign power and the changing mechanisms of legitimacy brought on by the rise of liberalism. Such ambiguity has been subsequently flattened out. This is in part due to her choice of genre. Since the historical legend held sway during the first part of the nineteenth century, it has led critics to label Asensi's legends as residual apolitical Romanticism, foregoing a wider discursive horizon.

The Romantic Roots of the Legend

In her mapping of Asensi's literary influences, Díez Ménguez highlights many junctions with historical legends popularized during the first half of the nineteenth century by José Zorrilla and Gustavo Adolfo Bécquer. The latter's *Leyendas* in particular casts a long shadow over future practitioners like Asensi. Published between 1858 and 1864 in periodicals, their subsequent popularity turned Bécquer's reimaginings of an idealised Medieval Spain into a byword for the genre. Yet the legend cannot be claimed as the exclusive domain of the conservative, but encompasses a spectrum of dissenting conceptions of the past and future of the nation. Published around the same time as Bécquer's work we find legends with very different ideological aims, such as *La dama de Amboto* ('The Lady of Amboto'; 1857) by Gertrudis Gómez de Avellaneda or Carolina Coronado's *La Sigea* ('Sigea'; 1854). Both female authors use the past as a platform to denounce the limited rights of women in the present. Coronado explicitly links the past to the present: 'han caído tronos, han pasado repúblicas, se han levantado imperios, y se han puesto en comunicación las gentes de los dos polos por medio de alambres' [thrones have fallen, republics have passed, empires have been founded, and the people from the two poles are communicating through wires] (Coronado 1854: 5). It is a modernity that makes the stalling of women's rights even more egregious.

By the time Asensi wrote her legends, nearly three decades later, the historical legend had been replaced by the Realist novel as the preferred vehicle to discuss this modernity. In this way, the decision of Asensi to compose legends implicitly voids her work of political content, as concluded — not unreasonably — by Díez Ménguez. Yet the legend continued to be cultivated throughout the century by the likes of Emilia Pardo Bazán, Vicente Blasco Ibáñez, Leopoldo Alas 'Clarín' and other stalwarts of late nineteenth-century narrative (Molina Porras 2013). It shows that the legends of Asensi were no atemporal oddities but instead formed part of a complex literary mosaic that the 'ism' labels tend to obscure or simplify. Still, the historical legend lacked the controversy that often accompanied the works of Pardo Bazán — seen as more in touch with their political reality. The latter was at the time engaged in a lively debate on the merits of Naturalism in the pages of the daily *La Época* ['The Times'] — the very same newspaper that published some of Asensi's legends that year.

Los Encubiertos and the Many Pasts

The legend of El Encubierto, as told by Asensi, takes place in 1526 and narrates the return of Don Lorenzo Valdés to his hometown in Valencia after years of absence, during which he has amassed a fortune in the New World. On his journey home, he notices that the local inn has changed owner, and upon enquiring is told by a group of children that this is due to a recent war, a reference to the Germanías conflict. He hears for the first time about the controversial El Encubierto, who had been one of the leaders of the uprising against the king before the Royalist authorities had him caught and executed. Lorenzo soon discovers that the war, and particularly the controversial capture of El Encubierto, has split his family into two camps. As a neutral observer, he hears both versions. First his older brother Antonio, one of the men who captured El Encubierto and brought him to justice, lays out his version of events. But before Antonio begins his tale, he pre-emptively discredits any other potential interpretations: '[l]a historia novelesca, en la que yo no creo — [...] ya te la contarán mi mujer, mi nuera o mi nieta; la real, hela aquí.' ['the novelesque story, the one I don't believe in — [...] my wife, my daughter-in-law or my granddaughter can tell you, you'll find the real one here'] (Asensi 1883: 13–14). By explicitly identifying his wife and other female relatives as acolytes of El Encubierto, Antonio claims objectivity at the expense of portraying these women as easily seduced by novelistic figures. Undermining female objectivity, Antonio insists that El Encubierto was just a conniving charlatan who sought power.

When Lorenzo, intrigued, queries the apparent familiarity of his narrator with the background of El Encubierto and his family tree — his brother had earlier alleged that nobody could ascertain the identity of the controversial leader — Antonio becomes agitated, a reaction that reveals his biased point of view and own emotional investment (Asensi 1883: 16). Antonio, as one who does not support El Encubierto, engages in vague innuendo, and avoidance of direct questions. In contrast, the sixteen-year-old Inés, a niece of Lorenzo, aligns herself as a fervent supporter of the now deceased leader. Her version is at odds with that of her grandfather Antonio, and she paints a completely different picture of El Encubierto, a depiction that resembles a hagiography in which he appears as a martyr and protector of the poor. Like her grandfather Antonio, she opens her story by first labelling other versions as fiction: 'Esa es una novela inventada por sus enemigos para desprestigiarle' ['That is a novel made up by his enemies to discredit him'] (Asensi 1883: 19). Likewise, when Lorenzo probes the veracity of her story, her passionate response gives her position away (Asensi 1883: 21).

As for El Encubierto himself, we never get to hear his version, as he is long dead by the time Lorenzo returns home. Yet he still exerts a strong influence on both his defenders and detractors, who keep his memory alive through the constant invocation of his name, together with their disagreements over his actions and legacy. Each of these depictions is vividly rendered to the extent that they still affect the actions of the living. In this respect, the legend of Asensi could be seen as echoing some of Zorrilla's work, specifically his historical drama *Traidor, inconfeso, mártir* ['Traitor, Unconfessed, Martyr'; 1849] on the figure of Sebastian I of Portugal, another popular variant of the returning king. This story centres on a baker who claims to be the Lusophone heir, dead in battle years earlier, a fact that did not deter several pretenders claiming his identity over the years. Yet in Zorrilla's version, the protagonist, with a contested pedigree like El Encubierto, remains similarly hidden from readers. Instead his importance is established through other characters who constantly allude to the mysterious figure, a technique that Asensi also employs to establish the centrality of the equally enigmatic El Encubierto (Senabre 1978: 36). However, unlike El Encubierto, the pretender in Zorrilla's tale not only shows up, but also dispels any doubts about his royal ancestry in the very last scene. Asensi takes it one step further and leaves her tale without its central character, who never materializes, leaving readers without closure.

The centrality of the two characters is reflected in the titles of both works. Zorrilla's *Traidor, inconfeso, mártir* can be read as a potted biography that summarizes the life of the protagonist as well as the different roles he fulfils. In a similar vein, Asensi's *El encubierto* refers to the eponymous shrouded one, although this might perhaps have been pluralized to *los encubiertos*, a term that would more accurately reflect the two competing portrayals presented to the reader throughout the story. A traitor to some and a martyr to others, Zorrilla's title could equally apply to the enigmatic figure who haunts the pages of Asensi's legend. In his study of El Encubierto, Cárcel christens this phenomenon 'encubiertismo' ('covertism'), that is, these attempts to articulate different social concerns projected onto the figure of El Encubierto (1981: 137–38).

A Controversial Pedigree

The phenomenon of *encubiertismo* has an extensive literary lineage, with adaptations traceable back to the sixteenth century,[6] though it is during the nineteenth century, with the rise of the liberal project, when often conflicting versions of El Encubierto, his significance and his legacy, start to multiply. The episode was repeatedly instrumentalised by everyone from progressive liberals to regionalists eager to discredit the authority of the reigning royal line by claiming it to be illegitimate. In his play *El encubierto de Valencia* ['The Cloaked One from Valencia'; 1840] Antonio García Gutiérrez backs El Encubierto's claims as genuine. The sympathies of Gutiérrez did not lie with the regime of Isabel II, as made patently clear in his poem *¡Abajo los Borbones!* ['Down with the Bourbons!'] composed after the dethronement of the queen in 1868.

Similarly some regionalists also rallied around the figure of El Encubierto, now fashioned as a Romantic hero who defends the downtrodden burghers and peasants of Valencia against an oppressive aristocracy and the centralist attempts of Carlos I. This version is found in the historical novel *El encubierto de Valencia. Leyenda histórica del siglo XVI* ['The Cloaked One from Valencia. Historical Legend from the 16th Century'; 1852], written by Vicente Boix. Others like Manuel Fernández Herreros saw a historical resonance between this revolt and more recent insurrections, such as the so-called Cantonal Revolution of the 1860s, which also unfolded in part of the Levantine region. This historical continuity is defended in *La Historia de las germanías de Valencia: breve reseña del levantamiento republicano de 1869* ['The Story of the Brotherhoods of Valencia: Brief Review of the Republican Rising of 1869'; 1870].

El Encubierto's portrayal as a champion of regional rights against a centralist government, together with his claims to descend from the legitimate male line, did not make him a popular figure amongst establishment historians of the later nineteenth century. Such claims were uncomfortably close to those held by supporters of the Carlist pretender and his heirs who had refused to accept the succession of Isabel II. It spurred historians like Manuel Danvila y Collado to refute any legitimacy ascribed to El Encubierto. Thus the version he promotes in his 1884 inaugural speech as a member of the Real Academia de la Historia ['The Royal Academy of History'] (1884: 47). Given this controversial pedigree, it is even more striking that Asensi chose to leave the true ancestry of El Encubierto unresolved, and is the only author to do so.

Instead the disputed pedigree of El Encubierto haunts Asensi's story, not only metaphorically but also literally, as an alleged apparition that returns each night to the room where El Encubierto was apprehended by his enemies. Although in disagreement about his origins, both Inés and Antonio vouch for the existence of this spectre. Intrigued by these apparitions, the neutral Don Lorenzo decides to sleep in this now cursed space in the hope he might disprove its supernatural dimension. After a fitful night plagued by oneiric sequences of a wounded white female figure, he wakes up to find that the bloodstains in the room — vestiges of the grim fate of El Encubierto — are present but freshly scrubbed, as if somebody had attempted to remove them. Don Lorenzo does not mention these irregular occurrences to his hosts, but decides to gather more evidence in his self-assigned role of Doubting Thomas before passing judgment.

Asensi hints at the involvement in these hauntings of the foster-sister of El Encubierto, driven to madness by her grief as she wanders aimlessly through the village decked in white (the colour of the Germanías). Raised together with her charismatic adoptive brother from childhood, she had become infatuated, and accompanied him in his campaigns — a loyal but lovelorn companion. Her tragic story had been introduced earlier by the young Inés as she painted her impression of El Encubierto. Faithful to this foreshadowing, Lorenzo wakes up the following night startled to discover the presence of a white-robed woman, oblivious to his presence as she attempts to remove the blood stains on the floor. The ghostly figure then slips through the open window, leaving a now terrified Lorenzo unable to return to sleep.

Later that day, it is revealed that the man who betrayed the whereabouts of El Encubierto to the Royalist authorities had been found hanging from a tree in an apparent suicide, on the very same day the shrouded one had been arrested and executed years ago. The traitor was commonly known in the village as Judas, and sold El Encubierto for 400 ducats rather than the proverbial 30 pieces of silver. So intrinsically linked with his betrayal has he become in popular imagination that he now functions strictly as an archetype — Inés is unable to recall his real name. Similarly, the bereaved and equally nameless foster-sister, already with one foot in the grave, as hinted at by her white ghostly appearance and complete disconnection from the world of the living, fulfils her inevitable Ophelia-like fate by drowning in the river. The blood-stains that had been the object of her nightly exorcisms have magically vanished, but the memory of El Encubierto still haunts the community. When we leave Inés, she has convinced Lorenzo to accompany her and her mother to a commemorative mass on the anniversary of the death of El Encubierto, an act that further cements his status as a martyr. After this revelation, the story ends almost abruptly, with no reflection on the events narrated, and no further clues towards the real identity of El Encubierto.

The story comes to a halt after the irruption of the supernatural has been dispelled, although one suspects that verifiable facts would not affect the unwavering faith displayed by adherents of either camp. It could be said that the subversion lies precisely in Asensi's neutrality and unwillingness to commit to a single interpretation, even the official version championed by historians like Danvila y Collado who claims El Encubierto to be a fraud. Asensi opts neither for the version presented by the men, nor for the contradictory one endorsed by the women, this impartiality almost dangerously implying that both versions are valid. Both will certainly remain so to their supporters in an ongoing disagreement that echoes the later clashes over the past that characterise nineteenth-century historiography. The potential of its unresolved ending and the uncertainty surrounding El Encubierto's pedigree lingers.

Although receiving equal treatment, the main difference between the two versions presented in *El encubierto* lies in the grade of agency experienced by each narrator, which seems to be related to their gender. While her grandfather Antonio took active part in his story as one of the men who apprehended and wounded El Encubierto, Inés has to content herself with the role of powerless witness in her version. She watches his capture from the window — 'Tío, yo ví desde mi casa el combate' [Uncle, I saw the fight from my house] (Asensi 1883: 23). It is a vantage point often adopted by Asensi's female characters, particularly conspicuous in her earlier work *Tres amigas* ['Three Friends'; 1880], where the three eponymous friends peer passively through countless windows, symbols of their confined domestic existence (Malin 2003: 104–05). Despite this demarcation between the public and private sphere, women are still affected by events instigated by men, as in the case of the execution of El Encubierto. Inés is reduced to the role of helpless spectator in an ambush coordinated by her male relatives, an incident that leaves her traumatized. The capture of El Encubierto leads to her estrangement from the most immediate male relatives in her family and she begins to harbour a certain animosity towards them (Asensi 1883: 24). Similarly the hauntings that take place in the family house illustrate the intrusion of politics into the confines of the private. According to a witness, the spectre 'penetraba por la ventana, aunque estuviese bien cerrada' ['penetrated through the window, even when well closed'] (Asensi 1883: 17). Asensi imagines the house haunted by a divisive figure that affects private power-dynamics even in death, and reflects in turn the tensions caused at a national level by the same incident.

It leaves the surviving women in the story, voiced by the young Inés, resigned to be silent witnesses at the window as history unfolds outside. They have to manoeuvre within these restrictions rather than risk the fate of the nameless foster sister. The only woman to cross the threshold between domestic and public by literally slipping through the window, she is punished with death for her openly disruptive behaviour.[7] The restrained Inés, who nonetheless insists in narrating to Lorenzo her conception of events, is reminiscent of the discreet writer herself. Asensi too was descended from a family whose male members actively shaped history whilst she had to watch from the sidelines. Excluded from political participation, she becomes instead a narrator like her character Inés, who in the act of weaving her own coherent version of events hopes to persuade her wealthy uncle to relay it to other men. It is a more indirect approach than the one championed by the foster sister but perhaps also a more realistic one. Such strategies lead Karen Offen to observe that '[h]istorical feminism offers us far more paradoxes and contradictions; it is about politics, not philosophy' (2000: xi). Yet such complexity should be recovered, if anything, to better understand our own complex modernity.

Occupying such neutral space leads later critics to remove Asensi from public debates, so that her surprisingly ambiguous ending remains under the radar. Instead of asserting one version as the truth, *El encubierto* can be read as a commentary on a political tribalism that might not be resolved any time soon, and which still haunted the country when Asensi decided to revisit this sixteenth-century legend. That this latent ambiguity could be subversive, or at least disorienting, is supported by a later edition of *El encubierto* published in 1905 by Edgar S. Ingraham, professor of Romance languages at Ohio State University, and aimed at Spanish language students. With this audience in mind, Ingraham added explanatory glosses that provided socio-historic context. Thus in a note on the genealogy of El Encubierto, the editor points out how '[t]he version given by Antonio, according to which he was an impostor, is the one generally accepted by historians' (Asensi 1905: 119). This dispels any unsettling ambiguity raised by its inconclusive denouement and curtails any potential polysemy in the process. Later assessments of Asensi have not restored this nuance, dismissing it, rather paradoxically, as an ahistorical historical legend. Rather than historicized, Asensi is essentialized as a passive guardian of the status quo in a teleological narrative of progress that does not include her. Asensi engages with her political reality obliquely if judged by modern parameters, an *encubierta* herself, and as a result she remains hidden. As we have seen, this was partly due to her decision to write a legend, a genre associated with Romanticism and the first half of the nineteenth century, at a time when the novel reigned as 'the literary mode most characteristic of our time' [la forma literaria más propia de nuestro tiempo] (Palacio Valdés and Alas 1882: 132) and was considered the more legitimate medium to discuss the nation. Asensi is a romantic in both the upper- and lower-case sense of the word: Romantic for writing a legend, and romantic because women's literary output often gets saddled with the label of 'personal'. Men, on the other hand, supposedly write Literature, concerned with universal themes, a deceptively neutral conclusion routinely denounced by feminist studies.

The political dimension present in the work of Asensi thus remains buried under several labels that conceal her engagement and palpable concern over the lack of female agency during a period that saw the consolidation of the constitutional model. Recovering authors like Asensi not only produces a more multi-faceted view of the nineteenth century, it reminds us that the fight for increased visibility was not merely the remit of a few pioneering supporters of the female vote, an anomaly amongst women otherwise content with the status quo. Instead female vindications are drawn from a more heterogeneous but also larger pool than traditionally portrayed. Since we are far from achieving gender parity in current political systems, which are direct descendants of nineteenth-century liberalism, such reminders remain sadly pertinent.

Bibliography

ARKINSTALL, CHRISTINE. 2014. *Spanish Female Writers and the Freethinking Press, 1879-1926* (Toronto: University of Toronto Press)
ASENSI Y LAIGLESIA. JULIA DE. 1876. 'A.S.M. el Rey D. Alfonso XII'. *Album poético dedicado a S.M. el Rey D. Alfonso XII y al Ejército con motivo de su entrada en la capital de la Monarquía* (Madrid: Imprenta Oficial)
—— 1880. *Tres amigas* (Madrid: Lit. e Imp. de la Biblioteca Universal)
—— 1883. *Leyendas y tradiciones en prosa y verso* (Madrid: Biblioteca Universal)
—— 1890. 'Tus cantares', *El Album Iberoamericano*, 14 December, issue 18
—— 1905. *Victoria y otros cuentos, por Julia de Asensi*; ed. with notes and vocabulary by Edgar S. Ingraham (Boston: D.C. Heath & Co)
BASTINOS, ANTONIO J (ed.). 1903. *Parnaso: Lectura selecta de autores contemporáneos en prosa y verso* (Barcelona: Librería de Julián Bastinos)
BÉCQUER, GUSTAVO ADOLFO. 2002 [1858–1864]. *Leyendas*, ed. Pascual Izquierdo (Madrid: Cátedra)
BOIX, VICENTE. 1921. [1852–1859] *El encubierto de Valencia. Leyenda histórica del siglo XVI* (Valencia: Imp. El Mercantil Valencia)
BURGUERA, MÓNICA. 2012. *Las damas del liberalismo respetable: los imaginarios sociales del feminismo liberal en España, 1834–1850* (Madrid: Cátedra)
CASTRO ANTONIO, ANA. 2010. *Julia de Asensi: el camarada* (Vigo: Trymar)
CORONADO, CAROLINA. 1854. *La Sigea: Novela original* (Madrid: Anselmo Santa Coloma)
CRUZ-FERNÁNDEZ, PAULA A DE LA. 2014. 'Embroidering the Nation: The Culture of Sewing and Spanish Ideology of Domesticity', in *Memory and Cultural History of the Spanish Civil War: Realms of Oblivion*, ed. by Aurora G. Morcillo (Leiden-Boston: Brill), pp. 249–84
DANVILA Y COLLADO, MANUEL. 1884. *La Germanía de Valencia: discursos leídos ante la Real academia de la recepción pública del Excmo. Señor Don Manuel Danvila y Collado el día 9 de noviembre de 1884* (Madrid: Tip. de Manual Gines Hernández)
DÍEZ MÉNGUEZ, ISABEL. 1999. 'Leyendas y tradiciones de Julia de Asensi y Laiglesia: una manifestación más del Romanticismo rezagado', *Anales de Literatura Hispanoamericana*, 28: 1353–1385

―― 2006. *Julia de Asensi (1849–1921)* (Madrid: Ediciones del Orto)
ESPIGADO TOCINO, GLORIA. 2010. 'El discurso republicano sobre la mujer en el Sexenio Democrático, 1868–1874: los límites de la modernidad', in *Género y modernidad en España: de la Ilustración al liberalismo*, ed. by Mónica Bolufer and Mónica Burguera (Madrid: Marcial Pons), pp. 143–68
FERNÁNDEZ HERREROS, MANUEL. 1870. *Historia de las Germanías de Valencia: Breve reseña del levantamiento republicano de 1869* (Madrid: Imp. de la Viuda e Hijos de M. Álvarez)
GARCÍA CÁRCEL, RICARDO. 1981. *Las Germanías de Valencia* (Barcelona: Península)
GARCÍA GUTIERREZ, ANTONIO. 1840. *El Encubierto de Valencia, Drama en cinco actos y en verso* (Madrid: Imprenta de Yenes)
GIES, DAVID THATCHER. 1994. *The Theatre in Nineteenth-Century Spain* (Cambridge: Cambridge University Press)
GÓMEZ AVELLANEDA, GERTRUDIS. 1871. 'La dama de Amboto'. *Obras literarias de la Señora Doña Gertrudis Gómez de Avellaneda. Colección completa.* Vol 5 (Madrid: Imprenta y Estereotipia de M. Rivadeneyra), pp. 147–56
HAIDT, REBECCA. 2011. *Women, Work and Clothing in Eighteenth-century Spain* (Oxford: Voltaire Foundation)
HOOPER, KIRSTY. 2010. 'Between Canon, Archive and Database: Spain's Women Intellectuals, 1890-1920, Notes on a Work in Progress', *Siglo diecinueve: literatura hispánica*, 16: 195-217
MALIN, MARK R. 2003. 'Of Beginnings and Endings, Prólogos y Despedidas: Julia de Asensi's Tres amigas.' *Confluencia* 19 : 103–11
MELLOR, ANNE K. 2000. *Mother of the Nation. Women's Political Writings in England 1780–1830* (Bloomington and Indianapolis: Indiana University Press)
MOLINA PORRAS, JUAN (ed.) 2013. *Leyendas del siglo XIX*. (Tres Cantos, Madrid: Akal, D.L.)
MUÑOZ SEMPERE, DANIEL. 2011. 'Historia como novela y novela como historia en *Ni rey ni Roque* (1835) de Patricio de la Escosura', *Bulletin of Spanish Studies* 88: 57–71
OFFEN, KAREN. 2000. *European Feminisms, 1700–1950: A Political History* (Stanford, CA: Stanford University Press)
PALACIO VALDÉS, ARMANDO and LEOPOLDO ALAS 'CLARÍN'. 1882. *La literatura en 1881* (Madrid: Alfredo de Carlos Hierro)
PALAU Y DULCET, ANTONIO. 1948–1977. *Manual del librero hispano-americano: bibliografía general española e hispano-americana desde la invención de la imprenta hasta nuestros tiempos, con el valor comercial de los impresos descritos* (Barcelona: A. Palau)
PAQUETTE, GABRIEL. 2015. 'Introduction: Liberalism in the Early Nineteenth-Century Iberian World', *History of European Ideas*, 41: 153–65
ROMEO MATEO, MARÍA CRUZ. 2008. 'Destinos de mujer: esfera pública y políticos liberales', in *Historia de las mujeres en España y América Latina: del siglo XIX a los umbrales del XX (vol III)*, ed. by Isabel Morant (Madrid: Cátedra), pp. 61–83
―― 2014. 'Domesticidad y política: Las relaciones de género en la sociedad posrevolucionaria', in *La España liberal, 1833–1874*, ed. by María Cruz Romeo & María Sierra (Madrid: Marcial Pons Historia; Zaragoza: Universidad de Zaragoza), pp. 89–130
SALLE, SARAH T. 2002. 'Revisiting El Encubierto: Navigating Between Visions of Heaven and Hell on Earth', in *Werewolves, Witches, and Wandering Spirits: Traditional Belief and Folklore in Early Modern Europe*, ed. by Kathryn A. Edwards (Kirksville, MO: Truman State University Press)
SCANLON, GERALDINE. 1986. *La polémica feminista en la España contemporánea (1868–1974)* (Madrid: Akal)
SENABRE, RICARDO. 1978. 'Introducción', in *Traidor, inconfeso y mártir*, José Zorrilla (Madrid: Cátedra), pp. 11–46

TOLLIVER, JOYCE. 2011. 'Politics and the Feminist Essay in Spain', in *A Companion to Spanish Women Studies*, ed. by Xon de Ros & Geraldine Hazbun (Woodbridge: Tamesis), pp. 243–56
YETANO LAGUNA, ANA (ed.) 2013. *Mujeres y culturas políticas en España, 1808–1845.* (Bellaterra: Universitat Autònoma de Barcelona)
ZORRILLA, JOSÉ. 1978 [1849]. *Traidor, inconfeso y mártir.* Ricardo Senabre (ed.) (Madrid: Cátedra)

Notes to Chapter 4

1. Spanish men had been granted universal suffrage in 1890 — no longer dictated by income, social status or other past restrictions. Attempts were made under the dictatorship of Primo de Rivera (1923–1930) to give women suffrage and the ability to run for office at a municipal level. There had also been several efforts to expand electoral laws as early as 1877, but women had to wait until the constitution of 1931 before they could vote in a democratic election.
2. Additionally, the researchers Christine Arkinstall (2014) and Gloria Espigado Tocino (2010) have uncovered a lively lineage of female republicans and free-thinkers who predate the Second Republic. Arkinstall also reveals a spirited exchange between Spanish left-wing women and their international counterparts.
3. Unless otherwise stated, all translations are my own.
4. Historians disagree on the exact number of Carlist conflicts, with some accounts claiming three while others like historian Jordi Canal identify two (2000: 128). At issue is whether the so-called *Guerra dels Matiners* ['War of the Early Risers'], which unfolded mainly in Catalonia between 1846–1849, is considered part of the Carlist canon.
5. The *Palau y Ducet Manual del Librero Hispanoamericano* ['The Palau and Ducet Manual of the Hispano-American Bookseller'] testifies to the popularity of this format, with over thirty pages dedicated to different *bibliotecas*, from the literary to the scientific (1949 Vol. 2: 227–50).
6. Diego Jiménez de Enciso (1585–1634), a Golden Age playwright, had already dramatized the story in his *El encubierto*, of unknown date.
7. David T. Gies (1994: 345) points out how 'these dishevelled women (usually dressed in white), symbols of social disorder or emotional chaos, are frequent in Spanish drama from the 1820s through the 1850s.'

CHAPTER 5

Undermining the Discourse of the Spanish Transition: Literary Approaches to Forgetting, Consensus and 'the New Spain'[1]

Leticia Blanco

The period immediately following the death of Spain's dictator Francisco Franco on 20 November 1975 is most commonly known as the 'Spanish transition'. The political process of transformation after this forty-year dictatorial regime is generally dated from the day of Franco's death to the election victory of the Spanish Socialist Workers' Party (PSOE) on 28 October 1982.[2] This was undoubtedly a period of 'transition', but the fact that it has been described in these terms rather than as, for example, a period of 'post-dictatorship' — a term recurrently used in countries like Argentina, Uruguay or Chile, to designate the years of their own transition to democracy — is significant, because it places the emphasis on its projected outcome, namely democracy, and consigns to oblivion Spain's recent history.

If I am drawing attention here to the importance of the name, it is because what concerns me is not something which some claim is historical fact, but rather the way history and its events are chronicled. Already in 1984, Águila and Montoro assert: '[e]l lenguaje que servía de vehículo al discurso político de la transición fue algo más que eso, un vehículo. De algún modo se puede afirmar que la transición fue lo que fue su discurso político, y viceversa' [the language used as a vehicle for the political discourse of the Transition was more than a mere vehicle. In a certain sense, we can say that the transition was what its political discourse was, and vice versa] (Águila and Montoro 1984: 1–2).[3] After 1982, once it was judged to have ended, the telling and re-telling of the transition to democracy — what Águila and Montoro assert to be at once process and discourse (henceforth referred to here as process/discourse) — became commonplace and, controlled by certain media and experts, grew into a myth: 'there is scarcely a story more mythologized by the intellectual clerisy than the story of the Transition' (Resina 2000: 5).

Until recently, the Spanish transition has mostly been purported to be a total success, with the 1977 amnesty as its cornerstone, so much so that it was proposed as an exportable political model. The media was crucial in casting the Spanish transition as a great feat to achieve democracy, and amongst the media, the newspaper *El País* played a leading role.[4] Its editorial described the amnesty as:

> un acto excepcional, justificado por la razón de Estado y por la necesidad de hacer borrón y cuenta nueva de acontecimientos tan cruentos y dolorosos para un pueblo como es una guerra civil, una guerra entre hermanos y una larga dictadura. La España democrática debe, desde ahora, mirar hacia adelante, olvidar las responsabilidades y los hechos de la guerra civil, hacer abstracción de los cuarenta años de dictadura.
>
> [an exceptional measure, justified by reason of state and the need to make a clean slate of such bloody and painful events for a nation as a civil war, a war between brothers and a long dictatorship. Democratic Spain must, from now on, look forward, forget the responsibilities and incidents of the civil war, set aside the forty years of dictatorship]. (*El País*, 15/10/1977)

Without making any explicit connection, the dictatorship was linked to the threatening memory of the war, and the necessity to forget the latter allowed both to fade into oblivion. According to this legitimizing view, the 1977 amnesty sealed a redeeming 'pacto del olvido' [pact of forgetting], brought fraternal reconciliation that became the ideology of a nonviolent and equitable 'consenso' [consensus]; and by encouraging society to wipe the slate clean and to look to the future, enabled the birth of a brand new Spain.

Along with the media, the new democratic institutions used art and cultural production as a means of legitimization and established a cultural paradigm that a group of analysts have recently called CT or 'Cultura de la Transición'.[5] In that period, literature was still 'investida de prestigio: es un discurso público que moldea' [invested with prestige: it is a public discourse that shapes] (León 2012: 90). In search of publishing opportunities and recognition, many writers adapted to the political project of cohesion and both supported and constructed the meaning of the process/discourse resulting, in the words of Juan Goytisolo, in 'una limitación y empobrecimiento de su ámbito literario, en una alborotada pero inane celebración del vacío' [a limitation and impoverishment of its literary scope, in an agitated but inane celebration of emptiness] (Goytisolo 1999: 55). In an article in 1988, Sanz Villanueva drew a parallel between writers and readers and affirmed: 'Uno y otro adoptan una actitud bastante escéptica, que evita la definición, que rehúye la confrontación y ensalza lo poco consistente' [both take a rather sceptical attitude, which avoids definition, shuns confrontation and extols the inconsistent] (quoted in Sanz Villanueva, 2013: 17). There were writers whose work might be critical in various aspects but did not directly challenge the narratives of the Transition — one of the most sophisticated examples of which is Javier Marías — while others had quite a different attitude towards the new socio-political situation and actively confronted the hegemonic discourse from a consciously critical perspective. Manuel Vázquez Montalbán calls this last group of writers, amongst whom he sees himself, *testimoniales*:

> Los que éramos testimoniales, los que como yo nos dedicábamos a reflejar la

realidad con un aspecto crítico, desde un aspecto crítico, lo seguimos haciendo y quienes no lo hacían, no quisieron hacerlo, porque seguiría operando sobre ellos el pudor de pensar que como la literatura no transforma nada, puesto que no influye nada sobre la realidad, no querían exponerse al ridículo de convertirse en *gurús* de una nueva situación, instrumentalizando la libertad para introducir ese mensaje crítico dentro de sus obras.

[Those of us who were testimonial writers, who devoted themselves like I did to reflecting reality in a critical way, from a critical angle, we continue doing so. Those who did not do it, who did not want to do it, because their modesty made them think that literature does not transform anything, or has no influence over reality at all, did not want to lay themselves open to ridicule by becoming gurus of a new situation, by capitalizing on freedom to introduce this critical message within their works.] (Vázquez Montalbán 1991: 20)

In reviewing the literary works of the Spanish transition, some critics of the period addressed the critical responsibility writers had in relation to the new parameters of freedom. They reproached writers who had claimed they would write 'finer literature,' were it not for censorship, failed to do so after Franco's death.[6] Interestingly, Rafael Conte of *El País* stated in one of his reviews that 'Las mujeres siguen un camino tan impertérrito como real. Dentro de sus imperfecciones son ellas las que parece que tienen algo que decir' [Women are following a path as unperturbed as real. Amongst their imperfections, they are the ones who seem to have something to say] (Conte 1985: 24). Despite admitting that these authors' narratives were essential for a desired and desirable renewal, Conte finished the article by returning to the previous reproof — that Spanish authors had nothing to say and had not fulfilled their potential even after censorship — and asked: 'Y ahora, ¿qué decimos?' [And now, what do we have to say?] (Conte 1985: 24). Apparently forgetting his own words, he paid no further attention to what women writers were actually saying, which would, theoretically, have answered his closing question.

It was common practice then for critics to segregate work written by women under the label 'feminine' and, because they wrote about love and relationships, under other disparaging tags like 'subjective', 'personal', 'intimate'. Paradoxically, they also demanded that these works introduce those same topics in accordance with the dominant culture's view of what women's literature should be.[7] Furthermore, critics often reduced measurements of their success to market sales, not referring to the quality of their work but treating them with the disdain that they thought mass cultural products deserved, even when someone like Conte acknowledged the importance of their contribution.

As a result, and despite the general impression that women have long become part of the canon, authors like Montserrat Roig, Esther Tusquets, Rosa Montero, Lourdes Ortiz or Carme Riera have been subject to mechanisms of invisibility and tend to be addressed separately from the literary and socio-political context in which male writers (or simply, 'authors') are usually studied.[8] Gender as a concept and tool of analysis is generally applied only when referring to women, creating an asymmetrical narrative that has negative consequences. Talking about 'women's literature' or 'feminine writing' when 'men's literature' or 'masculine writing' do not even exist is one of the mechanisms that perpetuates the exclusion of these authors' literature from the canon, while establishing a sub-canon. In 1984, Esther Tusquets declared:

> El hecho de ser literatura de mujeres nos ayuda, porque está de moda; a lo mejor vendes mucho y se escribe mucho sobre ti. Pero al mismo tiempo quedas muy catalogada, y no te tienen en cuenta cuando hablan de literatura en serio... Es un poco pesado que te encuadren y se hable en un programa de ti casi siempre en el apartado de las mujeres.
>
> [The fact that it is women's literature helps us, because it is fashionable; you might sell a lot and a lot is written about you. But at the same time you end up being categorized, and not taken into account when talking about serious literature... It is a drag to be stereotyped and spoken about in a TV programme mostly in the women's section.] (Quoted in Nichols 1995: 199)

Female writers were pigeonholed as a homogenous block and critics succeeded in belittling their achievements by obscuring their specificities, not drawing attention to the difference they represented.

What I want to address here is why *ellas*, women writers, had something distinct to say and what it is they were saying. I will do so by analysing the work of the five authors already mentioned: Roig, Tusquets, Montero, Ortiz and Riera, published between 1975 and 1982.[9] In their own characteristic styles, each contributed greatly to ideological and cultural renewal. Reading their works as *testimoniales* (understood as above: reflecting reality critically and endorsing literature's power to make substantive political interventions) and through a dialogue between them and the official discourse of the transition, I want to highlight their determination to contest the commonplaces of hegemonic contemporary history and to reveal that, far from forgetting, they offered a reflection on memory and a narration of memories that opposed the principles of the 1977 amnesty: they cast the civil war and the recent past in a different light, depicted the consensus as being not as robust as others asserted and the new Spain as suffering from a post-dictatorial hangover.

By the mid-1970s, there was a volatile mood in Spain, one that oscillated between long-standing hatred and new excitement over the recent economic, social and cultural enterprises intended to distance the country from the structures of the dictatorship. Spanish society was at a difficult turning point and it had to come to terms with a three-year civil war and the thirty-six years of dictatorship that followed, but how to find the right terms? When interpreting this event and its aftermath, serious conflicts between contradicting memories emerged at once. A hermeneutic battle to seize the past began.[10]

In this hermeneutic battle, the establishment engineered two coexisting action plans. One, as noted before, was to promote publicly via the amnesty a pact of forgetting that led people to believe that memories were harmful for the process towards democracy and it was only fair to silence them all. The second was to compose a master narrative that encompassed the key moments of political history.[11] Like all master narratives, this one sought to control the interpretation of the past (in other words, to have the past under control) creating what Ricard Vinyes calls 'buena memoria' [good memory]: a 'we-were-all-to-blame' memory imposed on society to explain the past once and for all. And in this sense, I agree with Ann Rigney, talking more generally about cultural memory, that '[t]o bring remembrance to a conclusion is de facto already to forget' (Rigney 2008: 345). In Spain, the past was eventually removed from public debates and 'people got used to replacing true memories with fake ones' (Pérez-Díaz 1999: 178) — the ones provided by the official discourse — and asked no more questions once the transitional process ended.

The State's double-action plan to monopolize knowledge (or ignorance) of the past ultimately failed. Firstly, the pact aimed for oblivion, but in the testimonies that have been (re)appearing in Spain since the late 1990s, there is no evidence of any forgetting or traumatic blocking of memory.[12] Instead, what we recognize in Spanish society's silence is lack of transmission, hesitation about whether or not to talk (see Labanyi 2007: 109). In Roig's *La ópera cotidiana*, young Mari Cruz points this out: 'Los viejos (...) Se negaban a transmitirme las palabras. Como si tuviesen las llaves de una cerradura misteriosa y no me las quisieran dar' [The elders refused to convey the words to me. As if they had the keys of a mysterious lock and would not give them to me] (Roig 1989: 177). Secondly, the master narrative of the official discourse sought to silence the debate, but was not able to account for the complexity of either past or contemporary events:

> Las historias generales con protagonistas tales como los estados, las naciones o los pueblos, siempre suelen manifestar unas pretensiones 'armonizadoras' y unas visiones unificadoras que les hacen incapaces de dar cuenta de la complejidad, diversidad y conflictividad del proceso histórico.
>
> [General histories with states, nations or peoples as the protagonists usually manifest 'harmonizing' pretensions and unifying visions that make them unable to account for the complexity, diversity and conflicts of the historical process]. (Ruiz 2002: 26)

The hermeneutic battle around memory has been reopened and determines who has the right and power to tell and interpret the past. It is by incorporating individual stories into the narratives of the period, and by attributing significance to the impact that the individual and the collective have on each other, that we dissolve the homogeneity of the process/discourse, allowing us to penetrate into the intricacies of Spanish history. At this juncture of personal and collective, private and public, gender may be a determining fact and useful tool of analysis. As Hirsch and Smith state: 'What a culture remembers and what it chooses to forget are intricately bound up with issues of power and hegemony, and thus with gender' (Hirsch and Smith 2002: 6), although they warn us: 'gender, like memory, must be grounded in context if it is not to remain an abstract binary structure' (Hirsch and Smith 2002: 7). A binary structure is found all too often in the works of critics: here, Juan Carlos Monedero highlights the importance of women's opposition to the pact of forgetting:

> Cuando echó a andar el nuevo régimen, no miramos a la Segunda República, no miramos a la guerra civil, no miramos al franquismo, y sólo buscamos el

reflejo narcisista, espejo frente a espejo, en una transición enseñoreada de la que sólo se podía aprender resignación y disciplina (es de justicia hacer salvedad de las mujeres, que muy pronto recordaron los grandes avances de que disfrutaron con el advenimiento de la Segunda República: voto, divorcio, igualdad de los cónyuges, capacidad contractual, despenalización del aborto, derechos laborales [...]).

[When the new regime got going, we did not look back at the Second Republic, we did not look back at the civil war, we did not look back at Francoism, and we only sought the narcissistic reflection, mirror to mirror, in a transition full of itself from which only resignation and discipline could be learnt (it is fair to make an exception in the case of women, who soon recalled the great step forward that they enjoyed with the advent of the Second Republic: the vote, divorce, equality of spouses, contractual capacity, decriminalization of abortion, labour rights.] (Monedero 2013: 58)

Note how the author keeps women out of the universal 'we' — who are 'we' then if I read it? Although I concur with the implications that gender was a decisive factor whenever people took up a stance on, for example, the rights of divorce or abortion, I disagree with the assumption that all women preserved the memory of the Republic and supported such matters, while all men turned their back on them, just because each were women and men respectively.

In Spain, the opposition to Franco's regime had been articulated in Marxist terms, and the Communist Party functioned for a long time as a political umbrella organization. In most countries in Europe, intellectuals had progressively abandoned orthodox Marxism. When the crisis into which Marxism fell after May 1968 reached Spain, the ideological project of many Marxist intellectuals (mostly men) collapsed. This is closely connected to the spirit of 'desencanto' [disenchantment]. Similarly to what was happening in Latin America, 'intellectuals began to doubt whether they could adequately reconstruct their national histories in a way that would help to plot directions for change' (Sommer 1988: 112). Most Spanish male writers who fought against Franco's regime abandoned the ideas of progress offered by the utopian master narrative of Marxism and started writing novels based on their own individual experiences and memories. As Ramón Buckley explains:

> a partir de 1968 se produce la desbandada de toda una generación de escritores unidos, hasta aquel momento, por su compromiso con el marxismo. Lo que se desintegraba para aquellos escritores, no era sólo una determinada ideología, sino el concepto mismo de la Historia. A partir de aquel momento, aquellos escritores se refugiarían en su propia historia (con minúscula), es decir, en su propia memoria.
>
> [beginning in 1968, a whole generation of writers who had been united, until that moment, by their commitment to Marxism, disbanded. For those writers it was not only a certain ideology that was disintegrating, but the very concept of history. From that moment on, those writers took refuge in their own histories (with a small 'h'), that is, in their own memories.] (Buckley 1996: xv)

They did not respond to the fall of the Marxist master narrative by building another, something that the fathers of the Transition endeavoured to do when Francoism ended (the 'buena memoria' mentioned above), but by substituting 'we' for 'I' in an autobiographical approach.[13] When describing testimonial literature by Latin American women, Doris Sommer distinguishes between the metaphorical nature of autobiography and the metonymical character of testimony. The metaphorical autobiographical voice replaces the whole of society, valuing 'marginality as a mark of personal distinctiveness rather than as a measure of political inequality' (Sommer 1988: 130) — precisely what the generation of authors to whom Buckley refers did. With a similar distrust of History, women writers tended to adopt metonymy instead, 'a lateral identification through relationship, which acknowledges the possible differences among "us" as components of the whole' (Sommer 1988: 108).[14] This is illustrated in the prologue Rosa Montero wrote when *Crónica del desamor* was reissued on the occasion of its thirtieth anniversary:[15]

> *Crónica del desamor* no fue nunca una novela autobiográfica (...). Pero sí es una novela estrechamente pegada a una realidad generacional. Un retrato en directo de aquellos años ardientes de la Transición. (...) esta novela la hemos escrito de algún modo entre todos.
>
> [*Crónica del desamor* was never an autobiographical novel (...). But it is indeed a novel closely attached to a generational reality. A live portrait of those ardent years of the Transition. (...) we have written this novel together in some way].
> (Montero 2010: 12–13)

Metonymy has the potential for resistance because it shifts an exclusive historiography into a legitimate space to incorporate the voices of many. Much closer to the testimonial than to autobiography, most Spanish women writers did not equate identity with individuality and spoke from a collective subject.

Marxist male intellectuals realised that their terms no longer fitted into the political framework — especially when even the Communist Party dropped them as the process/discourse of the transition was articulated in the new Constitution — so they changed them. Women who spoke for other women and exposed feminist claims were neither inside nor outside this framework. After clarifying that by the term 'mujer' he is referring to 'aquellos grupos que actuaban como sus portavoces' [those groups that acted as their spokesmen], Buckley argues that:

> la mujer es capaz de detectar los fallos de un proceso político en el que ella se siente 'convidado de piedra': la mujer 'toma la palabra', no sólo para expresar sus propias reivindicaciones, sino para ejercer una labor crítica con respecto a la transformación política y social que se estaba produciendo en España.
>
> [women are able to detect the failures of a political process in which they feel like an unwanted guest: women take the floor, not only to express their own demands, but to critically evaluate the political and social transformation that Spain was undergoing] (Buckley 1996: xv)

Women writers started to build a counter-discourse, coming to terms with people's unrepresentativeness in accordance with the trends across Western societies.[16] The objective of this 'history from below' was to:

> remover la conciencia de los ciudadanos ante la concepción de la historia cerrada, sin utopías (...) anclada en el orden que supone la relación con un

> pasado controlado, saturado de memoria y mitologías nacionales. Una historia pensada desde la libertad y la crítica que pretende restituir la complejidad del pasado y defenderlo como un valor en sí mismo.
>
> [stir the conscience of citizens before the conception of closed history, without utopias (...) anchored in the order that the relation to a controlled past involves, saturated by memory and national mythologies. History thought from a space of freedom and criticism that seeks to restore the complexity of the past and defend it as a value in itself.] (Peiró 2004: 278)

There is nowhere better than Franco's Spain for illustrating the creation of national mythologies. These reflections on historicity eroded both Francoist and anti-Francoist master narratives and opened spaces for testimonies and individual stories: an emancipatory narrative material that was at its best in fiction.

In any analysis of the earliest works of Roig, Tusquets, Montero, Ortiz or Riera, the fact that the authors are women is indeed meaningful. Their voices reveal 'el carácter "masculino" de la transición misma, de aquella "patriarquía" que continuaba vigente a pesar de haber muerto el "patriarca"' [the 'masculine' nature of the transition itself, of that 'patriarchy' that continued in force even though the 'patriarch' had died] (Buckley 1996: xiv). When the transition began, these authors focused on the continuity of the fiercely patriarchal structures that upheld the dictatorship and what these meant not only for them but for all others who lacked a voice. They recuperated hidden, underrated, excluded personal stories through literature, a privileged medium to re-present life and single out individual voices. Natalia, one of the two protagonists in *La hora violeta* — also the main character in the previous *Tiempo de cerezas* — , expresses this commitment: 'Me parecía que era necesario salvar con las palabras todo lo que la historia, la Historia grande, es decir, la de los hombres, había hecho impreciso, había condenado o idealizado' [I felt it was necessary to save with words all that history, big History, that is, men's history, had made inaccurate, had condemned or idealized] (Roig 1986b: 20). Roig exposes gender marginality and the fact that the moments of history that need to be uttered are not simply voiceless, but condemned or idealized, a consequence of both totalitarian and utopian master narratives.

Acknowledging the impossibility of producing a tabula rasa, 'estas autoras españolas abordan sin demoras un pasado traumático que es todo menos perfecto' [these female Spanish authors addressed without delay a traumatic past that is anything but ideal] (Reinstädler 2007: 132).[17] Their work incorporated a plurality of stories and, entering into women's domestic sphere, exposed critical elements that the official history omitted. But I would argue that they go further, that their ideological project creates a space where common people's histories merge with official History, rewriting and rethinking H/history. Their works incorporate 'sensory memory', a concept that Joan Ramón Resina defines as opposed to 'political history':

> It is possible to assert that political history privileges the narrative of change and transition, while the everyday is experienced as a denarrativized continuum, closer to biological than to historical time. A powerful social technology

detaches political events from the everyday and endows them with a dynamism that appears to inhere in them, producing the illusion that they and they alone are the contents of contemporary narrativity. (Resina 2000: 95)

What interest could these everyday individual stories have for society? The characters themselves are not sure. Mundeta, second of the three women in the grandmother-mother-daughter genealogy in Roig's *Ramona, adiós,* talks with an old man, member of FAI ('Federación Anarquista Ibérica'), in a hospital during the war and here is what she observes:

> Después de hablar mucho rato callé. [...] No entendía su curiosidad, su manera incisiva de preguntarme cosas de mi vida, cosas banales e intrascendentes. Pensé que qué le importaba. Que mi historia era breve y anodina al lado de la suya, llena de luchas, de huelgas, de ruido y de aventuras.
>
> [After talking for a long time I stopped. [...] I did not understand his curiosity, his incisive way of enquiring about things in my life, trivial and inconsequential things. I wondered what did he care. I thought that my story was brief and bland compared to his, full of struggles, strikes, noise and adventures.] (Roig 1992a: 155)

She measures her life against that of the old fighter exposing the opposition between 'sensory memory' and 'political history'. The common impression of banality that we see in Mundeta's words disappears when everyday experience is narrativized in these novels and conceived as being as much a part of history as 'political history'.

These literary works offer not only a narration of memories previously silenced, but also a reflection on memory and a different way of chronicling history as sensory memory gains prominence. In Montero's *Crónica del desamor,* Ana hesitates to write about what happens around her — 'Piensa Ana que estaría bien escribir un día algo. Sobre la vida de cada día' / 'Pero escribir un libro así, se dice Ana con desconsuelo, sería banal, estúpido e interminable, un diario de aburridas frustraciones' [Ana thinks it would be nice to write something one day. About everyday life / But to write such a book, Ana tells herself disconsolately, would be banal, stupid and endless, a diary of boring frustrations] (Montero 2010: 20/23). Nonetheless, her reluctance to write disappears and by the end of the novel she affirms that she ought to write:

> ese libro que ahora está segura de escribir, que ya no será el rencoroso libro de las Anas, sino un apunte, una crónica del desamor cotidiano, rubricada por la mediocridad de ese nudo de seda deshecho por la rutina y el tedio.
>
> [that book she is now sure about writing, that will no longer be the spiteful book of Anas, but a note, a chronicle of quotidian heartbreak, endorsed by the mediocrity of that silk knot undone by routine and boredom.] (Montero 2010: 258)

The book Ana plans, the one we have just finished by the time we read these words, consists of a series of apparently insignificant day-to-day events that affect numerous people and gain historical importance because, as we have seen, they are perceived as a shared testimony of the moment. History with a capital letter, as Roig defines it in *La hora violeta,* is incomplete and cannot (or should not) be understood as concluded until these intimate stories are incorporated.

While the discourse of the transition depicts the Second Republic as chaotic and deliberately confines the period to oblivion, these authors insist on its recuperation and offer an alternative image of the Republic as a truly exciting collective project in which everybody can participate. The sense of exhilaration remains at the centre of any description of the period between 1931 and 1939 and is mainly linked to the idea of political progress. Although this perception is not exclusive to female characters, it is the first time they seem fully aware of the political situation. Later in their lives, these characters will want to re-experience the truly democratic life that the Republic embodied, attempting to link it to the process of transition to democracy. In one of Riera's short stories, 'Sólo pude conservar una fotografía,' the protagonist calls for a bridge to connect the late 70s with the early 30s that creates a contrast with the years in between:

> Para mí lo era todo, todo lo que de bello y bueno había en aquel mundo que entre todos, habíamos comenzado a construir. Después de su muerte, la guerra, la victoria de los enemigos, cuarenta años de tragar bilis... [...] Toda mi vida pertenece a otra época, antes de la derrota y, sin embargo, ahora me doy cuenta de que debo unirla con esta que, por fin, empieza.
>
> [For me he was everything, everything that was beautiful and good about that world that we had started to build all together. After his death, war, the victory of the enemies, forty years of putting up with it... [...] All my life belongs to another era, before the defeat and yet, I now realize that I must join it together with this one that finally begins.] (Riera 1980: 82)

The need to link the pre- and the post-dictatorship relates to the potential for freedom and social agency that the first period had and the second ought to have. It also counters the idea that democracy in Spain emerged only (and for the first time) with the 1978 Constitution.[18]

As the historian Pedro Ruiz explains, narratives that recover the memory of the democratic past of the Second Republic, of those who fought for it and against the Franco regime, condemn the dictatorship and demand moral, political or legal reparation for the victims; by contrast, narratives in favour of leaving things as they were consider any claims of the Second Republic a dangerous rupture of the consensus reached during the transition. In any case, 'esos discursos reparadores o inmovilistas han de ser juzgados, no por lo que dicen del pasado, sino por los valores que defienden en el presente' [these restorative or stagnant speeches are to be judged not for what they say about the past, but for the values they defend in the present] (Ruiz 2007). Since novels do not imitate existing versions of memory, but re-produce the very past they describe, we can say that these literary texts re-create the Spanish Second Republic in order to make a correlation between the democratic space built by its government and the new possibilities after Franco's death. They bring unfulfilled expectations to their own present because '[d]eclarar in-significante lo que ya no es porque fracasó es una torpeza metodológica y una injusticia' [to declare in-significant what is no longer because it failed is a methodological blunder and an injustice] (Mate 2006: 47).

Our women writers often evoke the Second Republic in terms of that which failed to provide after its drastic and fulminant demise. In doing so, they recuperate the intentions of authors in exile like Constancia de la Mora, Clara Campoamor, Victoria Kent, Silvia Mistral, Federica Montseny and Felisa Gil who, in their testimonies — autobiographies, memoirs, diaries, chronicles or personal novels —, express their wish to 'consignar otra Historia, a través de la palabra, de luchar en contra de la realidad objetiva de una guerra perdida' [to record a different History, through the word, to fight against the objective reality of a lost war] (Samblancat 1997: 5). We find a similar commitment to filling in the gaps of historiographical writing. Words like these by Victoria Kent fully resonate in the novels examined here:

> Yo quiero no olvidar todo lo que hoy sé. Que otros hagan la Historia y cuenten lo que quieran; lo que yo quiero es no olvidar, y como nuestra capacidad de olvido lo digiere todo, lo tritura todo, lo que hoy sé quiero sujetarlo en este papel.
>
> [I do not want to forget everything I know today. Others may make History and tell what they want; what I want is not to forget, and since our ability to forget digests everything, it grinds down everything, what I know today I want to affix to this piece of paper]. (quoted by Samblancat 1997: 12)

In addition to marking the pivotal moment when the hopes of the Second Republic gave way to the curtailments of the dictatorship, the Civil War is described as parenthetical. Beyond being a calamity, it created what people saw as a desirable scenario in which to change a state of affairs that was unequal for many, such as those triumphant moments during the war when factory workers declared the workers' revolution in Barcelona and marched, at least for a while, in a taken city. Of all inequalities, these literary narratives attend predominantly to those caused by gender. There might be something disconcerting about women characters' enthusiasm for the war period but it can be explained in terms of the space and time afforded to them by the disruption war provoked. Judit, Natalia's mother in Roig's *La hora violeta*, writes in her diary (entry dated 30 March 1947):

> Añoro los días de la guerra pasados junto a Kati. No sé por qué pienso que fui tan feliz durante la guerra. Es extraño: fue la época en que vi más muerte y más tristeza y, a pesar de todo, fui feliz. Cuando Kati y yo, cogidas de la mano, paseábamos por una Barcelona *trastocada*.
>
> [I miss the days of the war spent with Kati. I do not know why I think I was so happy during the war. It is strange: it was the time I saw more death and sadness and, despite everything, I was happy. When Kati and I, hand in hand, strolled around a *disrupted* Barcelona.] (Roig 1986b: 128. Italics are mine)

A trait of the characters depicted living during the Second Republic is to feel as though they have an active role in history, that they are history-makers themselves, whereas such feelings are completely effaced in the same characters during the dictatorship: 'cuarenta años tan vacíos y tan estériles que se me han pasado como un ciclón, un ciclón que, de repente, me ha hecho encanecer, nada más' [forty years so empty and so sterile that flew past me like a cyclone, a cyclone that suddenly made me go grey, nothing else] ('Sólo pude conservar una fotografía' in Riera 1980: 82). The image of the cloistered woman forced to live a meaningless life recurs, as

Candela's mother — one of the many voices gathered by Ana, the protagonist and chronicler in Montero's *Crónica del desamor* — puts it:

> Casi cuarenta años juntos, desde que me casé a los veinte, virgen y niña. Sucedió todo muy rápido [...] Me acostumbré a ir quemando los días [...] reventada de cansancio y de rutina. Sabes, pasé tanto tiempo sin salir de casa [...] que llegó un momento en que me sentía incapaz de afrontar el mundo exterior. [...] Una mañana, de repente, me encontré casi en los sesenta, sin guardar recuerdos de mi vida.
>
> [Almost forty years together, since I married at twenty, a virgin and a child. It all happened very fast [...] I got used to killing time [...] knackered by fatigue and routine. You know, I spent so long without going out of the house [...] that there came a time when I felt unable to face the outside world. [...] One morning, all of a sudden, I found myself being almost sixty, without having memories of my life.] (Montero 2010: 215–16)

During the dictatorship women's memories are so worthless that they become non-existent. Thus, when it ends, remembering acquires a vital importance. In *La hora violeta*, Natalia is on an island in the Mediterranean reading the Odyssey. This choice is in no way fortuitous: to most critics, 'one of the principal functions of Odysseus's autobiographical story-telling is to keep his memory alive and, in the poem, memory is the sole defence against dissolution' (Porter 1999). Like Odysseus, most characters in the novels devote themselves to memory, to a constant process of remembering, in order to exist.[19]

The hegemonic discourse of the transition insisted that the process's success was based on collective agreement, and that it was precisely the fact of it being collective that made it infallible. At the same time, it constantly stressed that this agreement was only made possible by the good will of its few protagonists — such as Juan Carlos of Bourbon, Adolfo Suárez or Santiago Carrillo — who were identified individually in a narrative that heroized them. While the process/ discourse still maintains that those who ushered in the arrival of democracy were members of the political elite, a number of women writers viewed the compromise of consensus as a major sacrifice that claimed its victims. Disobeying the pact of forgetting and looking back to the activity of the clandestine political opposition and resistance movements during Franco's dictatorship, these novels rescue those who did not have the empathy of the official chroniclers, denouncing the exclusive nature of the process/discourse towards democracy. Elia, the protagonist of Tusquet's *El mismo mar de todos los veranos*, depicting university students taking part in demonstrations despite the dictatorship's physical repression (also described in great detail in Roig's *Tiempo de cerezas*), reminds us of those who set the process of change in motion:

> aunque no estaban todavía los tiempos maduros para nada [...] aquel encerrarnos sin proyecto ni propósitos y ver surgir por vez primera un tipo especialísimo de íntima solidaridad (aunque a la puerta aguardaban los grises y más allá, en la ciudad, en el reino, no se movía apenas nada) era terrible y hermoso y esperanzador.
>
> [although times were not yet ripe at all [...] that locking ourselves up without a project or purposes and seeing for the first time the emergence of a very special

kind of intimate solidarity (although policemen were waiting at the door and beyond, in the city, in the kingdom, hardly anything was moving) was terrible and beautiful and hopeful.] (Tusquets 1978: 62–63)

Remembering these acts of resistance reveals a commitment to memory and history and also to justice, and raises the hope for change.

The hegemonic discourse, in its will to confirm the achievement of this change, built the narrative of a brand new Spain, a recurrent phrasing that sought to erase the problem of the 'two Spains' which was tied to the ghost of the Civil War and the dictatorship.[20] This narrative insisted on the image of a brash, young, cosmopolitan nation that found its cultural counterpart in popular conceptions of the 'Movida'. The most visible way in which women authors denounced the fallacies of this narrative was by talking about love, gender, sex and sexuality, exposing and confronting the National-Catholic morality that conditioned people's sentimental education during the dictatorship.[21] These personal issues that concern us all were especially relevant to Spanish society as a whole in the post-Franco period and indispensable to a transition to democracy.[22] The death of Franco led to a period of cohabitation of old and new ways of life that triggered an urgent demand for narratives that accounted for the shifts in ideology and sensitivity. Women authors insisted on highlighting the set of norms imposed by Francoist sentimental education and formulated a sentimental counter-education, providing society with alternative behavioural models that would allow a true new Spain to exist. This sentimental counter-education was articulated by questioning power relations in the structures of romantic love, rebelling against established gender roles, exposing how the celebrated sexual liberation only favoured men, bringing to light homosexuality (especially lesbianism), or suggesting new ways of understanding masculinity (or better, masculinities).[23]

After 1975, the official discourse stated that the fathers of the Spanish transition led a historic process that succeeded, thanks to three principles — the pact of forgetting, the consensus, and the birth of a brand new Spain — , in bringing democracy to the country. The process became its discourse and every time its results were questioned, it was brought back and re-told with remarkable insistence. In the meantime, alongside people disobeying the pact and remembering, living in the margins of the proclaimed consensus and disbelieving the renovation of society, there were authors engaging with those people's stories that demanded to be told, writing counter-narratives to the process/discourse.

In line with the belief that a democratic society depends (amongst other things) on its historical memory, more and more researchers are currently examining the hegemonic discourse of the transition.[24] The historical memory movement: '*un fenómeno de reapropiación social de la capacidad de narrar desde muy diversas perspectivas y soportes aspectos de un pasado que reclama de nuevo atención o que parece estar todavía pegado al presente, aquí*' [a phenomenon of social reappropriation of the ability to narrate aspects of a past that demands attention again or that seems to be still stuck to the present, here, from very different perspectives and media] (Jerez & Sánchez 2014: 211. Italics in the original) has posed the question '¿De quién es el poder de contar?' [Whose is the power to tell?] (see Faber, Sánchez & Izquierdo 2010), demonstrating that the proliferation of subjective stories has a liberating effect in itself and expresses a constitutive equality of people's status as citizens.[25] If we want to question the myth of the process/discourse of the Spanish transition and recover its reality, we need to re-examine the canon, to recover and put in circulation as many stories in transition as we can, as an attempt to make 'un *ajuste de cuentos*' [a settling of stories][26] (Silva 2013: 16), to show that the dictatorship was much more than a political regime and the transition much more than the manufacture of a constitution. The more stories we have, the more we realize the complexity of the period, a complexity that the dominant process/discourse wanted to eliminate, but that is fundamental to (a healthy) democracy. Despite the intentions of the ongoing revision to multiply the stories, the lack of women's narrations is nevertheless shocking (not to say simply absurd), and when we find them, they are (again) often left out of the general analysis, confined in the 'feminine' sub-canon.[27] It is time to start making amends.

Bibliography

ÁGUILA, RAFAEL DEL and RICARDO MONTORO. 1984. *El discurso político de la transición española* (Madrid: Centro de Investigaciones Sociológicas)

AGUILAR FERNÁNDEZ, PALOMA. 1997. 'Amnistía al fin', Editorial of *El País*, 15 October 1977 <http://elpais.com/diario/1977/10/15/opinion/245718004_850215.html> [accessed 18 August 2016]

—— 2002. *Memory and Amnesia. The Role of the Spanish Civil War in the Transition to Democracy*. (New York: Berghahn)

BALIBREA, MARI PAZ. 2002. 'La novela negra en la transición española como fenómeno cultural: una interpretación', *Iberoamericana*, 2: 111–18

BENJAMIN, WALTER. 1999. *Illuminations*, trans. by Harry Zorn (London: Pimlico)

BUCKLEY, RAMÓN. 1996. *La doble transición. Política y literatura en la España de los años setenta* (Madrid: Siglo XXI)

CONTE, RAFAEL. 1985. 'En busca de la novela perdida', *Ínsula*, 464–65 : 1, 24. special issue 'Diez años de novela en España (1976–1985)'

ECHEVARRIA, IGNACIO. 2012. 'La CT: un cambio de paradigma', in *CT o la Cultura de la Transición. Crítica a 35 años de cultura española*, ed. by Guillem Martínez (Barcelona: Debolsillo), pp, 25–36

ERLL, ASTRID and NÜNNING, ANSGAR. 2008. *Cultural Memory Studies: an International and Interdisciplinary Handbook* (Berlin: de Gruyter)

FABER, SEBASTIAAN, SÁNCHEZ LEÓN, PABLO and IZQUIERDO MARTÍN, JESÚS. 2010. '¿De quién es el poder de contar? A propósito de las polémicas públicas sobre memoria histórica', *Viento sur*, 113: 70–73

FERNÁNDEZ-SAVATER, AMADOR. 2011. 'El arte de esfumarse; crisis e implosión de la cultura consensual en España,' *Público* (14/04/2011) <http://blogs.publico.es/fueradelugar/327/crisis-de-la-cultura-consensual-en-espana> [accessed 18 August 2016]

FUSI AIZPURÚA, JUAN PABLO. 1996. 'La reforma Suárez', in *Memoria de la Transición*, ed. by Santos Juliá, Javier Pradera and Joaquín Prieto (Madrid: Tauris), pp. 162–65

GOYTISOLO, JUAN. 1999. *Cogitus interruptus* (Barcelona: Seix Barral)

HERZBERGER, DAVID K. 1991. 'Narrating the Past: History and the Novel of Memory in Postwar Spain', *PMLA*, 106: 34–45

HIRSCH, MARIANNE and VALERIE SMITH. 2002. 'Feminism and Cultural Memory: An Introduction', *Signs*, 28: 1–19, Special Issue: Gender and Cultural Memory

Jerez Novara, Ariel and Pablo Sánchez León (eds). 2014. *Con la memoria de una república por venir. Conversaciones intergeneracionales sobre identidades antifranquistas y democracia* (Madrid: Ediciones Contratiempo)

Juliá Díaz, Santos, Javier Pradera, and Joaquín Prieto (eds). 1996. *Memoria De La Transición* (Madrid: Taurus)

Labanyi, Jo. 2007. 'Memory and Modernity in Democratic Spain: The Difficulty of Coming to Terms with the Spanish Civil War', *Poetics Today*, 28: 89–116

Labrador Méndez, Germán. 2008. 'Popular Filmic Narratives and the Spanish Transition', in *Post-Authoritarian Cultures: Spain and Latin America's Southern Cone*, ed. by Luis Martín-Estudillo and Roberto Ampuero (Nashville: Vanderbilt University Press), pp. 144–71

—— 'El Cristal de la Bola'. 2010. *Revista Mombaça*, 8: 5–10

León, Carolina. 2012. 'Libertad sin ira: qué fue de la crítica literaria (y cualquier otra) en la CT' in *CT o la Cultura de la Transición. Crítica a 35 años de cultura española* , ed. by Guillem Martínez (Barcelona: Debolsillo), pp. 89–100

Martín Gaite, Carmen. 1987. *Usos amorosos de la postguerra española* (Barcelona: Anagrama)

Martínez, Guillem. 2012. 'El concepto CT', in *CT o la Cultura de la Transición. Crítica a 35 años de cultura española*, ed. by Guillem Martínez (Barcelona: Debolsillo), pp. 13–24

Mate Rupérez, Manuel Reyes. 2006. '¿Existe una responsabilidad histórica?', *Claves de razón práctica*, 168: 34–39

—— 2006. 'Memoria e historia: dos lecturas del pasado', *Letras libres*, 53: 44–48

—— 2012. 'De la memoria a la reconciliación, una elipse incómoda', *Pasajes: Revista de pensamiento contemporáneo*, 40: 5–15

—— 2014. 'El historiador y la mirada de la víctima', *El Periódico* (17/06/14) <http://www.elperiodico.com/es/noticias/opinion/historiador-mirada-victima-3307547> [accessed 18 August 2016]

Monedero, Juan Carlos. 2013. *La Transición contada a nuestros padres. Nocturno de la democracia española* (Madrid: Catarata)

Montero, Rosa. 1981. *La función Delta* (Barcelona: Debate)

—— 1982. *Cinco años de país* (Barcelona: Debate)

—— 2010. *Crónica del desamor* (Madrid: Santillana Ediciones Generales)

Morán, Gregorio. 2015. *El precio de la transición* (Madrid: Akal)

Nichols, Geraldine C. 1995. 'Ni una, ni 'grande,' ni liberada: la narrativa de mujer en la España democrática,' in *Del franquismo a la posmodernidad : cultura española 1975–1990*, ed. by José B. Monleón (Madrid: Akal), pp. 197–217

Ortiz, Lourdes. 1979. *Picadura mortal* (Madrid: Sedmay)

—— 1981. *En días como estos* (Madrid: Akal)

—— 1982. *Urraca* (Barcelona: Puntual)

—— 1986. *Luz de la memoria* (Madrid: Akal)

—— 2010. *Pensar la escritura*, Morán Rodríguez, Carmen (ed.) (Valladolid: Universidad de Valladolid, Secretariado de Publicaciones e Intercambio Editorial)

Quaggio, Giulia. 2014. *La cultura en transición. Reconciliación y política cultural en España, 1976–1986* (Madrid: Alianza)

Peiró Martín, Ignacio. 2004. 'La era de la memoria: reflexiones sobre la historia, la opinión pública y los historiadores', *Memoria y Civilización*, 7: 243–94

Pérez-Díaz, Víctor. 1999. *Spain at the Crossroads. Civil Society, Politics, and the Rule of Law* (Cambridge, MA: Harvard University Press)

Porter, Roger, J. 1999. 'Convocation Talk' at Reed College, <http://www.reed.edu/humanities/hum110/odysseyconvocation1999.html> [accessed 18 August 2016]

Reinstädler, Janett. 2007. 'De la pizarra mágica a la cajita dorada: estrategias mnemónicas en tres autoras de la Transición española', in *Memoria literaria de la Transición española*, ed. by Javier Gómez-Montero (Madrid: Iberoamericana), pp. 119–35

RESINA, JOAN RAMÓN (ed.). 2000. *Disremembering the Dictatorship: The Politics of Memory in the Spanish Transition to Democracy* (Amsterdam: Rodopi)

RIERA, CARME. 1977. *Jo pos per testimoni les gavines* (Barcelona: Laia)

—— 1980 *Palabra de mujer: bajo el signo de una memoria impenitente* (Barcelona: Laia; trans. Luisa Cotoner)

—— 1982. 'Literatura femenina: ¿un lenguaje prestado?' in *Quimera*, 18: 9–12.

RIGNEY, ANN. 2008. 'The Dynamics of Remembrance: Texts between Monumentality and Morphing', in *Cultural Memory Studies: An International and Interdisciplinary Handbook*, ed. by Astrid Erll and Ansgar Nünning (Berlin: de Gruyter), pp. 345–52

ROIG, MONTSERRAT. 1980. *¿Tiempo de mujer?* (Barcelona: Plaza & Janés)

—— 1986A. *Tiempo de Cerezas* (Barcelona: Plaza & Janés). Translated by Enrique Sordo

—— 1986B. *La hora violeta* (Barcelona: Plaza & Janés). Translated by Enrique Sordo

—— 1989. *La ópera cotidiana* (Barcelona: Destino) Translated by Enrique Sordo

RUIZ TORRES, PEDRO. 2002. 'La historia en nuestro paradójico tiempo presente', *Pasajes: Revista de pensamiento contemporáneo*, 9: 17–30

—— 2007. 'Los discursos de la memoria histórica en España', *Hispania Nova, Revista de Historia Contemporánea*, 7 (2007). <http://hispanianova.rediris.es/7/dossier/07d001.pdf> [accessed 18 August 2016]

—— 2008. 'Los modos de producción del pasado', *Saitabi*, 58: 15–25

SAMBLANCAT MIR, NEUS. 1997. 'Las barricadas de la memoria: a propósito de algunos testimonios de guerra de mujeres exiliadas', *Guaraguao*, 2: 4–14

SANZ VILLANUEVA, SANTOS. 2013. 'Relatos del Postfranquismo: un apunte y diez fichas' in AA.VV. *El relato de la Transición. La Transición como relato* (Zaragoza: Universidad de Zaragoza), pp. 13–41

SILVA, EMILIO. 2013. 'El mito de la Transición no va a morir en la cama', prologue to Juan Carlos Monedero, *La Transición contada a nuestros padres. Nocturno de la democracia española* (Madrid: Catarata), pp. 13–16

SOMMER, DORIS. 1988. '"Not Just a Personal Story": Women's *Testimonios* and the Plural Self', in *Life/Lines: Theoretical Essays on Women's Autobiography*, ed. by B. Brodzki and C. Schenck (Ithaca, NY: Cornell University Press), pp. 107–30

SONG, H. ROSI . 2005. 'Tracing the Past: An Introduction', in *Traces of Contamination: Unearthing the Francoist Legacy in Contemporary Spain*, ed. by Eloy E. Merino and H. Rosi Song, (Lewisburg: Bucknell University Press), pp. 11–26

TSUCHIYA, AKIKO. 2003. 'Women and Fiction in post-Franco Spain' in *The Cambridge Companion to the Spanish Novel*, ed. by Harriet Turner and Adelaida López de Martínez (Cambridge: Cambridge University Press), pp. 212–30

TUSQUETS, ESTHER. 1978. *El mismo mar de todos los veranos* (Barcelona: Lumen)

—— 1979. *El amor es un juego solitario* (Barcelona: Lumen, 1979)

—— 1980. *Varada tras el último naufragio* (Barcelona: Lumen, 1980)

VÁZQUEZ MONTALBÁN, MANUEL. 1991. 'La novela española entre el posfranquismo y el posmodernismo' in *La rénovation du roman espagnol depuis 1975: actes du colloque des 13 et 14 février 1991*, ed. by Yvan Lissorgues (Toulouse: Presses Universitaires du Mirail), pp.13–25

VILARÓS, TERESA. 1998. *El mono del desencanto* (Mexico, D.F.: Siglo Veintiuno)

VINYES, RICARD. 2011. *Asalto a la memoria. Impunidades y reconciliaciones, símbolos y éticas* (Barcelona: Los libros del lince)

Notes to Chapter 5

1. This chapter was written with the support of HISPANEX (Programme for Cultural Cooperation with Foreign Universities of the Ministry of Education, Culture and Sport of Spain).
2. There have been different dates worthy of attention when framing the Spanish transition: some critics see the beginning of a transition when Opus Dei members reached the upper echelon of the Spanish government bureaucracy in the 1960s, since they interpret the 'technocratic' governance that followed as a modernization of Spain into a 20th-century industrialized capitalist economy; others state 1968, as a continental landmark in the lives of a whole generation in Europe; or 1973, year of the assassination of Prime Minister Carrero Blanco, the only figure who could have continued the legacy of Franco as it was. The end also shifts to 1986, second electoral victory of the PSOE, or even 1992, when Spain hosted the Olympic Games in Barcelona and the Universal Exposition in Seville, had Madrid designated European Capital of Culture, and celebrated the Quincentennial of Columbus's arrival in America. Some even claim it is not yet concluded. Nevertheless, 1975–1982 is a widely accepted frame for the political process of transformation.
3. All translations are mine (but not entirely — thanks to Gabriel Page for a last quick look).
4. During those years and for a long time afterwards, the newspaper *El País* was 'a hegemonic instrument for encoding and enforcing knowledges about Spain. No other has either the readership or the public status needed to challenge the mnemonic politics of this powerful opinion-shaper' (Resina 2000: 85). I understand and use this source as a privileged and influential instrument for creating knowledge and shaping public opinion.
5. The term CT is a collective construction proposed by the authors as a tool of analysis. It reads cultural reality in Spain from the belief that, in a democratic system, 'los límites a la libertad de expresión no son las leyes. Son límites culturales' [the limits to freedom of expression are not laws. They are cultural limits] (Martínez 2012: 14).
6. See the special issue: 'Diez años de novela en España (1976–1985)' of *Ínsula*, n° 464–65 (1985).
7. For the prescriptive/descriptive work of critics in relation to women's writing during the Spanish transition see Akiko Tsuchiya (2003).
8. Although by the time Franco died, this gender-labelling was especially acute in the country, it is not exclusive to the transitional period nor restricted to within Spanish borders. The gender labels still function and affect writers' works deeply. In 2015, Rosa Montero complained about the limiting effect they have on the interpretation of her novels: '[m]e fastidia mucho y lo he dicho muchas veces: que cuando una mujer novelista escribe una novela protagonizada por una mujer pues todo el mundo, muchas mujeres lectoras también, piense que está hablando de mujeres, mientras que cuando un hombre escribe una novela protagonizada por un hombre, todo el mundo piensa que está hablando del género humano. Yo no escribo de mujeres, escribo del género humano' [something that really annoys me and I have mentioned it many times is the fact that when a female novelist writes a novel with a female protagonist, everybody, including many women readers, thinks that you are talking about women, whereas when a man writes a novel starring a man, everyone thinks he is talking about the human race. I do not write about women, I write about the human race] (interviewed by Javier Gallego in the radio programme *Carne Cruda*, 23 April 2015).
9. The arguments presented here are based on the analysis of the following works: Esther Tusquets — *El mismo mar de todos los veranos* (1978), *El amor es un juego solitario* (1979), *Varada tras el último naufragio* (1980); Montserrat Roig — *El temps de les cireres* (1977), *L'hora violeta* (1980), *L'opera quotidiana* (1982); Carme Riera — *Te deix, amor, la mar com a penyora* (1975) and *Jo pos per testimoni les gavines* (1977), *Palabra de mujer*, (1980, Spanish re-edition of the original *Jo pos per testimoni les gavines* written by Carme Riera in Catalan. Most are direct translations, some are modified, and others were not published in the Spanish version); Rosa Montero — *Crónica del desamor* (1979), *La función Delta* (1981); Lourdes Ortiz — *Luz de la memoria* (1976), *Picadura mortal*, (1979), *En días como éstos*, (1981), *Urraca* (1982).
10. I take the concept 'batalla hermenéutica' from the philosopher Reyes Mate. In the interpretation of facts, ideologues can establish a collective imaginary that will justify one position or

another. Relating this to the concept of historical responsibility, Reyes Mate explains that in a hermeneutic battle what counts is not the interpretation of facts or figures but the later moral significance of this interpretation: 'Una cosa es contar los muertos y otra, comprender su significación. (...) La batalla hermenéutica no es sobre los hechos sino sobre su significación moral' [One thing is to count the dead and another, to understand their significance. (...) The hermeneutic battle is not about facts but about their moral significance] (Mate 2014). I think this concept is especially pertinent as the debate continues to stir passions and controversies.

11. According to the historian Ricard Vinyes, the problem lies precisely in the fact that '[el] Estado no suprime memorias: crea una memoria diciendo que no crea ninguna' [the State does not suppress memories: it creates a memory saying that it does not create any] (interviewed in Jerez Novara and Sánchez León 2014: 237).

12. In the late 1990s and early 2000s a new attitude towards the recent past emerged and questioned the perpetuation of this discourse of oblivion and the permanence of memory as a taboo. It had its most clear articulation in what is called 'recuperación de la memoria histórica', a movement that gathered strength with the generational intersection at the turn of the century, stimulated by 'the need for meaning that the third postwar generation projects on the war' (Winter 2012: 14). It most visibly materialized in the foundation of the 'Asociación para la Recuperación de la Memoria Histórica' (Association for the Recovery of Historical Memory) by Emilio Silva and Santiago Macías, an activist organization that collects oral and written testimonies of Francoist repression, and excavates mass graves in order to identify the bodies of its victims.

13. The seven political leaders who participated in the writing of the Spanish Constitution of 1978, four of whom had had relevant political and institutional positions in the Franco dictatorship, were all men and are usually referred to as 'the fathers of the Constitution.' I extend this term to all those men (journalists, critics, organic intellectuals) who wrote the transition controlling its discourse.

14. This distrust of historiography is very visible in novels like *Urraca* by Lourdes Ortiz. Here, the protagonist exposes the mediation of language in the account of factual events, thus the possibility of manipulation surfaces: 'Ellos escribirán la historia a su modo; hablarán de mi locura y mentirán para justificar mi despojamiento y mi encierro' [They will write history in their own way; they will speak of my madness and lie to justify my dispossession and my confinement] (1982: 12). The novel reflects on the constant struggle for power, or rather for the attainment of that power through narration.

15. Although Montero had decided some years earlier not to re-publish the novel, she confesses that people's requests made her change her mind. She emphasizes that those who wanted to see a reissue of the novel were not only the members of the generation who lived through the period and identified with the characters, but also their children, who felt the novel to be part of their own history.

16. In the 1970s and 80s, there was a global concern with promoting 'history from below', giving voice to the voiceless. It was then that memory was first acknowledged as a reliable source. It became the object of historical research and brought with it a new concept of subjectivity.

17. In this article, Reinstädler is referring specifically to Carme Riera, Esther Tusquets and Carmen Martín Gaite, but it applies to Montserrat Roig, Rosa Montero and Lourdes Ortiz as well. I do not comment on Martín Gaite's work because, although it was subjected to a remarkable change after Franco's death, she belongs to a different generation.

18. The historical memory debate has brought back the official discourse's reluctance to build bridges with the Second Republic, exposing the fallacy of a self-made democracy whose roots are to be found 'en el diálogo que desde los años 50 se entabló entre las partes divididas por la guerra de 1936–1939, y que concluyó finalmente en la Ley de Amnistía de 1977 y en la Constitución de 1978' [in the dialogue that, from the 50s, was held by the parts divided by the war of 1936–1939, and that finally concluded in the 1977 Amnesty Law and the 1978 Constitution] (Faber, Sánchez León & Izquierdo 2010: 71). On one hand, a democracy which acquires its foundations under a dictatorship comes across as a contradiction in terms. On the other, the validation of a democracy through its own inaugural events — the 1977 Amnesty and the 1978 Constitution — appears to be fairly arrogant.

19. 'Dedico todo mi interés a la memoria, me ocupo de ella meticulosamente y le consagro todo mi tiempo. La memoria lo es todo para mí' [I dedicate all my interest to memory, I deal with it meticulously and devote all my time to it. Memory is everything to me] ('Y pongo por testigo a las gaviotas', in Riera 1980: 34). We find an identical dedication to memory, the same interdependent relation between remembering and being, in a sixty-year-old Lucía, the protagonist of Montero's *La función delta*, when hospitalized in a clinic she starts writing her memoirs based on one determinant week thirty years before: 'Yo no tengo nada (...). Nada más que la memoria de aquellos años plenos, nada más que estos folios que voy rescatando del recuerdo y en los que juego a vivir' [I have nothing (...). Nothing but the memory of those full years, nothing but these pages that I am rescuing from memory and in which I play at living] (Montero 1981: 89). Remembering and living are intricately attached to such an extent that the recollection of memories becomes a self-asserting narration, says Tusquet's Elia: 'todo lo que me resta de vida centrado en [...] recontarme a mí misma por milésima vez las interminables, las inagotables viejas historias' [all that remains of my life focused on [...] retelling myself for the thousandth time the endless, inexhaustible old stories] (Tusquets 1978: 29). The act of remembering as a process of self-creation becomes performative, depending on the acts of telling or writing: 'A veces pienso que escribo esta historia para mí misma; que nadie, ni juglares ni poetas, la repetirán por los pueblos y las cortes. Pero, cada vez más necesito contar' [Sometimes I think I write this story to myself; that no one, minstrels or poets, will repeat it around villages and courts. But increasingly I need to tell it] (Ortiz 1982: 161).
20. In their effort to confirm that radical change, the analysts of the process/discourse, referring to Suárez's newborn administration, asserted that 'la voluntad democrática del nuevo Gobierno fue evidente casi de inmediato' [the democratic will of the new government was evident almost immediately] (Fusi 1996: 165), diverting the attention from the fact that most members had held posts of responsibility under the dictatorship and the institutions remained almost identical for years.
21. By sentimental education I refer to the complex social narratives around emotions that mainly affect the practices of love, gender, sex and sexuality. It is historically and culturally determined and lives in the deepest strata of the learning process where, though less visible, it influences all other spheres of life. Emotions are a central source of knowledge, and both reality and fiction condition the way of understanding and dealing with them. The adjective 'sentimental' was quite common during the Spanish transition, and we can easily find it in book titles like Vázquez Montalbán's *Crónica sentimental de la transición* (1985) or Montserrat Roig's *Breu història sentimental i altres contes* (1995), *De com s'inicia l'educació sentimental de Mundeta Claret i altres contes* (1998), and even her *Molta roba i poc sabó... i tan neta que la volen* (1970) was translated into Spanish in 1981 as *Aprendizaje sentimental*.
22. To better understand how National-Catholic norms imposed during the dictatorship had moulded people's understanding of love, gender, sex and sexuality, having the deepest impact on their day-to-day life, see the indispensable study *Usos amorosos de la posguerra española* (1987) by Carmen Martín Gaite.
23. This is a complex proposal with socio-political implications, the analysis of which is outside the scope of this chapter.
24. The 15-M movement marked a turning point in the understanding of 'democracy', social movements and civic engagement. Also referred to as the 'Indignants Movement', 'Take the Square' or '#spanishrevolution', it was a series of massive public demonstrations on 15 May 2011 that sprang up in fifty-eight cities all over Spain and lasted until October. People were summoned by social networks such as Real Democracy Now (*Democracia Real Ya*) to demand a real democratic system (their feeling of not being represented by any of the main political parties, put into words in the slogan 'No nos representan' [They do not represent us]), and to express their rejection of the austerity measures passed by the Government. It began to have visible impact on the political sphere in the municipal and general elections in 2015. Since then, new and old dissenting voices against the process/discourse of the transition have a bigger impact and the idea of not having ever reached a real democracy resonates much more.
25. It is no coincidence that this emerging democratisation of memory is forcing some pundits

to defend their interpretations, especially the ones concerning the transition to democracy in Spain. One of the most relevant historians engaged in this debate is Santos Juliá: '[N]o sé qué es defender la memoria histórica, ni siquiera sé qué es la memoria histórica' [I do not know what defending historic memory means, I do not even know what historic memory is], he stated in an interview after being awarded the National Prize for History 2005. He wrote his first opinion piece in *El País* the day that followed the electoral victory of the PSOE ('PSOE: de la taberna al gobierno', 29/10/1982) and has been a frequent columnist of this media since then. As part of *El País*, the historian became an influential opinion-maker who helped create the hegemonic discourse. He was the editor of *Memoria de la Transición* a volume that compiled all the articles that were published in *El País* from October 1995 to April 1996 and for twenty-six Mondays as a pull-out section dedicated to the commemoration of the transition. In the current debate, Santos Juliá maintains that there was neither silence nor forgetting and offers an alternative explanation to the pact of forgetting, using the expression 'echar al olvido' which, according to him, involves remembering the past to close it down, impeding in this way its interference with the process of making decisions for the future.

26. This is a play on 'ajuste de cuentas', meaning a settling of scores, and 'cuentos', stories.
27. The best example of this incomprehensible absence is Germán Labrador's otherwise brilliant work on the Spanish transition.

CHAPTER 6

Fascinated by Observation: Amalia Domingo Soler and Vicente Manterola's Debates on Spiritism in Late Nineteenth-Century Spain

Marta Ferrer

This chapter explores the changing relationship between science and religion and late nineteenth-century methods of observation[1] as portrayed in the debates on spiritism between the spiritist writer Amalia Domingo Soler (1835–1909) and the Catholic priest Vicente Manterola (1833–1891). In a series of sermons directed at Catholic devotees in Barcelona Cathedral, later published under the title *El Satanismo: O Sea, La Cátedra de Satanás Combatida desde la cátedra del espíritu santo: Refutación de la escuela espiritista* (1879) [*Satanism: Or, the Chair of Satanism refuted by the Seat of the Holy Spirit*],[2] the Piarist priest Vicente Manterola spoke out against the new science of spiritism. Manterola's speeches were heatedly rebutted by the spiritist writer Amalia Domingo Soler through the publication of a series of six articles published a year later under the title *El Espiritismo Refutando los Errores del Catolicismo Romano* (1880) [*Spiritism debunking the Errors of Roman Catholicism*]. Domingo Soler, a self-educated writer, was editor-in-chief of the spiritist weekly *La Luz del Porvenir* [*The Light of the Future*] (1879–1900), a journal published between 1879 and 1900 aimed at women which widely advertised Domingo Soler's arguments against Manterola. In her refutations, Domingo Soler praised William Draper's *History of the Conflicts between Science and Religion* (1876), the translation of which rekindled disputes between those who saw Catholicism as the main factor in Spanish decadence and the major obstacle to the development of science, and those who felt nostalgia for Spain's Early Modern empire.[3]

Spiritualism had originated in New York in 1848, and arrived in Spain thanks to the philosopher and educator Hippolyte Léon Denizard, alias Allan Kardec, during the 1860s, borrowing the name from the French *spiritisme* (espiritismo).[4] Spiritism, as Allan Kardec had articulated it, was both an observational and a moral science, which believed in the afterlife and in possible re-incarnation. As Arkinstall (2014) and others have argued, spiritism both in Spain and abroad presented itself as a universal panacea for the middle and lower classes, since it offered them spiritual redemption, progress and equality.[5]

In public speeches by both Manterola and Domingo Soler, spiritism was the umbrella under which they discussed topics including Catholicism, Spanish History, and more to the point, the nature of both miracles and spiritist phenomena and their scientific and doctrinal truth. The moment of these publications coincided with the well-known 'Spanish science polemics',[6] a series of highly politicized debates about the development of Spanish science and its place within Europe (Nieto-Galán 1999: 76). The debates within the *polémica* took three different strands, namely, the utility (or inutility) of Spanish science,[7] the comparison with other European nations, and the Black Legend of Catholicism during the age of the Spanish Empire, the last of which was rekindled during the early years of the twentieth century (Nieto-Galán 1999: 49). These theoretical debates have influenced Spanish historians throughout the twentieth century up to the present, as explained by Laín-Entralgo's (1963) enduring concept of the 'two Spains', according to which progressive political ideas from abroad fought against Catholicism. Historians of late nineteenth-century Spain have exhausted the possibilities of the famous *polemics* by examining the debate through political ideology. On the other hand, literary scholars typically study spiritism under the aegis of liberal politics, since much spiritist writing was produced by women who belonged to feminist associations.[8] Only recently have scholars challenged the dyadic position between science and Catholicism and between conservatism and liberalism by assessing literary works of science-fiction and cultural scientific practices, thereby both re-assessing the contribution of Spain to Western scientific knowledge and undermining well-established positions of liberalism against conservatism.[9]

In what follows, I will articulate a dialogue between spiritism and late nineteenth-century claims of objective observation, rather than focusing on spiritism's liberal and marginal input. According to Daston and Gallison (2007), the term 'objectivity' was used by scientists in the late nineteenth century who attempted to achieve a mechanical, restrained, and individualized series of practices. Attempts to cultivate objectivity caused great chagrin in literate spheres, since this policing of subjectivity generated a clear-cut division between the artist and the scientist (Daston 2007: 256). Taking Daston and Gallison's claims as a point of departure, late-nineteenth century objectivity should be seen as a strategy of legitimation for both Manterola and Domingo insofar as they propagated their theories of Catholicism and spiritism respectively by framing divine appearances as a test-case for objectivity.

This essay is divided into three parts. First, I will provide an overview of the rise of popular sciences in the second half of the nineteenth century and the entry of spiritism into Spain. Next, I will study the relationship between Manterola and Domingo Soler's theories of spiritism and the developments in astronomy. Third, I will prove how Manterola and Domingo's debates over the reality of miracles provide a central example in the struggles over the claims of objective observations. Miracles, I will argue, offered rich fodder from which to generate authority in religious and scientific debates. Both Catholics and spiritists not only took pains to approximate their views to modernity, but also linked their arguments with those articulated by astronomy and practices of scientific observation.[10] By giving spiritism a new framework within Hispanic Studies, this chapter attempts both to introduce potential ways of relating spiritism to contemporary phenomena like the proliferation of astronomic observatories and Catholic miracles, and to foreshadow a new set of cultural scientific practices beyond sterile debates like the *Polémica de la ciencia española*.

Popular Sciences and the rise of spiritism

During the second half of the nineteenth century, cultural phenomena on the borders of science were being mocked through sardonic material in the press and in popular literary stories.[11] From the second half of the twentieth century onwards, historians of science started to take these neglected practices seriously by arguing that their popularity in theatrical works had a counterpart in scientific lectures and serious publications in journals. The volume edited by Roy Wallis, *On the Margins of Social Science* (1979), was the first attempt to give these practices a historical value. By using the term 'pseudo-science', historians in Anglo-American academia separated such practices from hard sciences, that is, sciences which demonstrated their results empirically. This demarcation was more sociological than real, since as Thomas Kuhn argued in his *Structures of Scientific Revolution* (1962), much of what was considered a science was always open to modifications by upcoming generations of scientists. Later historians like Roger Cooter (1984) and Alison Winter (1998) challenged straight divisions between 'science' and 'pseudoscience' by respectively studying how phrenology and mesmerism imbued nineteenth-century British society and how they were praised by both amateurs and scientific authorities. In contrast to British and American studies, the failure to examine pseudoscientific practices in the Spanish context is remarkable, especially when such performative businesses produced specialized journals and triggered debate among ecclesiastical authorities.

The rise of spiritism in Spain and elsewhere derives directly from phrenology. Phrenology was the science of studying different human aptitudes through the various parts of the brain, and it was made popular in the 1840s thanks to Mariano Cubí's lectures at the Philharmonic Society in Barcelona.[12] While phrenology was attuned to the interest in physiology during the 1840s, spiritism flourished throughout the latter half of the century, when the practices of magnetic phenomena and brain-analysis started to be seen from a psychological outlook. Cubí's lessons quickly triggered publications by both critics and supporters.[13] An example of this was Jaume Balmés's series of 'Estudios Frenológicos' published in 1843 in the Catholic magazine *La Sociedad* (Menéndez Pelayo 1880: 917). Balmés, a Catalan apologist, expressed a wariness of phrenology because of its determinism and fatalism. Probably fearing censorship, phrenologists took pains to adapt their science to Catholic dogma.

From the 1860s phrenological practices waned thanks to growing interest in psychological research (Nofre Mateo 2005: 198). This shift helped phrenology to pave the way for the reception of spiritism during the 1860s and 1870s. Spiritism's ties with phrenology were based on the progressive reforms both sciences endorsed. In this way, Domingo Soler's praise for progressive reforms throughout different re-incarnations of the soul echoed what the phrenologist Mariano Cubí had sketched in his lessons three decades earlier, that is, a science for society in which each individual could make progress according to her or his mental attitudes.

While phrenology studied human physiology, spiritism was fashioned as a psychological science, much in tune with Wundt's psychological treatises and belief in the afterlife.[14] In his account of Spanish orthodox groups, Menéndez Pelayo claimed that spiritism had become particularly strong from the 1860s onwards because of the reception of French books by the spiritists Camille Flammarion and Allan Kardec. The scientific impetus of spiritism was highlighted by Flammarion's publication of the *Plurality of the Inhabited Worlds* in 1863. Flammarion, an amateur astronomer, gave spiritism a cosmic character by adding the argument that other planets of the Universe were inhabited by human reincarnations. As bizarre as Flammarion's assertions might sound today, *Plurality of the Inhabited Worlds* was translated into Spanish in 1873 and elicited both refutation and praise from the 1870s until the late 1890s. This period coincided with the rise of spectroscopic observations and the study of protuberances on other planets by the Italian society Spectroscopisti Italiani and by the Royal Astronomical Society in London. In Spain, it coincided with the erection of observatories and the first publications on the subject of astronomy, such as Linares's *La Vida de los Astros* (1877) and Arcimis's *El Telescopio Moderno* (1878).[15]

Catholic responses to the growing phenomenon of spiritism and its connection with scientific knowledge were popular from 1869 onwards, coinciding with the beginning of the Six-Year Revolutionary Period. The Spanish Glorious Revolution and the overthrow of Isabel II triggered new religious and printing laws, which ratified religious freedom and led to a flurry of anticlerical newspapers and booklets being published.[16] The short-lived revolutionary period resulted in the Restoration of both the monarchy and Catholicism as the official religion of Spain. However, José Cánovas, the first conservative leader of the Restoration period, discarded the law of 'religious freedom', ratifying the 1876 Constitution, which instead promoted religious tolerance.[17] This new bill was a compromise solution that did not satisfy either anti-clericals or Catholics, since it declared that any religion could be practised privately even though the public religion was Catholicism. Reactions against both the preceding religious freedom and the subsequent ambiguous religious tolerance raised concerns from Catholics, who saw both laws as dangerous challenges to Catholicism. An exemplary case of criticism against religious freedom was the canonist Vicente de la Fuente's political pamphlet *Sobre La Libertad Religiosa*, in which he labelled spiritism a Protestant and libertarian farce:

> El Catolicismo condena las ideas fatalistas, los sortilegios, la quiromancia, o inspección de las rayas de la mano, y otras ridiculeces comunes en la librecultista Francia, donde se reputan por industria [....] El espiritismo, superstición de las supersticiones, culto de Satanás, fanatismo horrible y devastador, que hace

sacerdote a un medio farsante, medio endemoniado, que lee por el espinazo, y hace mil actores de pretendido magnetismo, ha nacido entre los protestantes, entre ellos cunde y se practica (de la Fuente 1869: 221)

[Catholicism condemns fatalism, fortune-tellings, chiromancy, palm readings, and other absurdities which are commonplace in France, where religious pluralism is accepted, these absurdities achieve a higher status because of the business they generate. [...] Spiritism is the most dangerous of all superstitions, a Satanic cult, a terrible and devastating fanaticism, which makes priests fraudulent and possessed, and which both causes servitude to the Devil and produces thousands of practitioners of magnetism within Prostestantism]

De la Fuente not only criticized spiritism but also suggested that it was Satan who produced such hoaxes. A decade later, Manterola articulated a similar message in his sermons in Barcelona Cathedral. Manterola and de la Fuente were not denying spiritist phenomena, but giving them a source (Satan) that belonged to Catholic dogma, and thus installing spiritism in their doctrine. At the same time, growing concerns over the satanic character of spiritism could also elicit the contrary effect, that is, a flourishing interest in that new maverick belief. Such arguments were expressed ironically by Amalia Domingo Soler (1880: 17) in the prologue of her refutations of Manterola's speeches, in which she thanked him for his own dissemination of spiritism to the popular classes.

Spiritism's visionary character was similar to that provided by phrenology except for one fact: spiritism not only did not adapt itself to Catholicism but lampooned the Catholic Church for its numerous intransigencies throughout history. The fact that censorship laws were more relaxed from 1869 onwards probably made possible the publication of bold arguments against the Church.[18] The combination of a blind belief in progress and criticism of the Church became the backbone of Spanish spiritism:

Han aparecido mil y mil soles, innumerables sistemas planetarios, porque todas las grandes cosas tienen humildes principios, y de los visionarios que se han entretenido en ver danzar las mesas, han salido esos locos sublimes, esos genios que el mundo llama sabios, esas lumbreras de la ciencia y el sentimiento, esos apóstoles de la razón, esos profundos deístas llamados Allan Kardec, Pezzani, Flammarion, Victor Hugo, y tantos hombres ilustres cuyos nombres sería difuso enumerar. Es inútil que la Iglesia se quiera oponer al eterno adelanto del titán de los siglos. El progreso avanzará siempre, porque su destino aspira a la regeneración de la humanidad. Su lema es hacia Dios por la caridad y la ciencia. (Domingo Soler 1880: 13)

[Several thousand suns and planetary systems have appeared. Because great discoveries always have humble origins, a few of those visionaries who dallied about studying table-turning have now become wise geniuses who study both science and morality. These are apostles of reason and strong deists such as Allan Kardec, Pezzani, Flammarion, Victor Hugo, and other illustrious men who are not listed here. The Church uselessly hinders the eternal progress of the secular titan. Progress will eternally move forward as it aspires to humanity's regeneration. The motto of progress is 'Towards God through charity and science']

Catholic attacks on spiritism were contemporary with other criticisms that tried to establish a middle-ground argument between Flammarion's theories of the universe and Catholic dogma. In this way, the priests Niceto Alonso Perujo (1879) and Cayetano Fernández (1892) provided accounts flexible enough to accommodate Flammarion's arguments while arguing for the triumph of Catholicism over such theories. The fact that both Perujo and Fernández took pains not to condemn Flammarion's cosmological theory too harshly may be explained by the fact that Jesuit priests were deeply involved in the construction of astronomical observatories. As Ruiz-Castell (2008: 68) has demonstrated, the Jesuits' persistent interest in geophysical phenomena 'led to the establishment of different Jesuit geophysical research centres in the nineteenth century'.

Science of observation: astronomy and spiritism

The popularity of Flammarion's books in Spain not only triggered the dissemination of popular astronomy but also created common ground between literature, science, and religion. Manterola and Domingo's debates were surrounded by literary publications which used astronomy as a device to describe scientific reality. The figure of the polymath scientist embodied in the figure of an astronomer would be a common example of literary representation during this period. In both *La Familia de León Roch* (1878) and *El doctor Centeno* (1883), Pérez Galdós gave a sardonic view of the changing dynamics of science in Spain while criticising bourgeois values related to churchgoing, exultant worshipping, and the love of appearances. In both accounts, the science of astronomy is articulated as something new which might be combined with Catholic religion. This is particularly true in the ironic depiction of Ruiz Cienfuegos, one of the main characters of *El doctor Centeno* whose career as an astronomer is in tune with his Catholic worship. Valera's *The Illusions of Doctor Faustino*, published serially in the magazine *La España Moderna* between 1874 and 1875, embodies the ambiguous position of science during the period, in which imagination and experience were far from being opposed to scientific knowledge. No one represented better this overlapping of observance and imagination than the narrator of Valera's first novel, who wondered about the possibilities of seeing *au-delà* and believed in invisible objects:

> Even though I may see the heavens now like an immense space and the heavenly bodies separated from one another by enormous distances, beyond the reach of eyesight and a telescope, is there no room for me to imagine whatever I like and to believe whatever I wish? (Valera 1870: 19)

Manterola and Domingo were also drawn towards the science of observing the heavens for different ends. For Manterola, Flammarion's theory was acceptable when it was about the existence of other worlds, but he was against any kind of re-incarnated life on other planets. In his speeches, Manterola (1879: 69) introduced the language of astronomy and adapted it to Catholic dogma. In this way, he refuted Flammarion's argument about re-incarnated beings inhabiting other planets by alluding to opposing views, such as those provided by the French astronomer

Fraye. Later, Manterola used Moses' telling of Genesis to prove the connection between science and Catholicism, making use of Leonhard Euler's theories (1707–1783), whose work was widely adapted to explanations of Genesis throughout the nineteenth century:

> La tierra, interrogada por los sabios, nada dijo contra la veracidad de Moisés; y entonces la impiedad subió al cielo de los astros, con el impío propósito de declarar en contradicción manifiesta las declaraciones del Génesis con las leyes de la astronomía. Pero viene Euler sospechando primero, y demostrando después que el movimiento de la elíptica, lejos de ser progresivo, es undulatorio, y que sus oscilaciones se encierran en el estrechísimo espacio de un solo grado; y se desploma el edificio que los incrédulos iban construyendo sobre la base de las antiguas doctrinas de Arato. Y una vez más resultó Moisés vindicado por la ciencia. (Manterola 1879: 179)
>
> [When learned men studied the Earth none of them found anything against Moses's narratives of Genesis. However, because many men of science pinpointed the contradiction between Genesis and the astronomical laws when observing heavenly bodies, impiety started to flourish. Contrary to these theories, Dr Euler demonstrates that the elliptical movement, far from being sequential, is undulatory. The oscillations of the flowing movement embrace the unifying system. Therefore, the great edifice of incredulity towards Genesis, which was being built from Arato's doctrines, collapses. Once again, Moses is vindicated by science]

For Domingo Soler (1880: 34), astronomy was the perfect complement of spiritism insofar as it opened a door to the spiritist hypotheses of re-incarnation and belief in the afterlife, denying any possibility of finitude. Domingo Soler (1880: 64) claimed that astronomy still needed years to discover many invisible beings and that spiritists were like astronomers, since 'los espiritistas [...] tienen la obligación de ocuparse en todos los adelantos que tienden a engrandecer al hombre elevando su pensamiento sobre las miserias y las pequeñeces de la tierra' [they both had the obligation to develop the human being by raising her/his thought above earthly miseries and petty things']

According to Anduaga Engaña (2005), it was precisely around the late 1870s and the early 1880s that astronomical popular societies, such as the 'Sociedades Astronómicas de Camille Flammarion' together with publishing houses dedicated to astronomy began to flourish in Spain. These cultural factors surrounding the popularization of astronomy might have influenced both Manterola's and Soler's comments on astronomy in their respective Catholic and spiritist utterances.

Manterola and Domingo Soler used analytic observation to reshape Biblical passages. By couching Biblical passages in a language attuned to the public, they both took pains respectively to attack and to defend spiritism. A case in point of Biblical commentary was the episode of the Medium of Endor.[19] Manterola used this Biblical passage in order to prove the exemplarity of such an extraordinary phenomenon, which entailed divine punishment. In Manterola's narrative, Samuel was called not by the medium, but by God. Samuel's apparition and Saul's ensuing defeat by the Philistines was seen in Ecclesiastes and the Paralipomenon, Manterola remarked, as divine revenge against Saul's infringement of natural laws, since he had tried to invoke the dead by using a medium. For Domingo Soler (1880: 245), however, this Biblical passage was an example of spiritualism. Samuel's earthly apparition was evidence of life after death. In this vein, Domingo opened up spiritualist phenomena to natural causality and democratic views:

> No podemos quejarnos; los padres de la iglesia son todo lo explícitos que podíamos desear; queda bien demostrado que el alma de Samuel fue la que habló con Saul, y las almas de los que se fueron, señor de Manterola, son las que han hablado en todos los tiempos con sus evocadores; porque como para Dios no hay privilegiados, no le pudo conceder a Saul lo que, según la Iglesia romana, le ha negado a los demás hombres. (Domingo Soler 1880: 245)
>
> [We cannot complain. The Church Fathers have been as explicit as we expected. It is very clear that Samuel's soul spoke to Saul. In the same way, the souls of the departed, Mr Manterola, have always been communicating with us. Because true religion does not grant privileges, God must have granted the communication with the otherworldly to all of us, and not only to Saul]

By generating different theories on the basis of Biblical episodes such as that of the witch of Endor, both Manterola and Domingo fashioned themselves as public figures, combining orality and the press. Manterola saw the Biblical passage as a warning against the infringement of divine laws, while Domingo appropriated the same passage as an example of spiritist communication with the otherworldly.

Miracles as a test-case: the weight of tradition against impostures

In October 1858 in Seville, Catholic missions had used an earthquake in order to make inhabitants repent. According to the Catholic journal *La Cruz*, Jesuits were using a natural phenomenon as an example of divine punishment in order to instil pastoral guidance. While this phenomenon speaks of the rising power of the Church in Spain during the reign of Isabel II, it is also an exemplary case of how Catholics used natural events as evidence of divine presence which, in turn, was supposed to instil a series of devotional practices. Events like these became pervasive during the 1840s and 1850s thanks to the restoration of male religious orders, the creation of religious orders for women, and particularly, the articulation of popular belief in the shape of Marian devotion (Callahan 1984: 265). This was also encouraged by the different governmental regimes and personal tendencies, such as the enormous influence of Archbishop Antonio Claret, Isabel II's confessor, during the 1850s, and the politics of stabilization during the Canovist Restoration through the 1876 Constitution. Even during the Six-Year Revolutionary period, in which religious orders were banned, the pilgrimage to Zaragoza in 1872 was a huge success, attracting 60,000 Catholic devotees (Callahan 1984: 263). Based on political divisions, scholars of religion have generated a dyadic mapping of religious politics without leaving room for studies about how religious discourse was being articulated in relation to natural and scientific phenomena. In this way, Manterola, always considered under the rubrics of Carlism and Catholic intransigency, is here considered as a priest attempting to offer a nuanced version of Catholic miracles in tune with history and scientific discoveries.

In one of his speeches, Manterola claimed that miracles should not be taken literally, for in many saints' lives, their miracles were overblown. However, he claimed that a case of possession, in which an illiterate could speak a multitude of languages, was approved as a miracle not only by doctors but also by a Protestant:

> San Paulino, que aparte de su carácter de santo, vale mucho como historiador y hombre científico, y hombre de letras: En su vida de San Félix, nos refiere había visto con sus propios ojos un energúmeno o poseído del demonio, que se pareaba sin punto alguno de apoyo en las bóvedas del templo. El sabio Ferrel, médico de Enrique II, y el protestante Lak, ambos convienen en asegurarnos haber oído a un pobre hombre de pueblo completamente literato poseído por el espíritu malo, hablar todas las lenguas sabias sin haberlas estudiado jamás. (Manterola 1879: 277)

> [Paulinus, apart from his saintly features, is a worthy historian, man of letters and of science. In his account of St Felix, Paulinus narrates that he had seen with his own eyes a person possessed by the Devil who clashed with the temple's domes. Both the scientist Ferrel, doctor of Henry II, and the Protestant Lak agree upon having heard this poor yokel speaking learned languages without having studied them]

In her refutations of Manterola's speeches, Domingo Soler criticised such seeming possession as a hoax, proved scientifically by alluding to the cases of Loudun and Lourdes.[20] She remarked on newspaper clippings of miraculous scams both to debase the popularity of miracles and to differentiate them from spiritist phenomena. A case in point was the impersonation of a priest in Cervera, who had dressed up as the Devil. The episode had appeared in several newspapers in 1877, and Domingo Soler quoted some lines from the newspaper *El Globo*:

> Un ser indefinible, vestido de encarnado, se presentó ante la concurrencia [...] Ante semejante escándalo, un criado se hallaba en una pieza contigua, cogió un revolver, y entró en el lugar de la escena que venimos refiriendo. Como es consiguiente, quedó completamente aterrado a la vista del diablo; pero considerando que valía más matarle que ser muerto por él, le disparó tres tiros de boca de jarro. A los pocos instantes, la familia del difunto se encontraba cara a cara con el sacristán de la parroquia, disfrazado de demonio, con tres balazos en el pecho, y la espuma de la muerte en los labios. (Domingo Soler 1880: 157)

> [An undefinable being, dressed up in red, introduced himself to the popular crowd [...] A servant who was in the adjacent room took a gun and entered the crowded room. The servant shivered when he saw the impersonated Devil. Since he preferred to kill rather than be killed by the Devil, the servant shot three times. After some minutes, the crowd found out that the Devil shot was not the Devil himself, but the Parish priest disguised as a devil with three bullets in his chest and deathly foam on his lips]

In spite of the fact that miracles were sometimes exaggerated by authorities, Manterola remarked, the truthful character of most miracles was attested by scientific authorities around the world, as was proven in a case of a person who could speak several languages. On the other hand, Manterola (1879: 891) strived to prove the objective reality of miracles by distinguishing them from spectacular forms, such as the performances of the British spiritualist Mr Ong. For Manterola, extraordinary events that were not produced by God's grace were generated by Satan. This was the case of spiritist phenomena. Domingo Soler's refutations adroitly linked miracles to well-known scams and unmasked possession as mental illness proven by the authorities.

Miracles and polemics over their authenticity were commonplace within intellectual circles of apologists from the 1880s until the end of the century. In this vein, the apologist Agustí Arintero (1891) devised a more flexible narrative in which the Flood was explained by geological fact and marked the first extraordinary event on Earth at the hands of the Creator. Quoting Max Muller and nineteenth-century Assyriologists like George Smith, Arintero devised a narrative in which the Deluge was compared to other traditions and mythologies, such as the Biblical story of Izdubar.[21] As T. Masuzawa (2005: 57) has pointed out, Christian intellectuals used comparativism in order to prove Christianity was the prime religion, whilst they opened up new possibilities of thinking transversally about other religions. In this light, Arintero (1891: 142) used deductive reasoning and drew from a myriad of late nineteenth-century sources to fashion an account in which the one-time formation of loess, an aeolian material made of an accumulation of windblown sediment of which more coverings occur, proved to be a unique and extraordinary phenomenon. Arintero proved that the miracle of the deluge was compatible with what discerned knowledge of the natural world could reveal. Manterola, like the apologist Arintero, took pains to fashion a form of Catholicism in tune with scientific discoveries, while at the same time remarking on its extraordinariness. Domingo Soler, on the contrary, emphasized the common nature of spiritist appearances in contrast to Catholic miracles, many of which were the result of scams.

Conclusion

Spiritism, always considered as part of freethinking and marginal politics, has been posited in this essay as part of the struggle over scientific authority through objectivity. Spiritism's entry into Spain thanks to the psychological shift of phrenology was contemporary with the rise of astronomic observatories and the translation of Camille Flammarion's books, himself both an amateur astronomer and a spiritist. Whether criticizing or endorsing spiritism, Vicente Manterola and Amalia Domingo Soler's speeches embody a case in point of late nineteenth-century crisscrossing of religion and science. Their penchant for objectivity as an authoritative move is clear not only in their careful re-reading of Biblical passages such as that of the witch of Endor, but also in their analytic approach to miracles. Their narratives about the real or fraudulent nature of miracles were contemporary with the growing number of popular devotions and religiosity in the second half of the nineteenth century, reaching its peak during the Spanish Restoration Period (1875–1902).

Ultimately, Vicente Manterola and Amalia Domingo Soler's speeches seemed to be more similar than may have been expected. In spite of their very different purposes, they both disseminated the newest scientific experiments in astronomy and they used objectivity as a mode of legitimation for their own discourses. Thanks to the growing popularity of spiritism, Manterola felt compelled to discuss spiritism and astronomy in his sermons in Barcelona Cathedral. In turn, Domingo Soler and other spiritists who deemed Catholicism their biggest enemy established a dialogue between spiritism and the Catholic religion.

In tune with apologists such as Agustín Arintero, Manterola used scientific information, as it was through science that he forged a comfortable space for belief in a real existence that was beyond the reach of natural and empirical understanding. In contrast, Domingo Soler (1880: 385) strived to degrade Catholicism through a heated refutation of Catholic miracles, using the latest medical news and newspaper clippings that showed any kind of scandal. Her conclusion in particular, brimming with praise for science and reason, speaks of the porosity between science and religion that both spiritism and Catholicism maintained at that time.

Framing spiritism within a larger scientific discourse permits us to go beyond sterile assessments of the *polémica* and to re-assess the nineteenth-century search for objectivity as a common ground shared by science, religion, and culture more widely. More to the point, bringing spiritism into dialogue with Catholic orthodoxy not only entails the inclusion of spiritism within academic discourse, but also reconfigures Catholic culture itself. In other words, potential scholarship on spiritism opens a novel space for the research and the re-assessment of the cultural production of Catholicism, normally placed under the rubrics of conservative politics and Church history. In this vein, a potential site for research is sermons and apologetics, both of which were spreading Catholicism and taking into account spiritism. At the core of the study of spiritism and the subsequent revision of Catholicism, we would need to think about Hispanic debates which connect to other geographies, putting aside narratives of bare imports and influences from somewhere else.

Contrary to triumphant narratives of science, nineteenth-century popular scientific practices that were deemed 'pseudoscientific' or simply a 'hoax,' shed light on cultural anxieties and shifts in the perception of what science means. In this way, the dead-end of phrenology, spiritism and similar practices in the nineteenth century offer rich fodder to carry on interdisciplinary research. This scholarship touches not only upon science and religion but also upon the way knowledge was transmitted to the public and upon the different ways of marketing such knowledge, both of which were crucial in the context of the rapid expansion of the press in the nineteenth century.

As usually happens with every novel study on a little-known subject, potential research on spiritism and surrounding practices has its pitfalls. For instance, such a study risks delving blindly into a specific subject and neglecting to consider the reason for such study, prioritizing the fascination for excluded topics in culture. We should not forget that spiritist, religious, and scientific debates were happening elsewhere in Europe in the latter half of the nineteenth century. They were part of a diverse set of ongoing printing and oral practices that were aimed at a wider public before the separation of disciplines in the twentieth century, and so they were naturally multidisciplinary. In a period such as our own, in which multi-disciplinarism in the humanities prevails, the inclusion of spiritism into the canonic re-assessment of Hispanic Studies offers fruitful possibilities of dialogue with faculties outside the Hispanic circle, such as English, History, and Religious Studies.

Bibliography

ALAS, LEOPOLDO. 2003 [1892]. *Superchería* (Alicante: Biblioteca Virtual Miguel de Cervantes)
ALONSO PERUJO, NICETO. 1877. *La Pluralidad de los Mundos Habitados ante la Fe Católica* (Madrid: Imprenta de Gaspar Editores)
ANDUAGA ENGAÑA, AITOR. 2005. 'La Regeneración de la astronomía y la meteorología Españolas: Augusto Arcimis (1844–1910) y el Institucionismo', *Asclepio*, 52, 109–28
ARCIMIS, AUGUSTO. 1878. *El Telescopio Moderno* (Barcelona: Montaner y Simón)
ARINTERO, AUGSTÍ,. 1891. *El diluvio universal demostrado por la geología y la prehistoria* (Vergara: Imprenta del Santísimo Rosario)
ARKINSTALL, CHRISTINE. 2014. *Spanish Female Writers and the Freethinking Press, 1879–1926* (Toronto: Toronto University Press)
BALMÉS, JAUME. 1863. *La Sociedad. Revista religiosa, filosófica, política y literaria* (Barcelona: Imprenta de A. Brussi)
BOYD, CAROLYN P. 1997. *Historia Patria: Politics, History, and National Identity in Spain, 1875–1975* (Princeton, N.J. : Princeton University Press)
BRETÓN DE LOS HERREROS, MANUEL. 1845. *Frenología y magnetismo* (Madrid: Impr. De José Repullés)
CALLAHAN, WILLIAM. 2000. *The Catholic Church in Spain, 1875–1998* (Washington, DC: Catholic University of America Press)
COOTER, ROGER. 1984. *The Cultural Meaning of Popular Science: Phrenology and the Organization of Consent in Nineteenth-Century Britain* (Cambridge: Cambridge University Press)
CUBÍ, MARIANO. 1849. *La Frenología y sus glorias. Lecciones de frenología, fisionomía y magnetismo humano en completa harmonía con la espiritualidad, libertad, e inmortalidad del alma* (Barcelona: Impr. Hispana)
CUCHET, GUILLAUME. 2012. *Les Voix d'outre-tombe. Tables tournantes, spiritisme et société au XIX siècle* (Paris: Editions du Seuil)
DASTON, LORRAINE and GALISON, PETER. 2007. *Objectivity* (New York: Zone Books; Cambridge, MA: MIT Press)
DOMINGO SOLER, AMALIA. 1880. *El Espiritismo refuntando los errores del catolicismo romano. Colección de artículos* (San Martin de Provensals: Imprenta de Juan de Torrens y Comp.)
DRAPER, WILLIAM. 1876. *La Historia de los conflictos entre religión y ciencia*, trans. Augusto Arcimis (Madrid: Impr. de Aribau)
EDELMAN, NICOLE. 1995. *Voyantes, guérisseuses et visionnaires en France* (Paris: Librairie Universelle)
FERNÁNDEZ BREMÓN, JOSÉ. 2008. *Un crimen científico y otros cuentos* (Madrid: Lengua de Trapo)
FERNÁNDEZ, CAYETANO. 1892. *La Cruz y el telescopio; estudio sobre el supuesto conflicto entre la fe y la astronomía, con sujeción al tema primero de la sección científico-religiosa del tercer congreso católico nacional en Sevilla* (Seville: Rasco)
FLAMMARION, CAMILLE. 1863. *La Pluralité des Mondes Habités* (Paris: Didier)

FUENTE, VICENTE DE LA. 1868. *La pluralidad de cultos y sus inconvenientes* (Puebla: Imp. de N. Bassols)
GÓMEZ APARICIO, PEDRO. 1967. *Historia del periodismo español* (Madrid: Editora Nacional)
GONZÁLEZ DE PABLO, ANGEL. 2006. 'Animal magnetism in Spanish medicine (1786–1860)', *History of Psychiatry*, 17:3, 279–98
GONZÁLEZ LINARES, AUGUSTO. 1876. *La vida de los astros* (Madrid: t.p. Conde)
HORTA, GERARD. 2001. *De la Mística a les Barricades. Introducció a l'espiritisme català Del XIX dins el context ocultista europeu* (Barcelona: Proa)
KIPLING, RUDYARD. 2013. *Wireless* (London: Penguin)
KUHN, THOMAS S. 1962. *The Structure of Scientific Revolutions*, ed. by Ian Hacking. 4th ed., 50th anniversary (Chicago: University of Chicago Press)
LAÍN ENTRALGO, PEDRO. 1963. *Panorama histórico de la ciencia moderna*, ed. José María López Piñero (Madrid: Ediciones Guadarrama)
LOUZAO VILLAR, JOSEBA. 2008. 'La Recomposición religiosa en la modernidad: un marco conceptual para comprender el enfrentamiento entre laicidad y confesionalidad en la España contemporánea', *Hispania sacra*, 60: 331–54.
MANTEROLA, VICENTE. 1879. *El Satanismo; o sea, la cátedra de satanás combatida desde la cátedra del espíritu santo; refutacion de los errores de la escuela espiritista*, (Barcelona: Tip. de Espassa Hermanos y Salvat)
MASUZAWA, TOMOKO. 2005. *The Invention of World Religions, or, How European Universalism Was Preserved in the Language of Pluralism* (Chicago: University of Chicago Press)
MENÉNDEZ PELAYO, MARCELINO. 1880. *Historia de los heterodoxos españoles*, (Madrid: Librería católica de San José)
—— 1915. *La Ciencia española. Polémicas, proyectos y bibliografía* (Madrid: Tip. de la Rev. de Arch., Bibl. y Museos)
NIETO-GALÁN, AGUSTÍ. 1999. 'The Images of Science in Modern Spain. Rethinking *La Polémica*' in *The Sciences in the European Periphery During the Enlightenment*, ed. by Kostas Gavroglou (Dordrecht: Kluwer Academic Publishers), pp. 73–94
NOFRE MATEO, DAVID. 2005. 'Una ciència de l'home, una ciència de la societat: Frenologia i magnetisme animal a Catalunya, 1842–1854' (Barcelona: Universitat Autònoma)
OPPENHEIM, JANET. 1985. *The Other World: Spiritualism and Psychical research in England, 1850–1914* (Cambridge: Cambridge University Press)
OWEN, ALEX. 2004. *The Place of Enchantment: British Occultism and the Culture of the Modern* (Chicago: University of Chicago Press)
PEREZ GALDÓS, BENITO. 1888. *León Roch: A Romance* trans. Clara Bell (New York: William S. Gottersberger)
—— 2003 [1883]. *El Doctor Centeno* (Alicante: Biblioteca Virtual Miguel de Cervantes, 2003)
POE, EDGAR ALLAN. 1855. *Tales of Mystery, Imagination & Humour: and Poems* (London: H. Vizetelly)
RAMOS, DOLORES. 2005. 'Heterodoxias religiosas, familias espiritistas y apóstolas laicas a finales del s. XIX: Amalia Domingo Soler y Belén de Sárraga Hernández' *Historia Social*, 53: 65–84
RIEBER, ROBERT W. 2001. *Wilhelm Wundt in History: The Making of a Scientific Psychology* (Boston, MA: Springer)
RØDTJER, ROCÍO. 2015. 'Epistemological Myopia in José Fernández Bremón's 'Un Crimen Científico'in *Latin American and Iberian Perspectives on Literature and Medicine*, ed. by Patricia Novillo-Corvalán (New York and London: Routledge), pp. 64–84
RUIZ-CASTELL, PEDRO (ed.). 2008. *Astronomy and Astrophysics in Spain (1850–1914)*, (Newcastle: Cambridge Scholars)
SMITH, GEORGE. 1876. *The Chaldean Account of Genesis* (New York: Scribner, Armstrong)

TURNER, FRANK M. 1974. *Between Science and Religion; the Reaction to Scientific Naturalism in Late Victorian England* (New Haven: Yale University Press)
VALERA, JUAN. 2008 [1879]. *The Illusions of Doctor Faustino*, trans. Robert M. Fedorchek (Washington DC: Catholic University of America Press)
WALLIS, ROY (ed.). 1979. *On the Margins of Science. The Social Construction of Rejected Knowledge* (Keele: University of Keele)
WELLS, HERBERT GEORGE.. 1960. *Tono-Bungay* (New York: Heritage Press)
WINTER, ALISON. 1998. *Mesmerized : Powers of Mind in Victorian Britain* (Chicago : University of Chicago Press)

Notes to Chapter 6

1. I have in mind the conceptual framework of 'observation' of Jonathan Crary (1999), who argues that nineteenth-century rationalized observation was usually shaped by a whole set of anti-rational behaviours and attitudes due to new scientific, social, and anthropological studies. These studies affected both society and visual culture. In my approach to late nineteenth-century spiritism, I deviate from Crary's scope of anti-rational subjects in visual culture in order to argue that public claims over 'objective' observation (whether based on religion or scientific facts) were made biased by both Catholic and spiritist strategies.
2. All translations into English are my own.
3. In the prologue of Draper's *Conflictos entre Religión y Ciencia*, translated by the astronomer Augusto Arcimis, Nicolás Salmerón bemoaned the intransigence of the Spanish Catholic Church. Marcelino Menéndez Pelayo, on the contrary, highlighted Spain's glorious past and took pains to depict a more positive image of Spanish science.
4. In this essay, I use the term *spiritism*, translated into Spanish as *espiritismo*. Studies of Anglo-American spiritualism and French spiritism can be found in Janet Oppenheim (1985), Alex Owen (2004), Nicole Edelman (1995) and Guillaume Cuchet (2012).
5. As well as Arkinstall, see Gerard Horta (2001) and Dolores Ramos (2005).
6. This series of political debates is widely known under the phrase in Spanish 'polémica de la ciencia española'.
7. See Marcelino Menéndez Pelayo, *La Ciencia Española (Polémicas, Proyectos y Bibliografía.* 4. ed. (Madrid: Tip. de la Rev. de Arch., Bibl. y Museos, 1915).
8. Amalia Domingo Soler herself, along with Ana López de Ayala and Belén de Sárraga, created the Autonomous Society of Women in Barcelona in 1891. For more information about the links between spiritism and feminism, see Christine Arkinstall (2014) and Dolores Ramos (2005).
9. For a re-assessment of the place of science fiction within Spanish modernity, see Geraldine Lawless (2011) and Rocio Rødtjer (2015) For a study of scientific practices, see Nieto Galán (1999) and David Nofre Mateo (2005).
10. In the nineteenth century, astronomy belonged to a group of sciences called 'observatory sciences', including cartography, geodesy, and meteorology. The construction of observatories became a common global trend in nineteenth-century Europe. These buildings devoted to scientific observation juxtaposed activities of many kinds, being the place of work not only of scientists but also of philosophers and a number of Jesuits. For information about astronomy and Spain see Pedro Ruiz Castell (2008).
11. See Manuel Bretón de los Herreros, (1845) José Fernández Bremón (2008) and Leopoldo Alas (2003). For sardonic views of mesmerism and other pseudo-sciences in America and England, see Edgar Allan Poe (1855) H.G. Wells (1960) and Rudyard Kipling (2013).
12. See Mariano Cubí (1849).
13. The roots of Anglo-American spiritualism and the connections with Mesmerism and Phrenology can be seen in Oppenheim (1985). For the change of medical trends from phrenology to spiritism in Spain, see González de Pablo (2006).
14. For the origins of scientific psychology by Wilhelm Wundt, see Robert W. Rieber (2001).
15. See Pedro Ruiz-Castell (2008).

16. See 'Constitución de la Nación Española votada definitivamente en la sesión del día 1 de Junio de 1869' (Madrid, Calle del Izquierdo, 1869). Isabel II reigned from 1833 to 1869, when the Six-Year Revolutionary Period starts.
17. An overview of the 1876 Constitution and the aims of Cánovas to restore a stable Catholic monarchy can be found in Carolyn P. Boyd (1987).
18. See Pedro Gómez Aparicio, *Historia Del Periodismo Español* (Madrid: Editora Nacional, 1967).
19. Also known as the Witch of Endor, the passage narrates the divine punishment of King Saul after commanding the medium to summon the prophet Samuel's spirit. Samuel, who is concerned about the battle against the Philistines, learns that God has abandoned him and David will be his successor. This episode appears in I Samuel, 28.3–25, and allusion to it became a commonplace narrative during the latter half of the nineteenth century among spiritualist, socialist, and radical circles across Europe and America.
20. 'Sus adversarios creen oponerle algún argumento irrefutable, cuando después de haber hecho muy eruditas investigaciones sobre los convulsionarios de Saint-Medard, los Caminados de Cévennes, o las religiosas de Loudon, han llegado a descubrir en ellos hechos evidentes de superchería e impostura que nadie niega' (Domingo Soler 1880: 12) [His adversaries have articulated an unanswerable argument after erudite research about the epileptic cases of Saint-Medard, the walkers of the Cévennes, and the nuns of Loudun. [Doctors and scientists] have discovered undeniable hoaxes and impostures]
21. In 1872, the British Assyriologist George Smith discovered the legend of Izdubar, who was believed to be the biblical Nimrod. This coincided with the discovery of the Deluge texts, which were used as an observational and scientific explanation against the latest Darwinist theories about the origin of species and the descent of man. See George Smith (1876).

CHAPTER 7

Facha if you do, coward if you don't? The Problematic Canonicity of Francoist Authors in Post-Franco Spain

David Jiménez Torres

'Ganaron la guerra pero perdieron los manuales de literatura' [They won the war but they lost the literature textbooks] (Lucas 2015: 51).[1] This statement by the writer Andrés Trapiello is emblematic of a discourse on the canonicity of authors linked to the Spanish extreme right of the twenties, thirties and forties, that is, those poets, novelists, playwrights and essayists who adopted a critical position towards the Spanish Second Republic (1931–1936), supported the *nacionales* led by General Franco during the Spanish Civil War (1936–39) and contributed to the Francoist dictatorship's (1939–1975) cultural and ideological legitimation; authors whose place in the canon of contemporary Spanish culture has been, since the coming of democracy in the late 1970s, fraught with controversy.

My aim in this chapter is to outline the discourse that since the mid-1980s has vindicated the inclusion of these authors within the Spanish canon, as well as the counter-discourse that has arisen in response to it. I will also explain how these discourses have been influenced by wider debates on Spain's recent past, and particularly (since the late 1990s) on the recuperation of the Second Republic's 'historical memory'. Throughout this, we will see how the canonicity of right-wing authors has been inextricably linked to political and social issues, while also addressing, though in rather oblique ways, questions of literary analysis and criticism.

The right margins

'Algunos dejaron huella en calles con su nombre, otros en estelas, alguno en estatua y otros tantos en libros que merecen más lectura. Pero a la mayoría ni se les lee, ni se les recuerda demasiado.' [Some left their mark on streets bearing their name, others in monuments, one or two in statues and many others in books that deserve to be read more often. But most of them are neither read nor remembered very frequently] (Lucas 2015: 50). This statement, extracted from an article published in 2015 in the centre-right newspaper *El Mundo*, refers to the current fortunes of a group of authors that -according to the same article- included José Martínez Ruiz ('Azorín'), Camilo José Cela, Josep Pla, Luis Rosales, Julio Camba, Agustín de Foxá, Gonzalo Torrente Ballester, Álvaro Cunqueiro, Rafael García Serrano, Eugenio d'Ors, Leopoldo Panero, Dionisio Ridruejo, José María Pemán, Luis Felipe Vivanco, Rafael Sánchez Mazas, Eugenio Montes, Ernesto Giménez Caballero, and César González-Ruano.

As readers familiar with twentieth-century Spanish literature will already have noticed, the authors included in this list embody a wide array of different styles, literary careers and political options. The list lumps authors who are best-known for their non-fictional output (like Azorín, Pla, Camba, d'Ors or González-Ruano) together with poets (Panero, Ridruejo, Vivanco) and novelists (Cela, Foxá, García Serrano). In terms of politics, it brings together classic conservatives (Azorín), liberals (Camba), monarchists (Pemán), and members of Spain's fascist party, Falange Española (nearly everyone else, though even here there were many different modes and degrees of identification with its project). As for literary careers, it includes authors who by the 1930s were established names and those who were at that point penning their first works. More significantly, the list links those who granted a tacit support to the *nacionales* and the dictatorship with those who played an active part in bringing about the war and legitimating the regime. In other words, the line-up includes authors whose connection with Francoism is, as far as their literary oeuvre is concerned, fairly accidental, and others whose careers were inextricably linked with the dictatorship's cultural politics.

Despite this heterogeneity, however, the article makes clear that these authors share a common denominator: the fact that their place in the canon of contemporary Spanish literature would have been adversely affected by their links with the Francoist regime. As the piece's subtitle declares, 'cuando se cumplen 40 años de la muerte de Franco, la mayor parte de los escritores que dieron cimiento intelectual al fascismo y el falangismo en España permanecen silenciados' [forty years after the death of Franco, the larger part of those writers who supplied the intellectual foundations for fascism and falangism in Spain remain silenced]. These authors would thus have been excluded from contemporary bookshelves and reading lists on grounds of political prejudice rather than literary merit.

For reasons of scope I will not inquire into why these authors have been marginalized from the mechanisms of canon-formation, including university syllabuses and reprints of their works, but rather into the explanation provided for it.[2] Indeed, the narratives that are provided nowadays on the marginalization of Francoist authors can be considered as the continuation of a discourse that has its roots in the early- to mid-80s.

Between December 1983 and January 1985, a number of authors and critics wrote in the centre-left newspaper *El País* (the newspaper with widest circulation in Spain, and an important player in the cultural market through its cultural supplement Babelia and its links to the Alfaguara publishing house) about the need for Spanish readers to rediscover those authors whose lives and works had been linked to the

Francoist regime.[3] Figures like Pere Gimferrer, Andrés Trapiello and Juan Manuel Bonet claimed that the anti-Francoist consensus that had coalesced in Spanish high culture from the 60s onwards had led to the marginalization of authors linked to Francoism, both in terms of their place in the canon and their availability in the book market. It was claimed that the works of Foxá, Sánchez Mazas, Ridruejo et al. were, by the 1980s, out of print and very difficult to find, whereas those of authors linked to anti-Francoism (whether Republican symbols like Federico García Lorca, long-exiled figures like Ramón J. Sender, or leaders of the 'internal exile' like Miguel Delibes) had benefited from fresh critical attention, new editions and stagings, and even film adaptations. A vast swathe of contemporary literature was therefore, the argument continued, being excluded from the canon, creating a distorted image of the past (according to which Spanish literature of the mid-twentieth century was uniformly anti-Francoist) and refusing authors the possibility of being judged on the quality of their work rather than on their political sympathies.

The political context played a part in this call for a rethink of Spanish culture's relationship with Francoist authors. Following the failure of the attempted military coup of February 1981, and the election victory of the Socialist Party in 1982, the new Spanish democracy seemed finally to be on a firm footing; the process of political, social and cultural Transition that had culminated with Felipe González's election as prime minister appeared to signal the defeat of the *nacionales* forty years after the end of the Civil War. It therefore seemed that the anti-Francoist *Kulturkampf* of the 60s and 70s could be relaxed in favour of a more organic and inclusive cultural 'normalisation', allowing for the Spanish canon to be based on literary rather than political criteria (this presupposed, of course, that such a thing was possible, or that gauging what is 'literary' is a straightforward matter; more on this later). Trapiello exemplified this point of view when he wrote about Foxá's fervently pro-*nacionales* novel *Madrid de corte a cheka*: '¿Quién piensa en 1936? Ha pasado, como pasaron las otras guerras, civiles y carlistas. Se las llevó el tiempo. Y sólo permanecen algunos nombres y algunas de sus obras. El de Foxá, seguro. El de su novela, siempre.' [Who thinks of 1936? It is over, just as the other civil and Carlist wars are over. Time has washed them away. And all that remains are some names and some of their works. Foxá's, for certain. His novel's, forever.] (Trapiello 1984).

These arguments elicited a vehement contestation from academic Julio Rodríguez Puértolas, one that would become highly influential and which thus deserves discussing at certain length. In his two-volume *Historia de la literatura fascista española*, Puértolas surveyed and anthologized Spanish 'fascist' authors from the 1920s to the 80s. The quotation marks are warranted by the author's rather loose notion of what constitutes a fascist author:

> todo aquel que de un modo u otro puso su pluma y su pensamiento al servicio [...] del régimen político surgido de la sublevación militar contra la Segunda República [...] Y también, claro está, a quienes antes de esa fecha formaban parte de las organizaciones que propugnaban la destrucción de la democracia y la creación de un Estado autoritario, así como a quienes después de la muerte del general Franco [...] intentan, o un regreso al viejo sistema, o simplemente manifiestan una ideología antidemocrática. (Rodríguez Puértolas 1986: 9)

> [all those who, one way or another, put their quill and their intellect at the service [...] of the political regime that resulted from the military rebellion against the Second Republic [...] And also, of course, those who prior to that date belonged to organizations that called for the destruction of democracy and the creation of an authoritarian State, as well as those who after the death of General Franco [...] are either attempting a return to the old system or simply displaying an antidemocratic ideology.]

This definition is not only of questionable analytic value, given how it overlooks the large gulfs that separated, say, authoritarian monarchists like Pemán and revolutionary fascists like Ledesma Ramos; it also sidesteps the debate that has always surrounded the issue of Francoism's ideological nature.[4] Puértolas's credibility as an analyst of fascism was also called into question by his discussion of post-1975 Spanish culture, in which he considered the lampooning of Felipe González's government or a favourable attitude towards the USA as positions that were 'claramente fascistas, o neo-fascistas' [clearly Fascist, or neo-Fascist] (Rodríguez Puértolas 1986: 806).

As for the canonicity of Francoist authors, Puértolas took issue with recently-published articles in *El País*, as well as with Trapiello's reissuing of novels like *Rosa Krüger*. Puértolas argued that Francoist authors had never disappeared from the Spanish canon, and he ascribed the ongoing revival of fascist literature to 'nostalgia y seguramente algo más' [nostalgia and surely something else]; for him, Trapiello's openness to reissuing fascist novels was 'lamentable' [pitiful] and merely a 'más refinada' [more refined] way of keeping fascist culture alive in Spain (ibid. 11, 13). Moreover, he found it difficult to understand how a recent overview of twentieth-century Spanish novels had seen fit to include works by Francoist authors (ibid. 13 n. 2).

Of course, Puértolas's work itself also granted visibility to Francoist authors. The 1,200-page anthology that made up the second volume of his work, in particular, offered readers the chance to peruse selections from over forty years of 'fascistic' literature. Puértolas's intentions, however, were radically different from those of his antagonists. He was moved by his indignation at a current state of affairs that, as he saw it, had allowed Francoists to continue being important players in post-Franco Spain:

> Buena parte de aquellos fascistas convencidos, que tuvieron importantes cargos de responsabilidad política en más de un caso y que en sus obras manifestaron todos con acuidad excepcional su entrega a la causa del fascismo, hoy, tras un proceso de conversión, ocupan puestos de importancia en el nuevo régimen parlamentario y otros -los más- se identifican simplemente con el sistema democrático actual. [...] Viene a la mente lo ocurrido con los conversos del judaísmo durante los siglos XV y XVI. (Rodríguez Puértolas 1986: 10)

> [A good number of those true fascists, who in more than one case held important roles of political responsibility, and who in their works manifested with exceptional skill their commitment to the cause of fascism, today, after a process of conversion, occupy some important roles within the new parliamentary regime, and others –the larger part– simply identify with the current democratic system [...] What happened with the converts from Judaism during the 15th and 16th centuries comes to mind.]

Puértolas's visibilization thus operated as an 'outing', a public shaming of old 'fascists' whose conversion to or acceptance of democratic values he perceived to be insincere; or, in the case of authors who were already dead, it worked as a shaming of those who attempted to vindicate their place within the Spanish literary canon. Puértolas's was therefore a critical visibilization, one that aimed to achieve retributive and symbolic justice. Rather than aiming for inclusion, it compiled a literary blacklist that would result in cultural, political and even social exclusion (whether of those authors who were still alive or of those critics who tried to vindicate their work). Another academic, José-Carlos Mainer, would later refer to this type of visibility as a 'Nuremberg castizo' [homegrown Nüremberg] (Carbajosa and Carbajosa 2003: xvii).

Puértolas's questioning of the motives adduced by Trapiello and Gimferrer (labelling their positions as mere Francoist 'nostalgia') also turned their call for normalizing the Spanish canon on its head. By presenting the attempt to include Francoist authors within the canon as a surreptitious attempt to re-fascistize Spanish culture, Puértolas assumed a framework of civic urgency that required continuing with the anti-Francoist *Kulturkampf*. In other words, the calls for cultural normalization were construed as evidence that democratic culture remained far from 'normal'. This dovetailed with a vindication of the primacy of ideology and (some version of) ethics in literary analysis, as the canon needed to take into account 'la verdad histórica' [the historical truth] of authors' political affiliations (Rodríguez Puértolas 1986: 13). The results of this type of focus became explicit in Puértolas's analysis of fascistic texts: where Trapiello could extol *Madrid de corte a cheka*'s striking, avant-garde imagery, Puértolas focused solely on the way in which the text portrayed the historical events which led to the Civil War (ibid. 235).

Puértolas's outlook also displayed an ambivalent attitude towards the visibility of Francoist authors. On the one hand, and as indicated by his criticism of efforts to keep Francoist novels in print, Puértolas wished for 'fascist' works to become progressively harder to find. Only once the presence of these authors and their works ceased to contaminate Spanish culture could the latter consider itself 'normalised'. But on the other hand, and as the mere publication of his overview and his anthology demonstrated, the construction of a truly democratic Spain required a Francoist 'Other' against which the former's political values and cultural canon must be constructed; an 'Other' that must be at least somewhat visible in order for this construction to take place. How Francoist authors could be made invisible enough not to contaminate democratic Spain while remaining visible enough to help in the formation of an anti-Francoist culture, are difficulties that Puértolas did not address. Nor was the question of how normality could be arrived at via an open-ended state of exceptionalism.

Puértolas's likening of old fascists to Jewish converts at the time of the Inquisition also underlined some of the troubling assumptions and consequences of his method. On the one hand, this Inquisitorial approach ruled out the possibility that some evolution away from fascism may have been entirely sincere, even in the case of authors who, by the 1970s, had a long career of anti-Francoist activism (e.g.

Dionisio Ridruejo). An interpretive problem of great relevance to the history of Spanish culture of the 40s, 50s and 60s (why authors who were Falangists in their youth moved progressively towards anti-authoritarian positions) was thus explained away in a rather ham-fisted and unsatisfactory manner.

More generally, one has to wonder at the critical solvency of systematically casting doubt on the personal motives of authors whose arguments run counter to one's own, and the treatment of such arguments as decoys to disguise a personally culpable situation. It is unclear to me how such a methodology could advance scholarship in any kind of good faith, or whether it could make room for a reader who was more than just a passive recipient of propaganda. I can imagine, for example, that a critic adopting Puértolas's outlook would find it easy to cast doubt on the sincerity of my own arguments in this chapter and ascribe them to the fact that my father is (ludicrously, in my view) listed by Puértolas as one of the exponents of post-1975 'fascist' literature. In this type of criticism, the arguments I have developed over the previous paragraphs would therefore, and necessarily, have been surreptitious rhetorical flourishes by which I would be distracting the unwary reader from my own, always/already culpable personal situation. Such a reader would — I continue to assume — be expected to stop reading and put aside this chapter once that revelation had taken place. Yet those readers who trusted their own capacity to discern the validity of specific arguments, and wished to read on, would exemplify some of the limits inherent to Puértolas's approach.

As a final point on this first stage of the Spanish controversy over Francoist authors, we should note that it also seemed to contain an unvoiced opposition between writers and academics. It is perhaps not a coincidence that it was writers like Trapiello and Gimferrer who tried to vindicate Francoist authors on the basis of craft, while academics like Puértolas criticized them on the basis of discourse. It would be simplistic to argue that professional writers will always examine literature through the lens of craft, while academics will always be more attuned to its discursive elements; it is evident that theoretical-critical projects, as well as standards of what authors consider to be good literary craft, are historically contingent and have fluctuated throughout time. But in a fluid cultural-critical context like Spain's, in which perspectives put forward by professional writers and perspectives put forward by career academics are likely to interact and thus, potentially, to clash, we would do well to consider whether these clashes may not have been, at least on occasion, driven by the sets of conditions placed on their reading tastes by their very different professions.

New paradigm, old arguments

The late 1990s saw the appearance of a social and cultural phenomenon that would shape, in many ways until the present day, how Spaniards related to their recent past. This was the call for a recuperation of the 'historical memory' of the Second Republic, both in terms of vindicating that regime's status as the reference point for contemporary Spanish democracy, and in terms of bringing to light the experiences of Republicans who had been defeated during the war and persecuted during the dictatorship. The practical demands associated with this movement included the removal of any remaining symbols of dictatorship from public spaces and the opening of mass graves containing the bodies of Republicans who had been executed during the war or postwar repression. Academics were also called upon to research and denounce the repression unleashed by the *nacionales* during the war (now labelled by some as 'genocide' and as a 'Spanish Holocaust') and silenced by the regime that followed; and to break with the scholarly paradigm of a Civil War in which both sides were at fault, replacing it with another that laid blame directly on the Spanish right of the 20s and 30s. These calls were framed as the steps necessary to liberate Spanish democracy from the crippling 'pact of silence' that, it was argued, had been imposed during the Transition in order to integrate the old Francoist regime into the new system, thus guaranteeing the latter's stability.[5]

The call for the recuperation of 'historical memory' and its diffusion in new public symbols, school curricula and cultural politics met, in turn, with powerful opposition. A number of scholars and commentators argued that there had never been a 'pact of silence' (understood as an artificial blocking-off on the part of the elites of the Spanish people's desire to remember the Civil War) but rather a collective decision by all Spaniards to forsake the Civil War as a reference point for the politics of post-Francoist Spain. Delegitimizing the Transition, it was claimed, would mean a breakup of the pact-based consensus between the heirs of the victors and the heirs of the defeated on which contemporary Spanish politics was founded, and bring about a return to the division that caused the Second Republic's downfall. It was also pointed out that a uniform 'memory' could neither (epistemically) be salvaged from the multiple and conflicting memories of individuals, nor (ethically) be imposed on them by the State; and that even if this were possible or desirable, the 'historical memory' of the Republic overlooked the serious democratic deficit of, and the many crimes committed by, some defenders of the Republic.[6]

This new and fractious debate impinged on the canonicity (or otherwise) of authors associated with Francoism, by questioning the attitude that Spanish society had adopted after Franco's death towards the cultural foundations of his regime, as well as by placing a weighty civic demand on the appraisal of Spain's recent past and its transmission to new generations. Nevertheless, it is clear that, as far as the literary canon went, the debate remained firmly within the parameters that had been established in the mid-80s.

This is attested to by the fact that calls for the inclusion of Francoist authors in the canon have continued to claim that, after the dictator's death, these figures would have been deliberately marginalized for political reasons: the literature of Francoist Spain would be 'olvidada o menospreciada por algunos tratadistas como si no hubiera existido' [forgotten or looked down upon by some authors as if it had never existed] (Martínez Cachero 2009: 9). The critic's or researcher's task would thus be to forsake these prejudices, in the name not only of scholarship but also of ethics: Martínez Cachero (2009: 10) has written of the need to 'guardar la mayor objetividad e independencia ideológica posibles, condiciones ciertamente necesarias si tratamos de hacer historia verdadera y no panfletaria' [maintain the highest possible objectivity and ideological independence, which are necessary conditions if we wish to make true rather than propagandistic history]. Trapiello (2002: 18), for his part, has continued to speak of the 'obligación moral del escritor de transitar todos los caminos de la literatura, incluidos aquellos interceptados por un "prohibido el paso"' [writer's moral obligation to traverse all the paths of literature, including those that are marked with a 'no entry' sign]. In this context, authors have repeatedly labelled each other's decision to write about Francoist authors as 'valiente' [brave] (e.g. González Cuevas 2003: 19; del Rey Reguillo 2005: 278; Lucas 2015: 50).[7]

Another claim of the mid-80s that has been repeated during the 'memoria histórica' controversy is the compatibility between political condemnation of Francoism and aesthetic praise of authors who were linked to that regime. Carbajosa and Carbajosa (2003: xvii, xix) have stated that 'no se puede escribir una historia antifascista de la literatura fascista' [one cannot write an antifascist history of fascist literature], as 'el tribunal de las letras dicta sentencia en otro lugar que el de la historia' [the tribunal of letters makes its rulings in a place different from that of history]. The discourse that vindicates the canonicity of Francoist authors has thus hinged on the notion that, while aesthetics does not rule supreme over politics, it constitutes its own sphere of values and is thus able to dictate a different canon from it.

Yet another argument that has been repeated in the new century is the notion that a 'normalised' Spanish culture would have to make room for authors who had been influential during at least three decades of its recent history. Again according to Carbajosa and Carbajosa (2003: xviii, xxvi), 'la cultura española, "normalizada" presuntamente para bien, mal admitiría una exclusión' [Spanish culture, which has been 'normalised' presumably for the better, would hardly admit an exclusion], given how 'estos escritores son una rama de un tronco que es el común de una cultura, la española del primer tercio de siglo' [these writers are one branch from the tree trunk that is the whole of a culture, that of Spain in the first third of the century]. The project is therefore framed not as one of substitution but of addition, of amplification: after a proper appraisal of Francoist authors, 'las transformaciones en el canon son casi insignificantes. [...] El canon no ha sufrido otra alteración que la de ver aumentada su nómina, no el orden de importancia' [the changes to the canon are almost insignificant (...) The canon has suffered no alteration other than a broadening of its line-up, and not a change in its order of importance] (ibid. xviii).

However, I would argue that the proposal for a literary canon built on (some sense of) literary merit does more than simply expand the line-up of authors to be studied: it also includes new criteria for exclusion. After all, this new canon would hinge on a criterion which would allow some works to be more considered more successfully 'literary' than others; a criterion that does not seem to operate in genre- or style-neutral ways. It is noticeable, for example, that calls for a canon based on literary merit seem particularly unfavourable to those non-fiction writers whose style tends towards the classical and the argumentative instead of the avant-garde and expositive. This explains the vindication of authors such as Foxá and the relegation of figures like Laín Entralgo or Ramiro de Maeztu. That the vindication of the former is to the detriment of the latter is made clear by Trapiello's judgment on Foxá's current fortunes in the Spanish canon:

> [Foxá es] uno de los que ganó la guerra y perdió los manuales de la literatura. En el último *Diccionario de literatura española e hispanoamericana* [...] se le dedican veinticinco frías líneas [...] la mitad de las que se emplean, por ejemplo, para Laín, o una sexta parte, a ojo, de las dedicadas a Maeztu. (Trapiello 2002: 465)
>
> [(Foxá is) one of those who won the war and lost the literature textbooks. In the most recent *Dictionary of Spanish and Latin American Literature* (...) he is discussed in twenty-five cold lines (...) half the number devoted, for example, to Laín, and roughly a sixth of those devoted to Maeztu.]

The implicit argument here is that a novelist, poet and diarist like Foxá, with his avant-garde style and literary pyrotechnics, is more deserving of a place within the canon than sober essayists like Maeztu or Laín. The point is emphasized in comparison with another novelist, Ramón Pérez de Ayala: 'no se puede hablar de la literatura de la época de la República y hacerlo de Marañón y Maeztu, por muy principales pensadores que sean. Se podría hablar de Pérez de Ayala, pero no de ellos dos' [one cannot talk of literature during the Republic and speak of Marañón and Maeztu, however important they may be as thinkers. One could talk of Pérez de Ayala, but not of those two.] (ibid. 280). Later on, Trapiello again demonstrates that a 'purely literary' canon requires at least a few casualties:

> Es comprensible que a Maeztu se le estudie dentro del pensamiento político español del primer tercio de siglo; ahora, que se le incluya dentro de la literatura española, en el mismo plano que sus ilustres amigos del 98, resulta un exceso [...] el lugar o casilla que le corresponde más exactamente [es] el del pensamiento político. (ibid. 130)
>
> [It is understandable that Maeztu should be studied as part of Spanish political thought in the first third of the century; but his inclusion within Spanish literature, and on the same plane as his illustrious friends from the generation of 98, is excessive (...) the place or pigeonhole that is more correctly his (is) that of political thought.]

The new canon being put forward is therefore built on an implicit understanding of what counts as 'literature', one where the place of stylistically sober, long non-fiction holds a rather marginalized status. This even leads its proponents to question the writerly status of figures like Maeztu: 'estaría por dilucidar si fue un escritor como [Unamuno, Valle-Inclán o Baroja] y no solo un agitador' [it is worth pondering whether he was a writer like (Unamuno, Valle-Inclán or Baroja) and not simply an agitator] (ibid. 26).

On this issue, it is worth noting how much Wadda Ríos-Font's discussion of the problematic place of the *roman à thèse* in literary studies can be applied to long non-fiction in the new criteria being put forward by Trapiello. Departing from Stanley Fish's argument that the literary is a historically-constructed category on the basis of partialities, values and beliefs, Ríos-Font (2004: 123) explains:

> If literature is taken to be language that is not merely communicative, then the discourses that it is opposed to are those that serve chiefly to communicate, to describe, to refer to, or to change a reality that is considered external to language itself.

This in turn explains the 'prejudice [...] against texts that are seen as primarily concerned with 'truth and persuasiveness' (*as* truthful or persuasive texts, and not necessarily as texts that are truthful or persuasive in a certain 'aesthetic' way)' (ibid. 128). For, again according to Ríos-Font, texts that are considered to be literary place readers in a reassuring position of interpretation, and thus of control:

> The vantage point of interpretation implies a power over the text, the power to accept or reject its premises [...]. 'Ordinary' language might drive us to buy something or vote for a certain candidate; literature can never be imperative. [...] A text that we understand as imposing a certain view on us (particularly one with which we do not agree) violates the principle of our readerly freedom, and thus invites rejection. Such is the case with the *roman à thèse* (ibid. 129)

Not only does this provide a lucid analysis of the marginalized place of the *roman à thèse* in criticism, but it also helps us understand the similarly marginalized place of lengthy non-fiction in proposals for a canon based on 'literary merit'. I would only add that the vindication of Francoist novels like *Madrid de corte a checa* from the point of view of aesthetics demonstrates that certain *romans à thèse* can, through the right type of critical operation, be stripped of their 'unliterariness' -their overtly persuasive intent- and framed as purely 'literary'. It is telling indeed that a line on the cover of the 1993 Planeta reprint of *Madrid de corte a checa* read as follows: 'Una de las mejores novelas sobre el ocaso de la monarquía, los años republicanos y el inicio de la guerra civil' [one of the best novels on the end of the monarchy, the Republican years and the start of the Civil War]. An avant-garde style is crucial to the success of this operation, but so is the comparison with other texts which would be literarily 'unsalvageable'. In other words, the critical operation that involves vindicating *romans à thèse* as, simply, *romans*, often hinges on the comparison of fiction with non-fiction, where the former has an existence beyond its attempt at persuasion while the latter does not.

On a different level, one could argue that statements about the need to arrive at an apolitical canon respond, paradoxically, to a particular political context; namely, one which emphasized democratic normalization and pluralism. A plural democracy in which both the heirs of the victors of the Civil War and the heirs of the defeated could compete on equal terms at the ballot box would logically require a cultural canon that included as much as possible from both the Francoist and the anti-Francoist traditions. This is not to say that Trapiello or the Carbajosas were responding to some political diktat, or that there was anything disingenuous about their pronouncements, but rather, and quite simply, that calls for a pluralistic canon are not driven so much by an absence of politics as by the triumph of a certain political imperative: that of a liberal, pluralistic and democratic system.

This consideration would give the lie to the argument that a vindication of Francoist authors can only respond to an anti-democratic political imperative; but it should also refute claims that vindications of Francoist authors are somehow devoid of political imperatives altogether. If they can appear this way it is, I believe, because the liberal political imperative frames itself as the absence of constraints (the well-known concept of 'negative liberty') or as the coexistence of options which appear to be mutually exclusive. One also guesses that at work here is a narrow understanding of the term 'political', which is posited -at least implicitly- as the rather ham-fisted exclusion of whole swathes of political options. But the fact that this is the understanding of 'politics' being espoused by the likes of Puértolas does not mean that it is the only way in which politics can operate in literary analysis. Pluralistic inclusion is not an overcoming of politics but rather a specific political option. I would thus argue that Trapiello, Martínez Cachero and the Carbajosas were not aiding in the configuration of a non-political canon but rather in the creation of a liberal canon; not liberal in the sense of privileging works that exhibit a liberal ideology, but rather in the sense of being animated by the pluralistic principles present in liberalism.

These, however, are not the kind of criticisms that have been levelled at proponents of the canonicity of Francoist authors. Rather, critics of this position have tended to remain within the parameters laid by Puértolas. Becerra Mayor, for example, has given new currency to the argument that the pretence of critical objectivity is merely a disingenuous disguise through which 'el autor [...] pretende disimular su posición ideológica' [the author (...) pretends to disguise his ideological position] (Becerra Mayor 2012: 37). Behind this disguise would lie either a pro-Francoist agenda or a culpable aloofness that critics must proceed to 'desenmascarar' [unmask] or 'delatar' [denounce] (ibid. 37).[8] Focus is thus, and once again, displaced from the internal coherence and validity of arguments and instead centred on the presumed surreptitiousness of those who utter them. However explicitly critics like Gracia, Mainer or González Cuevas may criticize fascism or Francoism in their work, the very act of analyzing (and thus visibilizing) Francoist figures makes them liable to be portrayed as 'protector[es] de los fascistas reciclados' [protectors of recycled fascists], their works labelled as 'exculpatorio[s]' [exculpatory] and their efforts framed as part of a 'revisionismo neofranquista' [neo-Francoist revisionism] (Becerra Mayor 2012: 41, 40; López Villaverde 2014: 275).

This systematic suspicion might extend to the argument that aesthetic judgments can be self-sufficient from political ones. The distinction between politics and aesthetics that was outlined earlier is only addressed by the counter-discourse as a decoy by which fascism would be reintroduced in the Spanish canon. In the case of *Madrid de corte a cheka*, for example, 'el análisis literario [...] encubre (o mejor: desplaza) la cuestión ideológica con el propósito de introducir [la obra] en el canon de la literatura española contemporánea.' [literary analysis (...) hides (or rather displaces) ideological issues with the purpose of introducing this work into the canon of contemporary Spanish literature] (Becerra Mayor 2012: 44). The critical project put forward by the counter-discourse thus continues to be based on an *ad hominem* logic which posits that, in order to 'no errar en la lectura' [not misread], critics must 'considerar el contenido ideológico de la ideología del fascismo y analizar las consecuencias históricas de las palabras bellas al servicio de la inmundicia.' [consider the ideological content of fascist ideology, and analyse the historical consequences of beautiful words at the service of filth] (Ibid. 42). Aesthetics is thus reduced to the mere production of 'beautiful words'. And once again a problematic visibility is proposed for Francoist authors:

> No se trata de condenar al olvido las obras de los escritores del fascismo español. [...] El olvido no debe formar parte de nuestro proyecto. Al contrario, lo que se propone [...] no es sino leer la literatura fascista española en su radical historicidad, sin despolitizarla, sin extirparle nada. (Ibid. 44)
>
> [It is not about condemning to oblivion the works of Spanish fascist authors. (...) Oblivion must not be a part of our project. On the contrary, what is proposed (...) is merely to read Spanish fascist literature in its radical historicity, without depoliticizing it, without removing anything from it.]

Conclusions

The canonicity of authors who associated, however direct or obliquely, with the *nacionales* during the Spanish Civil War and with the Francoist dictatorship has been a topic of heated dispute in Spain since the mid-1980s. This dispute has led to the appearance of a discourse which claims that these authors have been marginalized for political reasons, and vindicates a new canon based on (a supposedly straightforward standard of) literary merit that would include these authors without implying a favourable stance towards Francoism. A counter-discourse quickly emerged, condemning the former points as closeted Francoism and vindicating political affiliation as the primary aspect that needed visibilizing in recent Spanish literature. This debate has been given new urgency since the late 1990s by the 'historical memory' controversy, but it has largely remained within the above-mentioned parameters.

Despite their differences, both sides of the polemic share the understanding that the Spanish canon is dependent on the configuration of a 'normalised', post-Francoist democratic culture. Where they disagree, of course, is on the issue of what constitutes 'normalization' after a forty-year dictatorship. Normalization could be understood as the imposition of either an anti-Francoist political imperative in canon-formation or a liberal-pluralistic one. And, as we have seen, these can often be at odds with one another.

Spain's cultural politics thus remain, forty years after the death of Franco, decisively interlinked with the divisions over the relationship the country should have with its recent past. These disputes, however, also conceal issues that are not specific to Spain, and which are more concerned with literary criticism than with history and ethics. A greater recognition of how these aspects underlie the Spanish polemic on the canonicity of Francoist authors would, in my opinion, revitalize a debate that has largely been entrenched in the same positions for nearly four decades, and which is often too acrimonious to be of much interest in advancing our understanding of literary studies. Strenuous efforts have been made in recent times by historians to situate Spain's difficult memory politics in a larger transnational context (e.g. in Rodrigo 2013 and Forcadell 2015). It would be useful if literary scholars could also situate the dispute over which texts from Spain's recent past deserve to be read today within larger transnational debates about what 'literature' is.

Bibliography

AGUILAR, PALOMA. 2002. *Memory and Amnesia: The Role of the Spanish Civil War in the Transition to Democracy* (New York: Berghahn)

BECERRA MAYOR, DAVID. 2012. 'El *revival* fascista o la redención por la vía estética', *Revista de crítica literaria marxista*, 6: 35–44

CARBAJOSA, MÓNICA and PABLO CARBAJOSA. 2003. *La corte literaria de José Antonio: la primera generación cultural de la Falange* (Barcelona: Crítica)

DEL REY REGUILLO, FERNANDO. 2005. 'Pedro Carlos González Cuevas. *Maeztu. Biografía de un nacionalista español*', *Historia y política*, 13: 278–81

DEL REY REGUILLO, FERNANDO and MANUEL ÁLVAREZ TARDÍO (eds.). 2013. *The Spanish Second Republic Revisited: From Democratic Hopes to Civil War (1931–1936)* (Brighton: Sussex Academic Press)

FERNÁNDEZ RUBIO, ANDRÉS. 1993. 'La reedición de una destacada novela fascista española desata la polémica', *El País*, 28 February, 'Cultura' section <http://elpais.com/diario/1993/02/28/cultura/730854010_850215.html> [accessed 5 January 2016]

FORCADELL, CARLOS, MERCEDES YUSTA and IGNACIO PEIRÓ (eds.). 2015. *El pasado en construcción: revisionismos históricos en la historia contemporánea* (Zaragoza: Institución Fernando el Católico)

GALLEGO, FERRAN. 2014. *El evangelio fascista: la formación de la cultura política del franquismo* (Barcelona: Crítica)

GRACIA, JORDI. 2004. *La resistencia silenciosa: fascismo y cultura en España* (Barcelona: Anagrama)

GRAHAM, HELEN. 2005. *The Spanish Civil War: A Very Short Introduction* (Oxford: Oxford University Press)

GONZÁLEZ CUEVAS, PEDRO CARLOS. 2003. *Maeztu: biografía de un nacionalista español* (Madrid: Marcial Pons)

JULIÁ, SANTOS. 2003. 'Echar al olvido. Memoria y amnistía en la Transición', *Claves de razón práctica*, 129: 14–25

LINZ, JUAN JOSÉ. 1964. 'An Authoritarian Regime: The Case of Spain', in *Cleavages, Ideologies and Party Systems: Contributions to Comparative Political Sociology*, ed. by Erik Allardt and Yrjo Littunen (Helsinki: The Academic Bookstore), pp. 291–341

LÓPEZ VILLAVERDE, ÁNGEL LUIS. 2014. 'La cultura de la memoria. Nuevo balance bibliográfico', *Studia Histórica*, 32: 263–83

LOUREIRO, ÁNGEL. 2008. 'Pathetic Arguments', *Journal of Spanish Cultural Studies*, 9: 225–37

LUCAS, ANTONIO. 2015. 'La otra literatura (olvidada)', *El Mundo*, 27 November, 'Cultura' section, 49–52

MARTÍNEZ CACHERO, JOSÉ MARÍA. 2009. *Liras entre lanzas. Historia de la literatura 'nacional' en la Guerra Civil* (Madrid: Castalia)

PEREIRA, ARMANDO. 2003. *Una España escindida: Federico García Lorca y Ramiro de Maeztu* (Mexico: F.C.E. / UNAM)

PRESTON, PAUL. 2012. *The Spanish Holocaust: Inquisition and Extermination in Twentieth-Century Spain* (London: Harper Press)

RESINA, JOAN RAMON. 2005. 'The Last Look from the Border' in *Visualizing Spanish Modernity*, ed. by Susan Larsson and Eva Woods (Oxford: Berg), pp. 329–48.

Ríos-Font, Wadda C. 2004. *The Canon and the Archive: Configuring Literature in Modern Spain* (Lewisburg: Bucknell University Press)
Rodrigo, Javier. 2013. *Cruzada, paz, memoria* (Granada: Editorial Comares)
Rodríguez Puértolas, Julio. 1986. *Historia de la literatura fascista española* (Madrid: Akal)
Saz, Ismael. 2004. *Fascismo y franquismo* (Valencia: Universitat de Valencia)
—— 2012. '¿Dónde está el otro? O sobre qué eran los que no eran fascistas' in *El fascismo clásico y sus epígonos. Nuevas aportaciones teóricas* ed. by Joan Anton Mellón (Madrid: Tecnos), pp. 155–90
Trapiello, Andrés. 1984. '¿Quién piensa en 1936?', *El País*, 18 November, 'Babelia' supplement
—— 2002. *Las armas y las letras: literatura y Guerra Civil* (Barcelona: Península)

Notes to Chapter 7

1. All translations in this chapter are my own.
2. One scholar who has undertaken the type of painstaking quantitative research that would be required to address the former issue has found what she calls 'huge lacunae' in the Spanish canon, as regards 'any text that supports fascism' (Brown 2010: 116). Her conclusions, however, are derived from the very specific source of graduate reading lists at Hispanic Studies departments in US universities.
3. See Becerra Mayor (2012: 39–40) for full bibliographical details. A later summation of the arguments involved, which also brings other critics into the fray, can be found in Fernández Rubio 1993.
4. The most influential paradigms are currently those of Linz (1964), Saz (2004 and 2012), and Gallego (2014).
5. An overview of Spanish-language bibliography on the subject is provided in López Villaverde 2014. The classic work on the supposed 'pact of silence' is Aguilar 2002. The new historiographic paradigm being put forward is condensed in Graham 2005. Preston 2012 contains the most famous -and controversial- use of the term 'Spanish Holocaust'.
6. The classic criticism of the notion of a 'pact of silence' is Juliá 2003, with another critical view, from the realm of Hispanism, in Loureiro 2007. Historiographic contestation of the 'historical memory'-driven view of the Republic, in del Rey and Álvarez Tardío 2012. These publications have in turn generated an anti-revisionist backlash, of which Forcadell 2015 is a good example.
7. A label that might not be unwarranted, given the discouragement that at least one researcher received from archivists when he decided to research the work of the journalist and essayist Ramiro de Maeztu (Pereira 2003: 13).
8. The 'culpable aloofness' charge has been levelled with particular ferocity at the bestselling novel *Soldados de Salamina* (e.g. Resina 2005: 344).

CHAPTER 8

The Unfortunate Case of Heritage Screen Media: Dismissal, Denial and Definition

Laura J. Lee Kemp

Within the context of Spanish screen media, the term 'heritage' remains ill-defined and under-explored. There is no equivalent term within the Spanish language to describe the concept, so despite some lively contemporary debate, the 'heritage' genre has remained firmly adhered to its English origins and the notion of genre itself has been constructed negatively throughout Spanish cinema history as a way of pushing back against the 'functional definition of genres adopted from American and European cinemas' (Beck and Ortega 2008: 5). Yet this category of film and television productions continues to emerge in quite substantial numbers and they constitute a formidable presence within contemporary cultural production in Spain — a presence which is not reflected within the Hispanic canon, not least because these terminologies are born of an Anglo-American critical tradition that has established them as unworthy of serious academic attention. This opinion has understandably influenced scholastic trends within Hispanic studies, locating the investigation of popular screen media at the margins of the critical canon, where its visibility and cultural capital is limited. Productions located at the generic crossroads of 'popular' and 'heritage' — a category which applies to most contemporary film or television productions set during the Civil War or the early years of Francoism — are doubly marginalised within the canon. This chapter will explore how critical attitudes within Hispanic studies have been influenced by English and American scholastic trends, before giving a brief overview of the main strands of research currently being undertaken on this topic in the UK. The case will then be made as to why it is so important for popular screen media of this genus to gain more cultural capital and visibility within the Hispanic canon.

Spain has a rich tradition of *cine histórico* [historical cinema],[1] of films which are located in a defined historical era and focus either on the portrayal of a well-known event, or the depiction of a historical figure. Typified by lavish set and costume design and the use of narrative allegory, this genre first came to prominence in the 1940s and 50s. *Los últimos de Filipinas* (Antonio Román, 1945), which is set during the

1898 Spanish-American War in the Philippines, was used as a cypher for Francoist propaganda, a characteristic shared by many 'historical' productions which dealt with figures or events perceived to be of import to the formation of the new Spanish national psyche. *Sin novedad en el Alcázar* (Augusto Genina, 1940) inspired by events which supposedly took place in Toledo during the Civil War, was also wielded as a political tool by the Francoist government. A plethora of productions directed by the prolific Juan de Orduña also focus on historical figures or events, such as *Locura de amor* (1948), *Agustina de Aragón* (1950), *Alba de América* (1951), *La Leona de Castilla* (1951), and *Zarzuela 1900* (1959). These films form the body of work which is defined by the term *cine histórico* in Spain, described by Triana-Toribio as 'emblematic in the construction of a national cinema and a national identity after the Civil War' (2003: 47). Sally Faulkner, however, has argued against the notion of a homogenous period of state-influenced, pro-Francoist historical epics of the 1940s (2013: 45) and Steven Marsh has concluded elsewhere that 'it is both a commonplace and a falsehood... that Spanish cinema of the early Francoist period comprised exclusively nation-building propaganda exercises in the form of rewritten history and religious epic' (2006: 1–2). Yet this period of cinematic production continues to be recognised within the Hispanic canon as an era that was undeniably historically minded, and all descriptions of *cine histórico* are populated by these heavily-costumed epics.

More recent auteurist productions such as Erice's *El espiritú de la colmena* (1973), Saura's *¡Ay, Carmela!* (1990) and Aranda's *Libertarias* (1996) were the harbingers of the growing corpus of contemporary films and television productions that are in fact set during the Civil War and immediate post-war era. Marvin D'Lugo (1997) has defined this genre of political and historical revisionism as a 'recuperation industry'. Since the turn of the century, films dealing with similar subject matter have formed a body of work that continues to emerge and evolve, both stylistically and narratively. D'Lugo has argued that since 2000 there has been a renewed interest in recent Spanish history amongst the generation comprised of the grandchildren of war veterans, who now feel sufficiently distanced from the conflict to be able to discuss it (1997: 23). Indeed, since the beginning of the 21st century over twenty-five popular narrative films have been produced which are set in the period from 1930 to 1950 and have the Spanish Civil War as their temporal or narrative backdrop. Koldo Serra's fictional narrative set during the bombing of Guernica in April 1937 (*Gernika*, 2016) is, at the time of writing, the latest production to join this increasing number of films. Yet to frame this group of recent productions within the *cine histórico* bracket is problematic, as it disregards the importance of Civil War films as a sub-genre within the historical corpus. Nor does the term *cine histórico* engage with a critical tradition that has aligned the term 'heritage' with a more popular, middle-brow aesthetic that seeks to 'depict the past, but by celebrating rather than investigating it' (Vincendeau 2001: xviii). Within the Spanish cinematic corpus this strand of Civil War 'heritage cinema' has indeed played an investigative and arguably integral role in the so-called memory boom. Triana-Toribio has argued that:

> Producers and directors in the Zapatero years, more often than not, pursued 'quality projects' such as Civil War dramas, that pleased the gatekeepers who

were interested, for instance, in the *recuperación de la memoria histórica* [recuperation of historical memory] that had been recently enshrined in law (2014: 69).

However, a steady stream of productions have emerged since the end of the Zapatero government and its politically motivated subsidies, such as *De tu ventana a la mía* (2012), *Pa negre* (2012), *El tiempo entre costuras* (2013), *El año y la viña* (2013) and *Gernika* (2016). Taken in conjunction with the continued presence of the Civil War on Spanish television and the persistent output of popular publications dealing with the same subject matter, these productions represent a socially integrated trend that continues to sustain public engagement within Spain and abroad.

The influence of the English Heritage Tradition

Oliete-Aldea's recent article 'Places of Memory in the New Millennium: British Influence on Spanish Transnational Heritage Cinema and Television' recognises the mutually influential nature of the European film industry, claiming that 'the renaissance of the heritage film in Britain during the 1980s with its pairing of 'enterprise' and 'heritage' corresponds to a similar revival in Spain at the turn of the millennium, especially in the realm of TV productions' (2015: 179). 'Heritage cinema' was a term originally coined in the 1980s to describe a corpus of British productions that centred on presenting historical narratives in an idyllic, nostalgic fashion with high production values and an emphasis on costume design and detailed mise-en-scène. Films such as *A Room With a View* (James Ivory, 1985), *Chariots of Fire* (Hugh Hudson, 1981) and *Elizabeth* (Shekhar Kapur, 1998) were critiqued, most notably by the theorist Andrew Higson, as representing a propensity for middle- and upper-class cultural nostalgia, thereby neglecting a duty for cinema to engage with contemporary social issues of the time. Visits to National Trust properties increased in tandem with the release and popular reception of heritage films: this was termed 'heritage tourism' and it was booming in the 1990s, much to the chagrin of critics who claimed that the past was being reproduced in film and television as 'flat, depthless pastiche' (Higson 2006: 95). At the onset of the 1990s in Spain, visiting heritage sites became an increasing popular pastime amongst the newly solvent middle classes, who 'now had sufficient collective economic clout for domestic tourism to become a prized cultural commodity' (Wheeler 2014: 215). This trend continued to increase after the economic hardship of the late 2000s began to ease. Spanish tourism to Morocco has increased exponentially since the release of the hugely successful TV series *El tiempo entre costuras* (Antena 3, 2013), a costume drama set in Spanish Morocco during the Civil War and the Second World War. Just before the eagerly anticipated final episode was broadcast, Smith noted how 'on the main channel, news bulletins announced that travel bookings to Morocco had boomed since early episodes set in that country had been aired: viewers wanted to follow the steps (or stitches) of character Sira' (2014a). After the British, the Spanish are ranked second within Europe as the most prolific visitors of historical sights and monuments.

Yet the success of these UK productions amongst audiences at home and abroad led to what Vidal has termed an 'artificial divide' between critical discourse and public reception. By ignoring and denigrating the popular success enjoyed by these films, UK film criticism retreated from any contact with audiences and their desires or preferences, elevating itself above engagement with this new emerging genre. This approach has since been seen as a return to the rigid models of 1970s theory which entirely neglects to consider the response of audiences and their diverse nature when forming critical opinion (2012: 15). Claire Monk has described the left-wing academic response to films released at the height of Thatcherism as 'monolithic', a rigid approach which ignored the significant differences between these films at the textual level and was defined by a 'top-down reading perspective which distanced itself from the films and their audiences' (2002: 183). The alienation of critic from both product and consumer has also crossed national boundaries; not only is it reflected in some attitudes towards the Civil War heritage film within Spain, but it has also resulted in this collection of productions being relegated to the margins of critical debate and interest.[2]

Another similarity between the Hispanic and Anglophone critical debates lies in the polemical subject of historical 'truth'. Accusations of inauthenticity were levelled against the purported historicity of many British heritage productions, connecting the presentation of the past as spectacle to a loss of critical representations of history. The consumer consumption of an historic simulacrum came to represent a departure from the 'true' history born of academia, and fuelled the growing divide between popularist and scholarly approaches to the past. Similarly, as Loxham has recently highlighted:

> Truth as an absolute and possible aim pervades the rhetoric involved with the process of the recovery of memory and a side effect of this approach has been to imagine a scientific understanding of the past that considers fictional products as unworthy vehicles for the transmission of these memories and thereby of this history (2015: 4).

Quintana espoused this interpretation of history in a recent review of *La voz dormida*, in which he claims that 'the film brings to the surface an important historical drama, but the staging ultimately dilutes it with a series of clichés that merely serve to minimize it and betray the weight of the historical truth' (2014: 16). This insistence on the existence of an historical singularity has allowed a number of scholars to dismiss 'heritage' productions which do not accord with the homogenous academic view of the period or events they depict (*Las 13 rosas*, for example, has been reproved for portraying prison inmates wearing lipstick) (Smith 2012: 10). In relation to a civil conflict, the notion of truth is especially problematic as it further polarises the memories and experiences of both victims and survivors. To dismiss a fictional narrative because it does not rigidly adhere to a notion of events established by historians is to be unaware that historical fiction is simply, as described by Jerome de Groot, a caricatured illusion of authenticity. Some productions, it can be argued, attempt to present themselves as reflecting a historical 'truth', but this can be considered an added level of textual complexity which requires the viewer to be aware of the narrative's aspirations to authenticity whilst simultaneously situating it within a context of falsity. An ability to comprehend and enjoy this textual duality demonstrates, according to de Groot, that 'the consumer of [an] historical product has a complexity of engagement that is a level higher or more complex than that of the "contemporary" text' (2009: 182). It is unfair, therefore, to disregard the corpus of heritage screen media about the Civil War as either a market-driven trend or as unsuccessful attempts to uncritically 'recreate' events wholesale. Heritage cinema and television requires a level of spectatorship that is nuanced, engaged and critical.

The British heritage aesthetic was also accused of deploying a 'stable and conservative iconography', such as lavishly decorated stately homes and pastoral landscapes, to misrepresent and even mythologise national history in service to the national imaginary and an invented national identity (Vidal 2012: 47). Speaking with reference to *El tiempo entre costuras,* Smith has identified a new paradigm for Spanish television in the formally ambitious detail of the *mise en scène,* which creates a level of production quality that is still unusual in television (2015). In the UK critics denigrated this level of material detail as a distraction from what they considered to be screen media's main role, and the main criticism engendered by this accusation of 'pastiche' was that heritage cinema and television could not affect social change, that it was only capable of reflecting a contextual political landscape. A similar criticism has been expressed by Ángel Quintana with reference to a list of the most popular contemporary Civil War films, including del Toro's *El laberinto del fauno* and Villaronga's *Pa negre,* which are accused of 'imposing a mega-model for profitable super-production aimed at penetrating the Hollywood market' (2014: 13). This 'blindness' to the needs of the Spanish film industry in crisis and at risk from the infiltration of international models, claims Quintana, 'could halt the process of recovery and revision of [historical] memory in contemporary cinema' (2014: 13). José F.Colmeiro has also joined this debate by stating that some 'popularly acclaimed' Civil War heritage productions, such as *Los girasoles ciegos, Las trece rosas, Silencio roto, Libertarias,* or *El viaje de Carol,* 'all have the same look and feel of conventional heritage drama productions', which have made the difficult, traumatic period of history they chose to represent 'too palatable and too comfortable, thus neutralizing their potential as instruments for social intervention' (2011).

In opposition to this opinion, Oliete-Aldea's recent article credits heritage cinema with satisfying a desire to look for 'foundational myths' in Spanish cinema, 'especially as the Civil War created a deep wound in Spanish society, which has remained entrenched in the memories of Spaniards for several generations' (2015: 180). Belén Vidal (2012: 67) has delved a little deeper into the formal characteristics of Spanish heritage film and identified that it shares certain stylistic idiosyncrasies with cinema that deals with other traumatic conflicts of the twentieth century in Europe. She terms this return to 'traumatic national pasts' an 'important trend in European heritage film,' which 'elicits forms of collective memory through the images and sounds of the recent past, which is fictionally re-enacted in the present tense.' These 'images and sounds' are presented through the use of period objects and costumes in the *mise en scène*, combined with 'audiovisual textures' of photographs, newsreel footage and popular music (2012: 67). This combination of a modern spectacle impersonating the past with authentic soundtracks and visual footage from the era in question, provides a privileged site from which to reassess the relationship of past and present. Landsberg would interpret this intersection of two temporal locations as the 'suturing' of a prosthetic memory onto an audience with no first hand recollection of the situations being portrayed. Dealing with a conflictive, divisive and violent past, the depicted situations may enable audiences actively to engage with progressive narratives about the 'conflicts at the heart of inheritance' (2004: 2). As Vidal has noted, 'it is the focus on textures of memory, rather than direct political commentary, that constitutes the basis for what Svetlana Boym calls "reflective nostalgia": a nostalgia whose affective power creates spaces for critical thinking' (2012: 68).

Spaces for Critical Thinking

A number of themes have made themselves prevalent amongst heritage productions released since the turn of the century. Narratives which focus on the role of women during and after the war have found an outlet in productions such as *Silencio roto* (Armendáriz, 2000), *You're the one* (Garci, 2000), *Las 13 rosas* (Martínez-Lázaro, 2007), *De tu ventana a la mía* (Ortiz, 2012), *La voz dormida* (Zambrano, 2011) and *Iris* (Vergés, 2004). The longstanding generic convention of using the child witness figure to explore the isolating traumas of the war and encourage audience identification, termed *cine con niño* [child cinema], has been further developed in films such as *El viaje de Carol* (Uribe, 2002), *El laberinto del fauno* (del Toro, 2006), *El espinazo del diablo* (del Toro, 2002), *Los girasoles ciegos* (Cuerda, 2006) and *Pa Negre* (Villaronga, 2010). A number of light comedies have emerged, such as *El año y la viña* (Cenzual Burley, 2013), *El portero* (Suárez, 2000) and *El bosque* (Aibar, 2013), an interesting approach to the treatment of national trauma and historical memory which deserves further investigation. There are also, of course, productions which do not fit neatly into these categories, such as the tale of a group of refugee children fleeing to Russia in *¡Ispansi!* (Iglesias, 2010), or the homoerotic exploration of religious fetishism in *El mar* (Villaronga, 2000). Literary adaptations, still perhaps the hallmark of a 'quality' heritage production as designated by the 1983 Ley Miró [Miró Law], dissect these categories. Yet within the Hispanic canon, and excepting the two del Toro productions, very little critical attention has been paid to this collection of works. Some productions have been referred to as works that 'ultimately surrender to the tenets of melodrama' and as such, are incapable of articulating 'genuine strategies' that would allow their audiences to participate in discourses of memory; an opinion reminiscent of the 'top-down' reading perspective of the rigid 1970s criticism of heritage productions within the UK (Quintana 2014: 16). It might be more productive, given the undeniable popularity of this genre within Spain, to concentrate on exactly why the symbiosis of melodrama and Civil War narratives continues to play such a visible role within popular memory discourses.

Laura Mulvey has argued that melodrama, when used in conjunction with a realist composition as it so often is, can be instrumental in enabling the expression of trauma and suffering beyond the quotidian confines of realism. When something happens which demands that the transparency of realism be replaced by something a little more self-conscious and attention-seeking, melodrama can step in:

> Realism and melodrama are, in different ways, stylistically important for dramas of social oppression and injustice. Realism records the state of things, without stylistic intrusion into a representation of the norms of everyday life and its fragile survival strategies. These are conditions that lack buffer zones or safety valves; misfortune or error can quickly mutate into disaster leaving its victims struggling to comprehend, unable to articulate clearly their suffering or the strain that leaves close relationships fissured. It is here that melodrama serves its purpose and the cinema takes on an expressive function that responds to both the intensity of the crisis and its protagonists' desperation (2010: 8).

Despite the acuity of this relationship between trauma and melodrama, as identified by Mulvey, the genre has been rejected as being incapable of effectively representing traumatic events. Likewise, realist aesthetics have been similarly dismissed as inappropriate, ineffective and unsuccessful. Mimetic trauma theory states that a traumatic experience incapacitates a victim's cognitive abilities, so that the experience never becomes part of their normal memory system (Leys 2000: 298), and this is the approach still overwhelmingly adopted by literary and film criticism: trauma defies cognitive assimilation and therefore it should resist narrative or realist representation. Jo Labanyi has used this methodology to claim that the 'realist aesthetics adopted by most recent Spanish films about the Civil War suggest not only a concern to show off high production values but also a lack of concern with the question of how the past is transmitted' (2007: 439). Realist textual composition, as defined by Paul Julian Smith, uses a consistent colour tone with most shots taken at eye level with no privileged point of view. There are no inner-vision shots, no impossible shots (i.e from ceilings) and no symbolic shots. The camera is relatively static and the speaker is always in focus with a predominance of medium close-ups, most importantly no one addresses the camera and there are no interior monologues. Medium-duration takes dominate, taking place in real narrative time (no fast or slow motion). There are no flash-backs and no flash-forwards, and no self-conscious intertextuality or non-diegetic music (2009: 125). This is a very stringent definition that is not resolutely adopted by films such as *Iris*, *El bosque* or *El laberinto del fauno*, for example. However, Labanyi makes a convincing case for cinematic and literary productions that reflect the fissured, anti-narrative of trauma, rather than a multitude of productions born of 'a nostalgia industry re-presenting the war and its aftermath in the form of heritage style movies' (2007: 429). This corpus of productions is not without its representational issues, and an anti-mimetic stylistic approach would perhaps result in productions of a more artistically and socially challenging nature, but a large proportion of the current output within Spain does follow the realist textual composition model and is subsequently ignored by the critical canon. Labanyi's comment, therefore, serves to reflect the artificial divide which has emerged between critical discourse and public reception.

Hayden White has also claimed that 'Holocaustal events' resist representation through narratives of 'traditional humanistic historiography', as they cannot be adapted to fit onto a narrative arc which ends with any sort of closure or attempts to convey any meaning. It is impossible, according to White, to render Holocaustal events without 'enfabling' them: leaving them liable to fantasies of wholeness and health, fantasies denied by their very nature. Representation through collage and fragmentation would be more appropriate, he claims (1988: 1193). White's generalised supposition that all fictional narratives, by definition, adhere to this false blueprint of 'wholeness' is shared by Colmeiro, who has criticised a perceived tendency to reconstruct the past as a complete and melodramatic narrative arc that fails to acknowledge the traumatic fissures of the period in question. In reference to the series *Amar en tiempos revueltos,* Colmeiro has stated that 'the unproblematic transparent mimetic representation of the past, with its meticulously reconstructed *mise en scène*, and traditional linear structure, effectively sutures the discontinuities of the fragmented past, made out of silences and voids' (2011: 29). I do not wish to contradict Colmeiro's opinion, just as I do not mean to imply that all contemporary Civil War heritage productions are formally accomplished; yet these statements do not legitimise the exclusion of this body of work from the canon. As Pam Cook has so aptly noted:

> Critiques of nostalgia films condemn them for de-historicising the past, for creating a timeless zone outside social change and historical analysis. This implies a particular view of history and social changes, as though they are themselves free from subjective emotion and the processes of representation (2005: 16).

Heritage screen media constitutes a field of cultural production within Spain which is both popular and enduring; surely the decision and techniques used to suture the fissured past of the Civil War onto smooth melodramatic narratives deserve to be thoroughly researched.

In order to close the rift that has developed between popular reception and scholarly opinion, research into cinematic affect, melodrama and the emotional legacy of collective traumatic memory may help to illuminate what Oliete-Aldea has termed the 'emotional liaison between the past remembered and the time of its remembrance' (2015: 177). Martínez-Lázaro's account of the infamous thirteen roses, *Las 13 rosas* and Zambrano's adaptation of Dulce Chacón's *La voz dormida* have been criticised for being overly emotional, too reliant upon emotive affect, both melodramatic and heritage. Both films may be considered middlebrow productions which appeal to spectators with a cinematic and televisual background shaped by the formal properties of British heritage productions, and Oliete-Aldea notes that 'the dismissal of these two films by critics is rooted in the use of melodramatic generic conventions of Hollywood historical dramas as well as the careful and often romanticised *mise en scène* of British heritage productions' (2015: 182). Spanish cinema has a somewhat problematic relationship with genre, because it has traditionally been viewed as a restrictive Hollywood model that functioned in opposition to Spain's auteurist tradition. Melodrama is repeatedly denigrated and dismissed within the academic community for its adherence to the 'low culture' of romantic soap operas and 'women's novels'. Yet the public reception of melodrama in Spain is far more accepting, and indeed it is repeatedly celebrated by Spain's most illustrious auteur, Pedro Almodóvar. Melodrama forms an established part of folkloric culture, celebrated in flamenco and embodied by the *toreador*. The popularity of Latin American *telenovelas* in the peninsula is also perhaps emblematic of how the Spanish enjoy the spectacle of highly dramatized moral dilemmas and family conflicts, characterized by a performance aesthetic of overstatement. Within heritage cinema and television, melodrama serves both to universalise and modernise narratives that are localised and temporally specific at root. The primacy of emotional affect over regionalised social or political motives allows these stories to transcend national boundaries and to flourish within the transnational frameworks of production and reception that are so integral to European cinema in the twenty-first century.

Current research trends within heritage screen media

Writing in 2008, Beck and Rodriguez Ortega lamented that to date not one academic monograph dedicated to genre within Spanish cinema had been published, despite genre representing 'one of the most powerful and salient methods for constructing meaning in cinema' (2008: 2). Their edited volume does address new representational forms of melodrama; Carla Marcantonio argues that it has come to reflect a new transnational imagination within Almodóvar's cinema, and Belén Vidal establishes a convincing interpretation of melodrama as a new 'indie' genre within Coixet's later work. The cross-section of historical allegory and the horror genre, in films such as *El laberinto* and *El espinazo del diablo,* is also carefully analysed in separate chapters by Lázaro-Reboll and Acevedo-Muñoz. Yet the conjunction of melodrama and historical allegory is not addressed, and the word 'heritage' does not make a single appearance in the volume. Claire Monk has argued that there are too many sub-categories of 'genre' (such as melodrama, period costume, literary adaptations, picaresque and satire) contained within the designation of Heritage Cinema to allow it to be neatly categorised (2002: 176). Indeed, Altman cites the techniques of sub-categorisation as one of the attempts to display genre as 'neat, manageable and stable; (1999: 14). The heritage genre, however, is not a clearly defined entity with unchanging characteristics: it forms hybrids, mutants and cross-breeds at every turn. Therefore, Monk's definition of Heritage Cinema as a 'complex, hybrid and contradictory terrain' goes some way to explaining how a seemingly immiscible wealth of films which share very little in their aesthetic composition, narrative or directorial style can be painted with the same descriptive brush (2002: 176). Wheeler has recently noted that a selection of Civil War heritage films 'as ostensibly disparate as *Las 13 rosas, De tu ventana a la mía* and *La voz dormida* all marshal emotional affect from the viewer through identification with the martyrdom of female prisoners facing the reality and/or prospect of firing squads' (2014: 226). The deployment of affect is, I would argue, a characteristic shared by all of the contemporary films mentioned in this chapter. Formally and narratively, affect is invariably integral to the depiction of stories set during such a psychologically and culturally traumatic period of history, and perhaps it is the singular defining generic quality of Civil War heritage films.

Although popular narrative heritage cinema and television is currently situated at the margins of the Hispanic canon, debates over its classification and cultural validity continue to expand and a select group of researchers have begun to establish where some of the more prevalent tropes lie. Its importance to cultural memory narratives is one of the more established themes, and as the most prolific analyst of Spanish popular culture, Paul Julian Smith has written expansively on the theme of historical memory. He is also responsible for several instructive essays on the television series *Amar en tiempos revueltos* and *Cuéntame cómo pasó*, along with authoritative reviews of *El laberinto del fauno* (2007) and *Las 13 rosas* (2014b). Smith has established a definition of the textual composition of Anglo-Catalan serial productions (2009) and in a recent lecture he identified *El tiempo entre costuras* as belonging to a new wave of 'quality television', defined by formally ambitious production and direction techniques which are engaged in the telling of national narratives. However, in 2006 he noted that 'no one has raised the question or indeed the possibility of a Spanish heritage cinema' (2006: 101).

Wheeler's chapter 'Back to the Future: Repackaging Spain's Troublesome Past for Local and Global Audiences' in the edited volume *(Re)viewing Creative, Critical and Commercial Practices in Contemporary Spanish Cinema* seeks to establish the Spanish heritage canon within a political, industrial and aesthetic context. Focussing mainly on historical epics set during the Golden Age, Wheeler argues for a consistently transnational outlook amongst productions as far ranging as *Locura de amor* (de Orduña, 1948) and *Alatriste* (Díaz Yanes, 2006). There is a singular reference to contemporary productions set during or after the Civil War, in which these films are united under the banner of a 'baroque effect', characterised by the primacy of emotion and the use of paradigmatic 'Hispanic' images. Wheeler argues that productions such as *La voz dormida* and *De tu ventana a la mía* unwittingly resurrect techniques of the 1940s and 1950s that 'complicated, and arguably sabotaged, the emergence of heritage cinema in Spain' (2014: 226). In reference to the earlier examples of this category, introspective and arguably regional literary adaptations supported by the Ley Miró such as *Los santos inocentes* (Camus, 1984), Wheeler notes that these 'cinematic depictions of Francoism are nevertheless the closest equivalent to heritage cinema that Spanish cinema had to offer in the 1980s; a state of affairs which is indicative of Spain's (wilful?) exclusion from a major pan-continental cinematic trend...' (2014: 214). However, the emphasis he so rightly places upon the intra- and trans-national nature of other heritage productions can very neatly be transposed onto the generic category of contemporary Civil War films, which are not only dependent upon international production investment and market reception, but also seek to trans-nationalise the specific local trauma of the conflict by emphasising the primacy of emotive affect.

Loxham's article analyses the role of audio-visual media in the 'negotiation and representation of cultural memory', looking at the way *Cuéntame cómo pasó* has been continually engaged in sustaining and renegotiating narratives of memory within the public sphere. She argues that 'popular media forms deserve sustained critical attention with regard to the creation of memory in Spain, and should not be dismissed as simply vehicles for nostalgia or as spurious recreation of a brutal past' (2015: 4). Although their work is not specifically concerned with films set during the Civil War and post-war period, at the time of writing both Belén Vidal and Rob Stone are undertaking research that is more specific to Spanish and Basque heritage cinema respectively. Conversely, Archibald's *The War That Won't Die* (2012) is solely concerned with Civil War films, but again fails to address the wealth of popular contemporary productions within this remit. A number of influential essays have been written about the more auteurist productions listed above, such as Ann Davies's 'The Beautiful and the Monstrous Masculine: The Male Body and Horror in *El espinazo del diablo*' (2006) and Dean Allbritton's insightful reading of *Pa Negre* in 'Recovering Childhood: Virulence, Ghosts and Black Bread' (2014). However, there are a wealth of productions that have not received any critical attention whatsoever, productions made on much smaller budgets that have not benefitted from associations with influential directors or producers. Notable amongst them are *De tu ventana a la mía* (Paula Ortiz, 2012), a formally accomplished film that depicts three women living through some of the most tumultuous periods in Spain's recent history, shot with stunning cinematography; *El bosque* (Óscar Aibar, 2012), a quirky mix of fantasy and hyper-realism starring Maria Molins and Tom Sizemore that narrates a poignant tale of war-time secrecy and escapism, and *Iris* (Rosa Vergés, 2004) which stars Silke in a touching interpretation of feminine loss and survival during an unspecified conflict that demands to be interpreted as the Spanish Civil War. Even some of the more well-known productions, such as José Luis Cuerda's *Los girasoles ciegos* (2009) and Montxo Armendáriz's *Silencio roto* (2000) have attracted meagre amounts of critical research. In relation to televisual productions, only *Amar en tiempos revueltos* and *Cuéntame cómo pasó* have received any attention. Other historical series such as *El tiempo entre costuras* (Antena 3, 2013–14), *Gran hotel* (Antena 3, 2011–13) and *El secreto del puente viejo* (Antena 3, 2011–14) are, as yet, unbaptised in the critical arena.

A paradigmatic shift towards the counter-heritage

Why, therefore, should researchers be motivated to look towards the margins of the Hispanic canon? To engage in a paradigmatic shift towards forms of cultural production that have so far been deemed unworthy of attention? Writing in relation to Germany's cinematic attitude towards Nazism and the trauma it entailed, Elsaesser believes that historically-based films can offer opportunities for 'mastering the past', or for helping a culture to come to terms (in a strictly Freudian sense) with its history. Remaining within the confines of psychoanalysis, Elsaesser defends the possibility of mainstream genres to enable 'mourning work' if emotional identification is achieved between spectator and storyline (1996: 179). If an affective connection is realised, the heritage film can represent a new relationship between history, memory and the present. The construction of historical *mise en scène* allows the past to return through a manifestation of contemporary objects and technology. The distinction between past and present becomes blurred, leading to recognition that one can look backwards and forwards simultaneously, that 'contemporary identities evolve in connection with a changing sense of historicity' (Vidal 2012: 18). Far from dismissing popular narrative heritage productions as nostalgic pastiche, historically inaccurate clichés or low-brow melodrama, Elsaesser's more positive assessment of German heritage film can be transposed onto the Spanish case study. As established by Oliete-Aldea, heritage screen media may be understood as an international genre which although originating from British productions, is now in use across the globe. The supra-national and trans-national nature of film in the twenty-first century can be seen as a contextual framework for the heritage genre, which has continually shifting boundaries that allow it to engage critically with a myriad of historical events and temporal locations, often by stressing the pre-eminence of affective strategies over political or historical specificity. This globalising technique has engendered a wealth of criticism, especially from within Spain, and it is compounded by the critical dismissal of popular heritage screen media within Hispanic studies which is born of the legacy of British heritage productions. This refusal to engage with the term 'heritage' in a meaningful and productive way does not enable the Hispanic canon to move beyond the dichotomy of academia versus popularity which has relegated such a popular and prolific oeuvre of cultural output to the margins of our field, seriously limiting its cultural capital and exposure to students and young researchers. I would argue for a wider deployment of the term heritage, and I would argue for it in opposition to terms such as Spanish Civil War Film or *cine histórico*. Firstly, the former nomenclature restrictively disavows any cinema engaged solely with the pre- or post-war years, or with a temporal mix of eras. *Cine histórico*, on the other hand, is understood as a genre which was often politically manipulated for propagandist purposes, and was overwhelming focused on eras before the 1930s, making use of lavish sets and costume design often at the cost of critical allegory. *Cine histórico* was a hegemonic, often propagandistic and highly conservative mode of representation, a list of characteristics not shared by the current collection of films under consideration.

Contemporary heritage productions consistently echo the post-1980s generational discontent with the political consensus that led to the *Pacto de olvido* [Pact of Silence], which failed to make a clean break with the corporate and political inheritors of Francoism and also resolutely refused to condemn the atrocities committed against civilians by the regime. Perhaps in opposition to the Pact of Silence, contemporary heritage productions focus overwhelmingly on narrating the muted histories of the victims of Francoism and the horrors of state repression in the 1940s. Accordingly, it may be more apposite to use Higbee's descriptive of 'counterheritage' in reference to these films. Developed in order to describe a current wave of anti-colonial French-Maghrebi heritage productions, the term is:

> intended to highlight the way that such films draw on the iconography and representational practices of the heritage film — such as a self-awareness of the act of historical reconstruction and questions of authenticity– while

challenging dominant neo-colonial or 'anti-repentant' modes of re-presenting and memorialising the past (2013: 71).

In the same way that these Maghrebi productions seek to subvert or undermine previously dominant narratives of historical memory, contemporary Spanish productions also strive to challenge the hegemonic Francoist historiography of the war and the repressive effects of the transition upon discourses of historical memory and cultural trauma. It is a sub-genre dominated by female and childhood protagonists, Republican victims and Communist *maquis* [resistance militia]. In a similar vein, Sally Faulkner has argued that *Alatriste* 'seemed to prove that Spanish cinema was fertile terrain for the newly gritty post-heritage trend', which she aligns with an increased focus on previously silenced narratives of oppression and suffering (2013: 273). Yet irrespective of whether it is referred to as post-heritage, counterheritage or simply heritage, the broadening category of contemporary films about the Civil War and post-war period represent a substantial presence within Spanish cinema (through both national and transnational co-productions) that plays an important social role in the development and maintenance of historical memory and cultural trauma narratives. Recognition of this genus of screen media is long overdue, as is the recognition that the wealth of Anglophone critical scholarship on the heritage genre should be considered an asset to Hispanists working in contemporary film studies, rather than an excuse to dismiss a category of production which persists across the globe. Arguably, our own *critical heritage* should be used for the advantage of both Hispanic studies and film scholarship more widely.

Bibliography

ARCHIBALD, DAVID. 2012. *The War That Won't Die* (Manchester: Manchester University Press)
ALLBRITTON, DEAN. 2014. 'Recovering Childhood: Virulence, Ghosts and Black Bread,' *Bulletin of Hispanic Studies*, 91: 619–36
ALTMAN, RICK. 1999. *Film/Genre* (London: BFI publishing)
BECK, JAY, and VICENTE RODRIGUEZ ORTEGA (eds). 2008. *Contemporary Spanish Cinema and Genre* (Manchester: Manchester University Press)
COLMEIRO, JOSÉ. 2011. 'A Nation of Ghosts? Haunting, Historical Memory and Forgetting in Post-Franco Spain,' *452°F. Electronic Journal of Theory of Literature and Comparative Literature*, 4 <http://www.452f.com/index.php/jose-colmeiro.html> [accessed 15 September 2015]
COOK, PAM. 2005. *Screening the Past. Memory and Nostalgia in Cinema* (Oxford: Routledge)
DASTON, LORRAINE T., and PETER GALISON. 2007. *Objectivity* (New York: Zone Books)
DAVIES, ANN. 2006. 'The Beautiful and the Monstrous Masculine: The Male Body and Horror in *El espinazo del diablo* (Guillermo del Toro, 2001)', *Studies in Hispanic Cinemas*, 3: 135–47
D'LUGO, MARVIN. 1997. *Guide to the Cinema of Spain* (London: Greenwood Press)
ELSAESSER, THOMAS. 1996. 'Subject Positions, Speaking Positions' in *The Persistence of History: Cinema, Television and the Modern Event*, ed. by Vivian Sobchack (Oxford: Routledge), pp. 145–86
FAULKNER, SALLY. 2013. *A History of Spanish Film. Cinema and Society 1910–2010* (London: Bloomsbury)
DE GROOT, JEROME. 2009. *Consuming History. Historians and Heritage in Contemporary Popular Culture* (Oxford: Routledge)

HIGBEE, WILL. 2013. *Post-beur Cinema: North African Émigré and Maghrebi-French Filmmaking in France since 2000* (Edinburgh: Edinburgh University Press)

HIGSON, ANDREW. 2006. 'Re-presenting the National Past: Nostalgia and Pastiche in the Heritage Film', in *Fires Were Started: British Cinema and Thatcherism*, 2nd edn. ed. by Lester Friedman (London: Wallflower Press), pp. 91–109

LABANYI, JO. 2007. 'Teaching History through Memory Work: Issues of Memorialization in Representations of the Spanish Civil War' in *Teaching Representations of the Spanish Civil War*, ed. by Noel Valis (New York: Modern Language Association of America), pp. 436–50

LANDSBERG, ALISON. 2004. *Prosthetic Memory: The Transformation of American Remembrance in the Age of Mass Culture* (New York: Columbia University Press)

LEYS, RUTH. 2000. *Trauma: A Genealogy* (Chicago, London: University of Chicago Press)

LOXHAM, ABIGAIL. 2015. 'Cuéntame cómo pasó/ Tell me how it was: Narratives of Memory and Television Drama in Contemporary Spain', *European Journal of Cultural Studies*, 18: 1–15

MARSH, STEVEN. 2006. *Popular Spanish Film Under Franco: Comedy and the Weakening of the State* (Basingstoke: Palgrave Macmillan)

MONK, CLAIRE. 2002. 'The British Heritage Film Debate Revisited' in *British Historical Cinema: The History, Heritage and Costume Films*, ed. by Claire Monk and Amy Sergeant (London: Routledge), pp. 176–98

MULVEY, LAURA. 2010. 'Between Melodrama and Realism: Under the Skin of the City (2001)' in *Film Moments. Criticism, History, Theory*, ed. by James Walters and Tom Brown (Basingstoke: Palgrave Macmillan), pp. 8–11

OLIETE-ALDEA, ELENA. 2015. 'Places of Memory in the new Millennium: British Influence on Spanish Transnational Heritage Cinema and Television', *Studies in Spanish & Latin American Cinemas*, 12: 175–95

PRIETO, CARLOS. 2009. ´HARTOS DE LA GUERRA CIVIL,´ *Publico* <http://www.publico.es/culturas/hartos-guerra-civil.html> [accessed 16 July 2014]

QUINTANA, ÁNGEL. 2014. 'Anchors in Time: Historic Memory and Representation', *Hispanic Research Journal*, 15: 10–21

SMITH, PAUL JULIAN. 2006. *Spanish Visual Culture. Cinema, Television, Internet* (Manchester: Manchester University Press)

——2007. 'PAN'S LABYRINTH', *Film Quarterly*, 60: 4.

——2009. *Spanish Screen Fiction: Between Cinema and Television* (Liverpool: Liverpool University Press)

——2012. *Spanish Practices, Literature, Cinema, Television* (Oxford: Legenda)

——2014A. 'Letter from Madrid: Bienvenidos al Lolita y el tiempo entre costuras', *Mediático* <http://reframe.sussex.ac.uk/mediatico/2014/01/27/letter-from-madrid-bienvenidos-al-lolita-globomediaantena-3-el-tiempo-entre-costuras-boomerangantena-3/> [accessed 16 July 2014]

——2014B. 'Winners and Losers in Cinema and Memoirs: Emilio Martínez Lázaro's *Las 13 rosas* and Esther Tusquets' *Habíamos ganado la guerra*', *Bulletin of Hispanic Studies*, 91: 255–66

TRIANA-TORIBIO, NÚRIA. 2003. *Spanish National Cinema* (London: Routledge)

——2014. 'Residual Film Cultures: Real and Imagined Futures of Spanish Cinema', *Bulletin of Hispanic Studies*, 91: 65–81

VIDAL, BELÉN. 2012. *Heritage Film. Nation, Genre and Representation* (Chichester: Wallflower)

VINCENDEAU, GINETTE (ed). 2001. *Film/Literature/Heritage: A Sight and Sound Reader* (Basingstoke,: Palgrave Macmillan)

WHEELER, DUNCAN. 2014. 'Back to the Future: Repackaging Spain's Troublesome Past for Local and Global Audiences', in *(Re)viewing Creative, Critical and Commercial Practices in Contemporary Spanish Cinema*, ed. by Duncan Wheeler and Fernando Canet (Bristol: Intellect), pp. 207–33

WHITE, HAYDEN. 1988. 'Historiography and Historiophoty', *American Historical Review*, 93: 1193–1196

Notes to Chapter 8

1. All translations are my own.
2. For an example of this attitude within the Spanish media, see Carlos Prieto, ´Hartos de la Guerra Civil´ *Publico* (2009) <http://www.publico.es/culturas/hartos-guerra-civil.html> [accessed 16 July 2014]

CHAPTER 9

❖

The Gypsies According to NO-DO: The Image of Spanish Roma from Dictatorship to Democracy[1]

Lidia Merás

The Rom, Roma, or Romani people — the preferred terms for Gypsies today — were Spain's largest ethnic minority until two decades ago. This ancient, persecuted people, with a shared history in the Iberian Peninsula spanning more than five centuries,[2] has always stirred the imagination of writers and artists, who have fantasised about their unconventional lifestyle. Cervantes's mistrust of the Spanish Roma in *La gitanilla* (The Gypsy Girl, 1613), and Lorca's admiration for their traditional folk songs in his *Romancero gitano* (Gypsy Ballads, 1928) are two examples of the main attitudes of authors from the dominant culture towards Romanies. The *Calés* (or Spanish Roma) have been constantly regarded as the 'Other' and myths and misconceptions have often attended their portrayal as an ethnic group. As a result, their image fluctuates between idealized images of 'cheerful exoticism' linked to their artistic skills, and the most detrimental stereotypes. Paradoxically, despite their inherent 'otherness', the representation of *Calés* shaped Spain's national image, portraying it as a vibrant, lavish and orientalised country in travel books and tourist guides.

The study of Roma culture within the parameters of Hispanism has been hindered by the contradictory circumstance of a community embodying a certain idea of national identity while remaining alien in its own country. Unlike other minorities, their problem has not been invisibility, but quite the opposite. The overwhelming number of fabricated images of *Calés*, so powerful that many accept them unquestioningly as representative of real Romanies, have obscured their portrayal. Another factor that has prevented scholars from researching on *Calés* within the broader field of Hispanic Studies lies in the fact that 'traditional Romani culture is strictly oral, with no documents or scriptures that outline either the people's history or rules or the values that govern their lives' (Matras, 2014: 131). Furthermore, this oral tradition is often expressed in their own language (*Caló*), hardly ever accessible to non-Romanies unless they are devoted linguists. In sum, the relatively small body of criticism on the genuine cinematic representation of Roma culture in Spain is due to several methodological challenges and the additional need to engage with texts emerging from different disciplines, such as linguistics, sociology, anthropology and film studies. In contrast with the Jews, the other European minority with which we might trace some parallels, Romanies' historically deficient schooling, precarious socioeconomic status, and lack of access to media networks has hampered their involvement in demystifying Roma labels on screen. Therefore, depictions of them are customarily told from the same perspective, exposing the failure to engage with non-hegemonic understandings of Spain.

However misleading, filmic representations of Spanish Roma have been essential to the construction of Spanish national identity and can be traced back to silent films *Celos gitanos* (Gypsy Jealousy, Ricardo Baños, 1909) and *Amor gitano* (Gypsy Love, Segundo de Chomón, 1910), two early titles that evoke one of the most common storylines, that of fatal love, and which unambiguously embrace the Romantic Gypsy myth (Garrido, 2003: 122).

The long tradition of screen representation of Spanish Romanies has, however, only received academic interest in the past two decades. From different perspectives, Labanyi (1999), Garrido (2003), Charnon-Deutsch (2004), Nair (2006), Santaolalla (2005) and, more recently, Woods Peiró (2012) have dealt with ethnic stereotypes, Romanies' contribution to the construction of the nation, or to certain film genres. However, the focus in most of these works has been confined to cinematic representations within fiction, whereas little has been published on documentary films featuring Romanies. There is no comprehensive account of documentaries devoted to the depiction of *Calés,* only some isolated studies of specific and unrelated documentaries.[3] Hence the question of how Spanish Romanies have been represented on screen remains largely unexplored. In this sense, this research is a first attempt to broaden the scope of analysis of Roma images in Spanish media employing a fundamental historic source, the Francoist newsreel NO-DO. I will focus on the construction of the *Calés* archetype from a historical perspective. My aim is to reflect on the shifting cultural values in the representation of this group and demonstrate how certain stereotypes were tempered during Franco's dictatorship, while others reappeared or emerged in the 1970s as a response to the new challenges during the early years of the democracy. I will explore a key propagandistic tool of the Franco Regime, the NO-DO (short for '*Noticiario y documentales*', or 'news and documentaries').

The newsreel NO-DO ran in Spain between 1943 and 1981. Compulsory in cinemas until a few weeks before the death of General Franco in 1975, the newsreel was state-controlled and, for almost two decades, the sole audiovisual source of information for most Spaniards. As early as 1938, during the Spanish Civil War, the propaganda agencies working for Franco's forces had decided to allow private companies to produce fiction films to support their cause, but retained a state monopoly on the production of documentary images (Tranche and Sánchez-Biosca, 2001: 285). Such arrangements reveal the future government's aspirations to control non-fictional footage and employ it as a crucial medium of propaganda. Instituted on December 17, 1942, NO-DO never had a set of ideological guidelines which staff were required to follow; hence, as Rafael Tranche and Vicente Sánchez-Biosca acknowledge, it cannot be claimed that the newsreel represented the 'official image' of Spain. Yet NO-DO was founded 'with an explicit commitment to serve institutional tasks' (Tranche and Sánchez-Biosca, 2001: 196). Therefore, by analysing its online archive (Filmoteca Española/RTVE) it is possible to trace the evolution of the Roma archetype endorsed by Franco's dictatorship. NO-DO moulded the image of Spanish Romanies, although the newsreel was not alone in this task. Documentaries and fiction films provided alternative representations of this community. Both Edgar Neville's documentary *Duende y misterio del flamenco* (Flamenco, 1952) and Francisco Rovira-Beleta's musical *Los tarantos* (1963), to mention a couple of valuable films representing Romanies, combated adulterated versions of Roma folklore common in fiction films of the period. For instance, in his peculiar adaptation of *Romeo and Juliet,* Rovira-Beleta filmed in the shacks of Somorrostro, a deprived Gypsy neighbourhood in Barcelona which no longer exists. The *mise en scène* exposed the poverty of the inhabitants, many of whom were cast as extras, presenting an unflattering picture of the Roma slums that was conveniently purged in NO-DO episodes of the same period.[4] The importance of NO-DO documentaries lies precisely in the fact that they presented the 'authorised' image of the Spanish Roma during the years these newsreels were produced. In the following pages, I will outline the main characteristic of NO-DO's episodes and its relevance as a source for stereotypes. I will also analyse some of its illustrative episodes, describing the clear evolution in the depiction of the Romanies: from a pious community regarded as the cheerful and folkloric 'other' during the dictatorship, to the notable changes in their representation that came about in the early years of democracy.

With the motto 'The whole world brought to all Spaniards', NO-DO was primarily a source of news, but hardly ever current affairs, as until the 1970s its episodes would often be released in towns or villages months or even years after the event. The intention was for them to look timeless. Tranche and Sánchez-Biosca argue that, unlike the press or the radio broadcasts of the period, a defining characteristic of NO-DO was its lack of interest in politics or factual events. Instead, NO-DO documentaries showed traditional religious festivities, military parades, fashion shows, and the inauguration of construction works that the authors link to the dictatorship's aspiration to illustrate the solid and enduring bases of the new political order after the Civil War (2001: XII). In this regard, Sánchez-Biosca eloquently added that:

> Dans cette perspective, les actualités filmées jouèrent un rôle de première importance: elles déployaient un théâtre monotone peuplé de personnages presque omniprésents accomplissant des activités répétitives, dont le traitement mettait en évidence l'identité plutôt que les différences. Le fonds commun était une vision de l'Espagne comme nation éternelle (2015: 287).
>
> [From this perspective, newsreels played a key role: they depicted a monotonous theatre populated by almost ubiquitous characters performing repetitive activities, where the treatment highlighted identity rather than differences. It was in essence a vision of Spain as an eternal nation (...)].[5]

This idea is illustrated in part by the regular appearance on camera of Romanies on pilgrimages, as in the examples below. A certain amount of factual information was, however, required in the films in order to give a reason for the presence of Romanies, meaning that each film had to be tied to an event of specific relevance which justified the appearance of Roma people on the big screen. As a result, the clichés of the female Gypsy character as *femme fatale*, or the recurrent narratives of jealousy and passionate love that reach a violent climax common in fictional representations, are absent. NO-DO had the potential to provide a new approach to portraying Romanies, and indeed these documentaries depart from the plots that are typically found in fiction films. At least they suggested an inherent anthropological knowledge of clothing, customs and religious practices that, in principle, were not directly influenced by the stylized recreations in films devised for them by non-Gypsy filmmakers — even if this image was still not necessarily more truthful than the one provided by fiction films. Indeed, NO-DO displayed stereotyped images of Roma that were far from neutral and, since the newsreel was the main propaganda instrument of the Regime, these stereotypes were intended to have a great influence.

A devout race

If we consider how neglected the Roma community was until a few decades ago, it is perhaps not surprising to learn that there were only a small number of NO-DO episodes made about them: thirteen, to be precise. The first to mention the presence of Romanies was released relatively early (in 1945) and the last was broadcast in 1978. The scarcity of episodes featuring this community does not allow us to make a definitive statement about the significance of these figures, but the existence of only two episodes on *Calés* between 1945 and 1964 and the concentration of the rest between 1965 and 1978 might suggest that from the mid-sixties this minority became the focus of renewed interest and an increasing source of anxiety.

The first NO-DO documentary depicting Romanies in their own right (i.e. not as part of a spectacle addressed to non-Gypsies such as the 1945 episode) was devoted to the burial of Mimi Rossetto, a charismatic member of the Roma community elected 'Queen of the Gypsies'.[6] Although not entirely surprising, it is worth mentioning that, as would happen with a significant proportion of NO-DO episodes on Romanies during the following decade, the footage is set not in Spain but elsewhere in Europe.[7] Titled 'The Queen of the Gypsies has died — Burial of Mimi Rossetto' (1958), the episode is used as an excuse to draw attention to the 'bizarre' funeral rites of her people, as she died in a tent surrounded by hundreds of Romanies from all over Europe. The voice-over reports that Rossetto's tent will be burned and a cherry tree will be planted in its place; in addition, as a sign of mourning, men will grow their beards for six days. However, the audience is also notified about the Queen's compliance with the rites of the Catholic Church, a recurrent theme in the following documentaries. Most NO-DO documentaries of the sixties would stress the religious faith of Romanies and depict this group in constant pilgrimages such as 'Worship of the Gypsies for Our Lady. 5,000 Gypsies Arrive in Lourdes on Pilgrimage' (1965) or, the same year, 'The Gypsies with the Pope. Congregation in the Eternal City'. These episodes were followed by many others of similar titles, suggesting that the Roma's only important gatherings were related to religion.[8] The emphasis on the number of attendees in each, combined with the sparse information concerning their nationalities or parishes of origin — the voice-over never specifies whether there are any Spanish pilgrims in Lourdes or Rome — shows that Romanies are depicted as an indistinguishable mass, regardless of any distinct European origins among them. For instance, in the Lourdes episode, the film not only makes no distinction between *Manouches* (French Gypsies) and *Calés*, thereby endorsing a certain idea of cultural and ethnic homogeneity that denies even their nationality. Romanies are not considered Spaniards or French, but a people set apart from regular citizens. Incidentally, this assumption reinforces the belief that non-Roma Spaniards (or *Payos*) are ethnically just like other Europeans, although, as we will see, slightly better in moral terms.

The voice-over informs us that the French authorities do not allow Romanies to remain for more than 24 hours in the same place, a piece of information which inevitably draws attention to the 'hassle' of living together, and identifies difficult coexistence with Romanies as a European (not only Spanish) 'problem'.[9] Although tempered straight away to avoid sensitivities among neighbours ('Now they will enjoy a whole week in the home of Bernadette,' we are assured), the former statement seems to present Spain as a more indulgent country with regard to ethnic differences. Charnon-Deutsch has argued that such discourse was tactical, in order to show Franco's regime in a favourable light in the aftermath of the Second World War: 'Representing Spain as a place of tolerance where people were not killed because of their race clearly reflected a national project to rehabilitate Spain's repressive past during the Franco era' (Charnon-Deutsch, 2004: 219). Moreover, the emphasis on the idea of these borderless pilgrimages prevents the audience from learning about their typical living conditions in the slums and, without doubt, emphasises the view of Romanies as permanently itinerant, a misleading myth (at least in the Spanish case) with convenient implications.[10] If they are not settled then they cannot be considered full citizens, relieving the government of responsibility for their access to education and other social benefits.

The film that documents the pilgrimage to the monastery of Montserrat is another good example of the first type of NO-DO documentary featuring Romanies. Released in 1966, the Roma are here portrayed as a large group of docile and devout Catholics. However, while the footage shows a composed procession, the voice-over insinuates that their orderliness is only momentary: 'They come here not with the noisy joy of folklore,' we are told, 'but with the inner joy of a pious pilgrimage prepared by them.'[11] In other words, they manage to restrain their irritating customs but only because of the solemn nature of the occasion. Inside the temple, men in dark suits offer honey and other offerings to Our Lady while the voice-over describes them as *'una raza creyente que ansía liberarse de su injusta mala fama'* ['a devout race that longs to divest itself of its unfair bad name']. The episode clearly illustrates how the Roma community is depicted in a highly patronizing tone as a light-hearted, colourful and boisterous people.

Between 1965 and 1970, NO-DO highlighted their peculiar habits and alluded to certain distinctive elements — for instance, the size of their candles is constantly mentioned in the episodes from the sixties. However, all these documentaries aim to reassure non-Gypsies about the assimilation of Romanies through the Catholic faith, downplaying their reputation as petty criminals. For that reason, although the films still portray them as the 'Other', religion is emphasized as an important cohesive element; this implicitly reminds the non-Roma audience of their duty to tolerate their 'brothers'.

Broadcast ten days before Franco's death, one of the last episodes to feature a pilgrimage presents an interesting case study for the way in which it mixes the two contrasting NO-DO narratives concerning the Romanies. A similar title, alluding to a new European pilgrimage destination ('Nearly 3,000 Gypsies from Remote Corners on Pilgrimage to Rome'), creates the false expectation of another procession with devout Christians carrying enormous candles, but here the tone differs from previous documentaries. On the one hand, this episode seems more genuinely interested in documenting Roma ethnic and cultural diversity. Female attire and accessories are shown in close-ups; the 'anomaly' of a blond Gypsy girl is registered; and even the acknowledgement of a certain degree of evolution from their outdated customs is reported. On the other hand, rather than challenging the Romanies' bad reputation, the script takes for granted the Roma's innate criminal tendencies. In the two-minute clip, a group of men play cards '*hay que suponer que sin hacer trampas*' [We must assume they are not cheating] jokes the narrator, in the distinctive way NO-DO introduces humour not inherent in the images but added afterwards, seeking the complicity of the spectator.[12] Similarly, when a paunchy Roma wearing a cowboy hat emerges from a flashy car and approaches a modest caravan to drink a toast with family members, the remark is: '*Hay gitanos millonarios que bajan de lujosos deportivos y lucen indumentarias de elevado coste*' [There are Gypsy millionaires who get out of luxurious sport cars and wear expensive clothes']. In marked contrast with previous slanders, the news ends on a positive note, with Pope Paul VI surrounded by Roma children. The voice-over observes that His Holiness has addressed them with words of affection. The evident clash of antithetic discourses is left unresolved. The doubt concerning Romanies' honesty is blatantly exposed, but religion still operates, even if no longer as a cohesive element, at least to prevent social fracture. The rationale of these final images seems to be that you need to be as compassionate as the Pope to treat Romanies with benevolence.

A Gypsy in Parliament (1978)

Probably the most manipulative example of a NO-DO episode on the Roma is 'A Gypsy in Parliament', a documentary that depicts quite the opposite of what its title suggests. This film is one of those cases in which the audiovisual trumps the written message, and is fascinating because it revives nineteenth-century clichés about the

Roma, but also expands negative stereotypes exploiting contemporary fears. The lawyer and politician Juan de Dios Ramírez Heredia was the first Roma member of the Cortes, the Spanish Parliament, and would later become the first Romani member in the European Parliament. In June 1978, two months after his appearance in 'A Gypsy in Parliament', de Dios was to deliver a famous speech aimed at revoking three articles of the Civil Guard regulations, which discriminated against the Roma.[13] The repercussions of his historic speech would turn him into the most recognizable spokesperson for the Spanish Romanies — a credit that still holds, as the Head of Unión Romaní and his occasional appearances in the media.[14]

The portrayal of Juan de Dios seated in Parliament is clearly staged in opposition to the Roma cliché.[15] Smartly dressed in a dark suit, with excellent oratory and speaking in a formal register, these features show that he is different from the stereotypical Gypsy in appearance and speech. At first sight, he seems to embody an ideal of the assimilated and modern Roma. Presented as a role model for the largely illiterate Romani population of the time, he symbolizes certain aspirations towards social mobility. After all, he is a Gypsy who has made it to Parliament. But while de Dios denounces the marginalization of Romanies, a panning shot of empty seats stresses the isolation of the young politician in the Cortes. Completely alone, the deputy acknowledges that the Roma's marginalization is partly self-imposed but explains that it is a response to concerns about losing their threatened values. However, the film's editing does not allow the politician to explain which Romani values are worth protecting. The audience will remain unaware of the needs of Spanish Gypsies because the subsequent images of slums suggest that the only contributions the Romanies seem to offer are poverty and social exclusion.

Furthermore, the distressing notes of an organ on the soundtrack emphasize the negative connotations and associate the scene with the horror movie genre. One sequence, involving a group of women and children, is particularly telling. It is a hand-held shot, filmed at a considerable distance, as if the cameraman was recording a dangerous encounter with a monster. But this time the malign creatures are women, a few children and a starving dog. The association of the female Gypsy and the monster can be traced back to the nineteenth century in *Las mujeres españolas, americanas y lusitanas pintadas por sí mismas* (1881). Subtitled a 'Complete study of women from all levels of society', Blanca de los Ríos, writer and critic for the conservative periodical *Raza española,* depicts the Gypsy woman — to whom she attributes a 'sinister aura'– as having more 'infernal Machiavellianism' than her male partner.[16] Other negative stereotypes in the documentary include a pre-adolescent girl who mischievously winks at the camera, reinforcing the eternal myth of the ardent Gypsy woman; the group of idle youngsters who play the guitar and clap their hands; or, more interestingly, a smoking teenager whose defiance clearly personifies the new archetype of the *quinqui*.[17] *Quinquis* in particular would become hugely popular, appearing as main characters in fiction films such as *Perros callejeros* (José Antonio de la Loma, 1977) and *Navajeros* (Eloy de la Iglesia, 1980). His main features, however, updated the Roma typology found in Rafael Salillas's essay *Hampa. El delincuente español* (Criminals. The Spanish Delinquent). Originally published in 1898, *Hampa* is a seminal text in anthropological criminology, in which Salillas associates Roms with slyness, laziness, parasitism, and what the author defines as *psicología ladronesca* or 'thief psychology',[18] all qualities that can be recognised in the exteriors shots of 'A Gypsy in Parliament'.

At the end of the report, de Dios's vehement tone warns the audience that the requirements for integration imposed on the Romanies are not well received by them. The deputy concludes his speech by giving some figures about the number of Roma living in Spain and Europe while a final image of a donkey cart slowing down traffic on a main city road appears on screen. His final words sound threatening: there are millions of us and we are not going to change, we won't be assimilated. Furthermore since the speaker is a member of parliament, Romanies are now also power-holders and decision-makers.

The image of Romanies presented by NO-DO promoted the return of some of the most negative stereotypes about Romanies, as well as generating new ones. Stereotypes — primarily negative — multiplied during the seventies on the basis of new social concerns, introducing the association of the Gypsy with shanty towns, juvenile crime and marginalization. In the ethnically uniform Spain of the seventies, the Roma people were seen as an obstacle to social and economic development. Amid rapid urbanisation, accompanied by the growth of the middle classes during the 'economic miracle', the Roma remained on the impoverished peripheries, aggravating their marginalization.[19] As a consequence, they were turned into scapegoats symbolising a minority opposed to progress. Interestingly, when the nationalist agenda was still on the rise, issues of ethnic difference were minimised, whereas in the promising first years of the Spanish democracy, NO-DO fuelled the ancestral fears of the dominant group.

Representation of Romanies during the transition to democracy

The evolution of the image provided by NO-DO, then, can roughly be described as follows: following the portrayal of the Romanies as an exotic but innocuous group, during the dictatorship, the early years of the transition to democracy saw the multiplication of stereotypes, which had been avoided in previous decades. The newsreel disseminated the idea that the Romanies were dragging modern society down and started pushing the same stereotypes that for decades they had been trying to conceal. It was only with the arrival of television, in particular the documentaries *Rito y geografía del cante* (1971–1973) and *Los gitanos* (Luis Tomás Melgar, 1975), both shown on TVE-2 (now La 2), that more balanced depictions of contemporary Romanies emerged. As in many European countries during that decade, the second public channel was committed to the dissemination of 'high culture' and educational programmes and, consequently, less driven by entertainment and also less popular in terms of audience figures. *Los gitanos* in particular made explicit the discrimination against *Calés*.[20] Through several interviews with Romanies from Madrid, Barcelona and Seville, *Los gitanos* showed the appalling living conditions of Roma families as well as the prejudices that hindered their access to employment and education. Melgar's documentary also presented accusations of institutional indifference and exposed society's intolerance for the first time.

Once NO-DO lost its exclusivity in documenting the lives of Spaniards, and Romanies had the chance to express opinions about the reasons for their segregation, narratives imposed by the newsreel were no longer credible. Condescending portrayals of *Calés* began to disappear in the mid-seventies, as did documentaries that exclusively blamed Romanies for their social exclusion. Soon afterwards, the Spanish Roma experienced dramatic social changes after the implementation of the welfare system during the eighties.[21] Some of these measures (such as coerced urbanisation that in some areas created ghettos) were misguided, but overall eased access to decent housing, schooling for children, and better social protection for families.[22] While Juan de Dios's intervention was one of the last times the state-controlled NO-DO screened Romanies, other documentaries were, on the other hand, drawing public attention to Roma needs. It was evident than in the new democratic scenario it would no longer be possible to silence them, even if NO-DO made little effort to play its part.

Bibliography

[ANON.]. 1978. 'Apoteosis gitana en el Congreso de los Diputados', *El País*, 8 June 1978. <http://elpais.com/diario/1978/06/08/espana/266104810_850215.html> [accessed 2 March 2018]

CRUCES ROLDÁN, CRISTINA. 2012. 'Constructos audiovisuales sobre el flamenco. La perspectiva antropológica y la representación del ritual', *Revista Comunicación*, 10: 479–503

FUNDACIÓN SECRETARIADO GITANO, and EDIS EQUIPO DE INVESTIGACIÓN SOCIOLÓGICA (data collection). 2012. 'Spanish and Migrant Roma Population in Spain. Employment and Social Inclusion. A Comparative Study 2011' (Constanţa: Editura Dobrogea and Soros Foundation Romania). <https://www.gitanos.org/upload/74/09/Situatia_romilor_-_spanish.pdf> [accessed 2 March 2018]

CHARNON-DEUTSCH, LOU. 2004. *The Spanish Gypsy. The History of a European Obsession*, (Pennsylvania: Pennsylvania State University)

DE LOS RÍOS, BLANCA. 1881.'La gitana', in *Las mujeres españolas, americanas y lusitanas pintadas por sí mismas. Estudio completo de la mujer en todas las esferas sociales*, ed. by Faustina Sáez de Melgar (Barcelona: Juan Pons), pp. 589–95

GARRIDO, JOSÉ ÁNGEL. 2003. *Minorías en el cine: la etnia gitana en la pantalla* (Barcelona: Universitat de Barcelona)

LABANYI, JO. 2002. *Constructing Identity in Contemporary Spain* (Oxford: Oxford University Press)

MATRAS, YARON. 2014. *I Met Lucky People. The Story of the Romani Gypsies* (London, Penguin)

NAIR, PARVATI. 2006. 'The Regard of the Gypsy: Ramón Zabalza's gitano photographs and the visual challenge to the stereotype', in *Prácticas de poder y estrategias de resistencia en la España democrática*, ed. by Óscar Cornago Bernal, special issue of *Iberoamericana*, 24: 111-19

RODRÍGUEZ, ISIDRO. 2011. 'El proceso de inclusión de la comunidad gitana en España ¿un modelo para Europa?', *Revista Trimestral Fundación Secretariado Gitano*, 58: 48–51

SALILLAS, RAFAEL. 2004. *Hampa. El delincuente español* (Madrid: Victoriano Suárez, 1898; repr. Pamplona: Analecta)

SÁNCHEZ-BIOSCA, VICENTE. 2015. 'Le NO-DO ou la réussite politique du banal en Espagne', *Vingtième siècle. Revue d'histoire*, 127: 285–91

SAN ROMÁN, TERESA. 1997. *La diferencia inquietante. Viejas y nuevas estrategias culturales de los gitanos* (Madrid: Siglo XXI)
SANTAOLALLA, ISABEL. 2005. *Los 'otros': etnicidad y raza en el cine español contemporáneo* (Zaragoza: Universidad de Zaragoza; Madrid: Ocho y Medio)
TRANCHE, RAFAEL R., and SÁNCHEZ-BIOSCA, VICENTE. 2001. *NO-DO: el tiempo y la memoria* (Madrid: Cátedra and Filmoteca Española)
WASHABAUGH, WILLIAM. 1996. *Flamenco. Passion, Politics and Popular Culture* (Oxford: Berg)
WHITTAKER, TOM. 2013. 'Mobile Soundscapes in the *Quinqui* Film', in *Screening Songs in Hispanic and Lusophone Cinema*, ed. by Lisa Shaw and Rob Stone (Manchester: Manchester University Press). pp. 98–113
WOODS PEIRÓ, EVA. 2012. *White Gypsies: Race and Stardom in Spanish Musical Films* (Minneapolis: University of Minnesota Press)

List of NO-DO episodes on Romanies (in chronological order)

II Aniversario de la creación de NO-DO. Festival en la Palacio de la Música (15–01–1945), #107 B
<http://www.rtve.es/filmoteca/NO-DO /not-107/1467122/> [accessed 2 March 2018]
Ha muerto la reina de los gitanos. Entierro de Mimi Rossetto (12.05.1958), #801B
<http://www.rtve.es/filmoteca/No-Do /not-801/1486328/> [accessed 2 March 2018]
Devoción de los gitanos a la Virgen. 5000 gitanos llegan a Lourdes en peregrinación (27–09–1965), #1186
<http://www.rtve.es/filmoteca/NO-DO /not-1186/1469211/> [accessed 2 March 2018]
Los gitanos ante el Papa. Concentración en la Ciudad Eterna (04–10–1965), # 1187C
<http://www.rtve.es/filmoteca/No-Do /not-1187/1469208/> [accessed 2 March 2018]
Peregrinación a Montserrat. Dos mil gitanos de toda España (14–03–1966), #1210
<http://www.rtve.es/filmoteca/NO-DO /not-1210/1473984/> [accessed 2 March 2018]
Un belén gitano (25–12–1967), #1303
<http://www.rtve.es/filmoteca/NO-DO /not-1303/1486071/> [accessed 2 March 2018]
Peret y sus gitanos (16–09–1968), #1341A
<*http://www.rtve.es/filmoteca/No-Do /not-1341/1486397/*> [accessed 2 March 2018]
Los gitanos de todo el mundo en Zaragoza. Peregrinación al Pilar (30–09–1968) #1343B
<http://www.rtve.es/filmoteca/No-Do /not-1343/1486412/> [accessed 2 March 2018]
Folklore internacional gitano (04–10–1970), #1426
<http://www.rtve.es/filmoteca/NO-DO /not-1426/1486650/> [accessed 2 March 2018]
Gitanos polacos. Conjunto cíngaro "Krist Romano" (02–06–1975) #1690B
<http://www.rtve.es/filmoteca/No-Do /not-1690/1466879/> [accessed 2 March 2018]
Cerca de 3000 gitanos procedentes de muy remotos confines, en peregrinación a Roma. Cita en la ciudad eterna con motivo del Año Santo (10–11–1975), #1713A
<http://www.rtve.es/filmoteca/NO-DO /not-1713/1466910/> [accessed 2 March 2018]
Un Gitano en Las Cortes (24–04–1978), #1839A
<http://www.rtve.es/filmoteca/NO-DO /not-1839/1465389/> [accessed 2 March 2018]
Gitanos en Sevilla (25.07.1978), #1861
<http://www.rtve.es/filmoteca/No-Do /not-1861/1487648/> [accessed 2 March 2018]

Other audiovisual sources

Amor gitano, dir. by Segundo de Chomón (Chomón y Fuster, 1910)
Celos gitanos, dir. by Ricardo de Baños and Alberto Marro (Hispano Films, 1909)
Duende y misterio del flamenco, dir. by Edgar Neville (Flamenco, Suevia Films, 1952)

Los gitanos, dir. by Luis Tomás Melgar, TVE-2, 26 December 1975
Los tarantos dir. by Francisco Rovira-Beleta (Tecisa, Rovira-Beleta Films, 1963)
Rito y geografía del cante, dir. Mario Gómez, TVE2, 23 October 1971 — 29 October 1973
'Soy gitano', *Ochéntame otra vez*, TVE, 5 February 2015. <http://www.rtve.es/alacarta/videos/ochentame-otra-vez/ochentame-otra-vez-soy-gitano/2983558/> [accessed 2 March 2018].

Notes to Chapter 9

1. I am very grateful to Valeria Camporesi and Samuel Llano for their support, advice, and assistance in writing this text.
2. Their presence has been documented in the Iberian Peninsula since 1425 (see Matras, 2014: 136). According to the last estimation by Centro de Investigaciones Sociológicas (CIS), 453,788 Roma citizens lived in Spain in 2007 (quoted in Fundación Secretariado Gitano, 2011).
3. An exception is William Washabaugh's chapter on TV series *Rito y geografía del cante* (TVE2, 1971–1973) that introduced unknown Roma (and non-Roma) performers to mass audiences, offering an alternative to the degraded version of flamenco disseminated in fiction films under Franco (Washabaugh, 1996: 139–78). For more recent documentaries on flamenco, see Cruces Roldán (2012: 479–503).
4. Nominated for the Oscars, *Los tarantos* included Romani stars such as the dancer Carmen Amaya and the musician who popularised the Catalan rumba, Pedro Pubill Calaf 'Peret', a sign that the film was committed to showing authentic Romanies.
5. All translations are my own.
6. The first documentary that mentions Gypsies includes an excerpt of Mercedes Borrull's performance at Palacio de la Música (Madrid) during the second anniversary of NO-DO (1945). Known as 'La gitana blanca' (the White Gypsy), Mercedes Borrull belonged to one of the most esteemed families of Flamenco music.
7. Born near Bilbao to Hungarian parents, Mimi Rossetto died in Lendinara (Italy) on 3 May 1958. The event was also covered by a British Pathé newsreel and Tony Saulier, from Paris-Match. Her last days were photographed by Nicolas Tikhomiroff (Magnum Agency).
8. See links to these episodes after the bibliography.
9. 'Los municipios franceses no toleran a los gitanos más de 24 horas de permanencia en el mismo lugar. Ahora disfrutarán de una semana entera en la patria de Bernardette'. [French towns do not permit Gypsies to remain in the same place for longer than 24 hours].
10. According to Bernard Leblon, in the 17th century more than 80% of Spanish Romanies were already settled except in Catalonia (quoted in Charnon-Deutsch 2004: 168).
11. ['Vienen aquí no con la alegría ruidosa del folklore, sino con el júbilo interior de una romería piadosa preparada por ellos mismos'].
12. See NO-DO's introduction of humour in Tranche and Sánchez-Biosca (2001: 121).
13. An anonymous article in the newspaper *El País* praised Juan de Dios's rhetoric ('Apoteosis gitana en el Congreso de los Diputados', 8 June 1978).
14. His latest appearance at the time of writing this chapter was in *Soy gitano* (TVE, 5 February 2015).
15. Juan de Dios' formal attire was in all probability a concession to the camera, as it was during his speech on 7 June 1978. At the beginning of the speech he referred to his white shirt and tie, chosen in opposition to his usual coloured shirts and polka-dot scarves to avoid offending the susceptibilities of his colleagues in Parliament. The complete speech can be downloaded from Unión Romaní's homepage <http://www.unionromani.org>.
16. Blanca de los Ríos's vivid description of the monstrous Gypsy woman: 'Alta, escuálida, demacrada, sombría, huraña, atezada, zahareña, feroz; pero rodeada del misterio, ceñida como de extraño nimbo, cercada como de siniestra aureola; respetada por los hombres, atacada por las mujeres y temida por los niños; reconcentrada y selvática es la pitonisa de la raza: persistente realidad de la superstición primitiva y salvaje, símbolo vivo inconsciente e ininteligible de

un culto extraño' [Tall, skinny, gaunt, grim, sullen, tanned, aloof, fierce; but surrounded by mystery, encircled with a strange nimbus, surrounded by a sinister aura; respected by men, attacked by women and feared by children; lost in thought and jungle fortune-teller of the race: persistent reality of a primitive and wild superstition, thoughtless and unintelligible living symbol of a strange cult']. Needless to say, the entry devoted to the Roma woman in the book was not written by the group member claimed, the sole exception in the book (1881: 595).
17. According to the RAE Dictionary, the term *quinqui* defines a 'persona que pertenece a cierto grupo social marginado de la sociedad por su forma de vida' ['person belonging to a marginalized social group because of their way of life']. Although *quinquis* were not necessarily Romanies, Roma petty criminals such as legendary El Vaquilla (Juan José Moreno Cuenca), were associated with this term. On *quinqui* cinema see Whittaker, pp. 98–113.
18. See Salillas (2004: 22, 29, 286 and 376).
19. On Roma marginalization see San Román (1997).
20. However, it is worth noting that *Los gitanos* (TVE-2, 26.12.1975) was soon broadcast on the first channel in order to reach a wider public.
21. '[...] *en 1978 más del 75% de los hogares gitanos eran infraviviendas y hoy el 88% de las familias gitanas habitan en viviendas normalizadas y tan sólo queda un 4% de familias gitanas que malviven en chabolas [...]. Si en 1986, la mayoría de los niños gitanos estaban fuera del sistema educativo, hoy todos están escolarizados y finalizan los estudios primarios, si bien hay una altísima tasa de abandono escolar en Secundaria.*['(...) in 1978 more than 75% of Roma households were substandard and today 88% of Roma families are living in standardized homes, and only 4% of Roma families struggle in shacks (...). Whilst in 1986 most Roma children were not in education, today they all finish primary school, although there is a very high dropout rate in secondary'] (Rodríguez, 2011: 49).
22. These policies eventually turned Spain into a model country for the integration of its Roma population, although a lot still needs to be done, according to Rodríguez (Rodríguez, 2011: 49).

CHAPTER 10

Constructing a Feminist Room of Her Own: The Marketing and Reception of María Xosé Queizán

Jennifer Rodríguez

María Xosé Queizán (Vigo, 1939) is a self-identified feminist writer from Galicia. Queizán has had a prolific fifty-year career in Galician literature, beginning in 1965 with her novel *A orella no buraco*, and, as will be discussed later in this chapter, is a pioneer in the field, paving the way for future generations of Galician feminist women writers, such as Teresa Moure (Montforte de Lemos, 1969) and María Reimóndez (Lugo, 1975).[1] However, despite her significant contributions to Galician literature, Queizán's work has largely been met with silence. Helena Miguélez-Carballeira states for example that, 'o sistema recibira daquela cunha acollida inhóspita ou cun silencio enxordecedor' [The system gave her an inhospitable welcome or she was greeted with a deafening silence] (2007: 75).[2] Though the twenty-first century has seen an increased awareness of Queizán through reviews of her latest novels on literary blogs and the publication of two books containing in-depth analyses of her work,[3] this visibility tends to be localized in her home town of Vigo and traceable to the publishing house, Xerais.[4] Indeed, Queizán is rejected by traditional Galician cultural institutions, such as the *Real Academia Galega* (RAG), as is evidenced by the failure of a campaign to obtain Queizán a seat at the academy in 2011. This chapter will examine how Queizán has negotiated this complex space to create and work within a 'feminist room of her own'.[5] In addition, it will look at the visibility of Queizán within and outside this feminist literary community, as well as analysing the tensions between the nationalist and feminist impulse in Galicia exemplified by Queizán's failure to enter the RAG.

From the very beginning of her literary career Queizán presented herself as a pioneer willing to subvert the norms of the Galician literary field. Though her first novel *A orella no buraco* (1965) — which tells the story of a man who lives on a bench and keeps warm by placing his ear in a hole in the bench — followed the *Nova Narrativa* literary trend, it made Queizán the first woman since Francisca Herrera Garrido (1869–1950) to write a novel in the Galician language and the only woman within the *Nova Narrativa* generation of writers.[6] Thanks to the legacy of the prolific poet and metonym of Galicia, Rosalía de Castro, Galician women writers had traditionally been associated with poetry and usually began their careers in this genre (March: 1986); by choosing to start her literary career in the prose genre Queizán was subverting the association of women with writing poetry.

After the publication of *A orella no buraco*, Queizán is notably absent from the Galician literary scene while attending university. When she returns in 1977, her work takes on a markedly feminist tone with essays such as 'A muller en Galicia' (1977) and the novel *Amantia* (1984), a work of historical fiction about the fourth-century Galician religious figure Prisciliano and a group of learned women. Queizán's commitment to a feminist discourse has continued into the present day; however, it is to the *Nova Narrativa* generation of writers mentioned above that academics such as Vilavedra (2010) refer when situating Queizán within the Galician literary community. As Kirsty Hooper points out, the novel is one of the few of Queizán's works that is not considered to be concerned with gender and sexuality (Hooper: 2011, 283) and is also one of the few books of Queizán's that is not published by *Xerais*.[7] The publishing house concerned is Galaxia, which, as Hooper states is 'the publishing house most closely linked with the Galician literary establishment and the post-civil war renaissance of Galician literature' (2011, 283). Thus, in the case of *A orella na buraco*, the prestigious status of Galaxia gives the book, and Queizán, added cultural capital. In addition, the image of Queizán as a pioneer and forerunner of contemporary Galician literature leads to many critics favouring her first, ground-breaking work rather than her subsequent feminist endeavours. Furthermore, with her first novel, Queizán adheres to the rules of the literary field and those of the *Nova Narrativa* generation, whereas some of her later work challenges some of its taboos and patriarchal structures.[8]

However, in response to the marked lack of visibility received by her work and that of other Galician women writers, Queizán carved out new spaces for herself and other women writers within Galician literature. In 1983 Queizán created the feminist literary journal *Festa da Palabra Silenciada*. The poignant title — Celebration of the Silenced Word — reveals the objective of the journal: to give visibility to writers, particularly women writers, who had previously been ignored; it also has clear feminist implications, as it challenges the established Galician literary canon. Sharon R. Roseman states, for example, that 'Festa da palabra silenciada challenges the problematic utilization of both female writers and passive female imagery in the construction of a Galician national identity' (1997: 45). This is evidenced by the vindication of women writers whose reception and authorial image had been skewed by patriarchal readings, such as the legacy of Rosalía de Castro, which is discussed in the first issue. The importance of this feminist journal cannot be understated, since as well as creating a space for her own work to be reviewed, Queizán also released unpublished work of women writers, such as the poem 'Penélope' (1992) by Xohana Torres, which has since been published and whose final line 'Eu tamén navegar' [I also to navigate] has become a feminist motto and has been used intertextually by other Galician women poets.[9] In this journal, Queizán also introduced feminist theories from French and British writers, such as Simone de Beauvoir and Virginia

Woolf. Quotations from such texts in the journal were often the first time these important feminist texts had been translated into Galician. Queizán is a pioneer in this respect for effectively creating a Galician feminist 'room of their own' where women writers could operate and achieve recognition.

In addition, Queizán took advantage of the feminist community in her home town of Vigo in order to further the construction of a 'feminist room of her own', and is one of the key figures in creating the strong feminist tradition in Vigo. In 1978, for example, Queizán created her own women's group in Vigo called *Feministas Independentes Galegas* (FIGA) and it is this group that edits the feminist journal, *Festa da Palabra Silenciada*.[10] This strong feminist activity continued into the late twentieth century. As Martínez-Quiroga states in her chapter on María Reimóndez's novel *O club da calceta*,

> Vigo holds a tradition of fostering the creation of associations in which women demand their rights both as workers and feminists. A good example is the 'Asociación de Mulleres Dorna' which was created thirty years ago in the working-class neighbourhood of Coia (Martínez-Quiroga 2015: 52).

This feminist tradition in Vigo has persisted and is evident in the twenty-first century with the recent establishment of a Chair of Feminist Studies in Vigo in 2000, the *Cátedra Caixanova de Estudos Feministas*. As the name suggests, the chair is funded by the *Caixanova* bank and receives 36,061 euros annually to give lectures and conduct research on feminism. Thus, Vigo, a Galician feminist centre which has strong grassroots feminist movements, offers Queizán, a self-identified feminist, the perfect platform from which to work.

Indeed, the most significant factor in the marketing and reception of Queizán is her home town, Vigo. Queizán has strong ties to the city and, most interestingly, the majority of her press coverage originates in Vigo. In the Galician daily *Faro de Vigo*, for example, Javier Mosquera makes clear just how strong these ties are. He states, 'María Xosé Queizán está unida a Vigo no sólo por nacencia sino por un amor a la ciudad que le ha llevado a declarar que no podría vivir en otra ciudad de Galicia' [María Xosé Queizán is linked to Vigo not only by birth, but also through a love for the city that has led her to state that she could not live in any other Galician city] (*Faro de Vigo*, 10/03/13). Indeed, Queizán started her career by writing articles for the Vigo-based daily *El Pueblo Gallego*. In 1959, Queizán created *El Teatro de Arte y Ensayo* of the *Asociación de la Prensa de Vigo* and after formative trips to Paris and Santiago de Compostela, she returned to Vigo in 1979 to teach Galician language and literature at the *Instituto de Bachillerato Alexandre Bóveda de Vigo*. She is also the director of the *Galería de Arte "Roizara" de Vigo* and Vice-president of the *Concello Municipal da Muller de Vigo*.[11] Further, the publishing house *Xerais*, which has published the majority of Queizán's work since its foundation in the 1980s, is based in Vigo. Queizán also works with the *Consello de Mulleres* in Vigo and has helped to create a theatre community in the city. Thus, Queizán has gained prestige through her close ties to, and role in creating, many of the social and cultural institutions of the city and has carved out a place for herself within the local cultural establishment.

However, Queizán's prestige in Vigo is a double-edged sword. In 1998, for example, the *Asociación de Escritoras e Escritores en Lingua Galega* (AELG) in conjunction with the *Consello da Cultura* awarded Queizán one of their highest accolades, 'Escritor/a na súa terra' [Writer in his/her land]. This annual award pays homage to Galician writers whose home towns have played a significant part in their literary careers. These writers are awarded the letter 'E', activities are planned in their honour and a tree is planted. In Queizán's case a park in Vigo was also named after her. To commemorate this event, a small sign was erected and a stone engraved with an extract from one of Queizán's poems 'Fóra de min' from *Fóra de min* (1994) was placed at the location.[12] A magnolia tree was also planted, in reference to the aforementioned poetry extract. The detailed planning of the ceremony and the high honour bestowed upon Queizán in 1998 is indicative of the prestige she had accrued within Vigo up to this point. The park is a narrow strip of land situated on Isaac Peral Street, a busy main road in the city overlooked by large blocks of flats. In 2013, land bordering the park was used to build a tunnel for the high-speed AVE trains. Thus, this park in Vigo is indicative of Queizán's standing as it demonstrates that while Queizán is recognized in her home town, by a small minority, her level of recognition has its limits. It also demonstrates the complexity of Queizán's literary persona in that she is rendered both visible and invisible at the same time.

This is noted by Kirsty Hooper, who draws attention to the fragmented reception of Queizán's work. She states that '[f]or many years Queizán was the most canonical (i.e., the most read, reviewed and studied) of contemporary female novelists, but note the changing pattern of publication of her novels. She is now strongly linked with *Xerais*, but *Xerais* does not publish all her works, and even those that they do publish receive differing treatment' (2011: 282). Hooper goes on to discuss the lack of critical attention to two of Queizán's works, the civil war narrative *Amor de Tango* (1992), based on real events from her home town of Vigo, and *A semellanza* (1988), which Hooper aptly describes as the story of 'a young man coming to terms with his homosexuality in a hostile society' (283). Hooper suggests that the author's gender, and the reluctance of Galician scholars and critics to talk about gender and homosexual characters and themes, has contributed to the silence surrounding these two works. Hooper notes in particular that *A semellanza* did not even receive attention from the feminist critics who usually respond to Queizán's work.

On a more optimistic note, Queizán's *Amor de Tango* has been discussed by John Patrick Thompson in his article 'A Tango of Lost Democracy and Women's Liberation: María Xosé Queizán's Feminist Vision in Amor de Tango' (2008). In addition, *A Semellanza* is discussed in Bar Cendón's book chapter 'Ousadías sexuais na escrita de María Xosé Queizán' (2011), while Rodríguez Rodríguez (2013) provides a thorough, in-depth discussion of the novel in terms of identity formation through the theories of Robert J. Stoller, Gayle Rubin and Judith Butler (176–201). Though Hooper does refer to Thompson's article in her book chapter, she does not address the language that Thompson uses to describe Queizán's approach. In the abstract to his article, for example, when discussing cultural heritage he states that 'María Xosé

Queizán aggressively reveals the reactionary elements that this heritage contains and proposes a new nationalist canon, ideology and praxis' (2008, 343). The use of the word 'aggressively' reinforces the image of Queizán created by other academics such as González Fernández and Vilavedra, who use military vocabulary to describe her. In a recent article in *El País*, for example, Vilavedra includes Queizán in a list of Galician women writers that she argues were 'pioneiras, case francotiradoras' [pioneers, almost snipers] (quoted in Cuiñas 2010).[13] González Fernández paints a similar picture of Queizán when she refers to her as a 'zapadora' or sapper, a soldier who builds trenches or tunnels to undermine enemy positions (2005: 25). The image of a soldier on the battlefield paints a violent picture of Queizán's approach to the Galician literary field. *Amor de Tango* is also the subject of a review by Kathleen N. March in 1993, a year after the book's publication. March discusses the quality of Queizán's language, stating that it is 'quiet, descriptive, yet controlled Galician' and also refers to her 'taking a stand' for Galician democracy (1993: 806). Though March's analysis of Queizán's language softens the image of the militaristic feminist conjured by the academics mentioned above, her reference to Queizán 'taking a stand' is in line with other portrayals of the writer as a metaphorical fighter.

For other academic references and analyses of Queizán's other works, we must look to specific feminist spaces and the work of feminist academics. In the edited volume *Breve historia feminista de la literatura española VI* (2000), María Camiño Noia makes reference not only to *A orella no buraco*, but also Queizán's other narrative works, such as her second novel *Amantia* (1982), which was also heralded as her first feminist fictional work by feminist critics (249–50). In addition, Camiño Noia situates Queizán within a female literary tradition from Francisca Herrera Garrido (1868–1945) to one of the youngest writers of the time, Navia Franco Barreiro (1973-) (2000: 249–50). In the same volume, Mónica Bar Cendón devotes the final section of her chapter on female Galician playwrights to Queizán, particularly her play *Antígona, a forza do sangue* (1989) (230–34). Bar Cendón also refers to Queizán's stance as a feminist and adds that this, in addition to her prolific literary career, makes for 'un caso insólito en la literatura gallega' [an exceptional case in Galician literature] (230). Bar Cendón's reference to Queizán as a 'caso insólito' suggests that the national literary canon is incompatible with overt feminist stances and that feminist writers do not usually go on to have long-standing literary careers.

Also in the same volume, Helena González Fernández discusses Queizán's poetic work and her influence on the Galician literary sphere within her chapter on Galician women poets. González Fernández argues convincingly that Queizán's commitment to feminism and making feminism compatible with the Galician national project, her use of irony as a deconstructive strategy in her poetry, and her projects to vindicate silenced or forgotten writers make her '[l]a figura más destacada de la literatura feminista gallega [...]' [the most prominent figure of Galician feminist literature] (2000, 205–06). She adds that 'María Xosé aborda una escritura volcada hacia afuera, comprometida, rabiosa y a menudo cáustica' [María Xosé tackles a writing pushed outwards, committed, furious and often aggressive] (2000, 206). The familiarity with which González Fernández refers to Queizán is reminiscent of the way in which writers refer to Rosalía de Castro and therefore suggests a high level of respect.[14] In addition, the violent language used to describe Queizán's approach to literature is in line with González Fernández's abovementioned reference to Queizán as a 'zapadora'. It is worth noting here, however, that González Fernández situates Queizán within a specific feminist literary tradition and not within the literary sphere as a whole. This reinforces the notion of Queizán's feminist stance being incompatible with the national canon, while being integrated within the feminist literary (sub-)canon.

In more recent years, two publications have been devoted to Queizán's work: *Cara a unha poética feminista: Homenaxe a María Xosé Queizán* (2011) edited by Manuel Forcadela and María Camiño Noia, and *Feminismo e innovación en la narrativa gallega de autoría femenina: Xohana Torres, María Xosé Queizán, Carmen Blanco y Teresa Moure* (2013). The former edited volume was published in Galicia by *Xerais* and features essays and interviews in which academics and writers engage with Queizán's work and feminist position from different analytical perspectives. In her analysis of Queizán's work Rodríguez discusses the themes of maternity, alternative sexualities and the search for identity in relation to Queizán's narrative. Though these two publications are markedly different in tone, as the former is a homage to Queizán and the other an in-depth analysis of her work, they are an indication of the increasing awareness of Queizán's work both within and outside Galicia.

Outside Vigo, *Xerais* and the feminist literary community, however, Queizán is still not recognised by key institutions, such as the *Real Academia Galega* (RAG). In 2010, the death of Olga Gallego, a female member of the *Real Academia Galega*, left a vacant seat. On 14 September 2010, the *Concello Municipal da Muller* announced that they would support Queizán as a candidate for the seat. However, a candidate needs the backing of three existing members of the institution. Accordingly, on 30 September 2010, a general letter was sent to all members of the *Real Academia Galega*, from the *Concello Municipal da Muller* making a case for Queizán and encouraging academicians to give her their support. At this time the *Concello Municipal* also launched a public petition online. Despite the hundreds of signatures on the public petition, and despite extensive press coverage for the campaign, not a single member of the Academy supported Queizán's candidacy. On 29 June 2011, after almost a year of campaigning, the *Concello* sent a second letter to all academicians further outlining their argument and imploring them to support Queizán as a candidate. However, María Xosé Queizán received no response.[15]

On 15 September 2011, Queizán sent a well-written letter to the *Concello Municipal da Muller*, in which she thanked all those who had supported the campaign, but asked them to stop campaigning as it was by now obvious that 'non se ía producir tal ingreso' [It would not produce such an entrance] (2011). In the letter, Queizán states that she never wanted to be a member of the RAG and, in anticipation of comments that this statement was only made because it was now certain she would not be accepted as a member, she adds, '[...] tampouco me importa que non o crean' [...nor does it bother me if you do not believe me] (2011). In addition, Queizán references two other high-profile women writers from turn-of-the-century Galician literature, who were also not elected to the RAG: Emilia Pardo Bazán and Rosalía de Castro. Queizán made her opinion of the RAG clear when she stated that 'Nesa Casa [...] predomina o imaxinario masculino' [In this house [...] the masculine imaginary dominates] and adds that it ignores both male- and female-authored feminist theory, stating that '[o]s libros onde se amosa esa herdanza intellectual, nondeben figurar nas bibliotecas nin nas mentes dos ilustres académicos' [The books which relate this intellectual heritage should not appear in the libraries or in the minds of the illustrious academicians] (2011). At the end of the letter she adds a strongly worded message to Galicians: 'Pretendín demostralle á cidadanía que me propuxo que a Academia será o ultimo que cambier na sociedade. Aínda que vaian introducindo algunha muller a conta gotas como quen regala unha flor' [I am trying to show to those who put my name forward that the academy will be the last thing that changes in society. Though they are introducing some women little by little like those who present a flower as a gift] (2011). However, while Queizán is intent on distancing herself from the institution, she adds that 'teño un vínculo coa Academia co que sempre me identificarei: a lingua galega' [I have one link to the academy with which I will always identify: the Galician language] (2011).

It has been necessary to include many of Queizán's own words above to illustrate properly her position in this case. In her letter, Queizán clearly sets herself against the RAG, which she asserts is patriarchal, unwilling to accept feminists or feminist approaches to literature. This reinforces the notion mentioned earlier in this chapter regarding the tensions between the national literary canon and the feminist literary canon. Queizán's overtly feminist stance and the image of her as a pioneer, an agent for change with a perceived aggressive attitude in her approach to literature and politics rendered her incompatible with the RAG's more conservative approach and led to the failure of the *Consello de Vigo's* campaign for her membership of the institution.

Queizán demonstrates solidarity with her feminist supporters, and further reinforces her position as a feminist writer, through her extensive references to feminist theory throughout the letter. In addition she demonstrates her connection to Vigo, referring to the *Concello Municipal da Muller de Vigo* as 'Concello da miña cidade' [Council of my city] (2011). Finally, Queizán makes clear exactly which issues preoccupy her: 'as literarias, as culturais, e o activismo feminista' [the literary, the cultural, and feminist activism] (2011). This letter is significant for analysing Queizán's authorial persona, as it gives an excellent summary of her image and of how she portrays herself. In other words, it demonstrates her commitment to feminist activism, while also incorporating her dedication to the Galician language and, to some extent, to a form of national identity. She also insists on the close link between herself and her home town of Vigo. Finally, and perhaps most importantly, she demonstrates her stance against central, and what she perceives as patriarchal, literary and cultural institutions, such as the RAG. The day after Queizán sent this letter to the *Concello Municipal da Muller de Vigo*, she sent it to the director of *Xerais*, Manuel Bragado, who subsequently posted it on his blog, demonstrating that the intended recipients of the letter were not only her supporters, but also the general public. In addition, the support that Queizán receives from her publisher *Xerais*, particularly from one of the highest-ranking members of the company, is illustrative of Queizán's authority.

This chapter has demonstrated the mixed responses Queizán's authorial persona and work receives in Galicia and beyond, as well as the mixed reception, tensions between the Galician national and feminist canons, and the portrayal of Queizán as a pioneer and, at times, even a violent, quasi-military figure. However, critics and academics often fail to mention that Queizán still produces literary texts and continues to push the boundaries of Galician literature, while working alongside women writers whom she has helped to inspire and for whom she has created a place. The most recent example of this is the publication of her latest book *Son noxento* (2015). The novel, narrated by internal monologue, tells the story of a paedophile and how his actions led to his subsequent incarceration. Throughout the novel the main character frequently uses expletives. Assuming that the subject matter as well as the use of swear words will shock readers, Queizán appears to provide an explanation in a short prologue. However, she offers no justification for the way she has written the book. She states that, '[s]ei que non só o comportamento, senón o vocabulario do libro é abominable. [...] As palabrotas e blasfemias que ten o Noxento na punta da lingua, conforman un discurso eticamente indigno' [I know that not only the behaviour, but also the vocabulary of the book is abominable. [...] The profanities and blasphemies that Noxento has on the tip of his tongue shape a discourse that is ethically shameful] (2015, 3). Queizán's acknowledgement that the novel's discourse is 'ethically shameful' indicates that she intends to provoke the reader into reacting. Her denouncement of the main character's wife as also being shameful for being complicit in his actions and the statement that readers will find themselves laughing when reading certain parts of the novel are sure to spark discussion and debate, demonstrating how her work continues to court controversy in the twenty-first century and making both Queizán and her work intriguing subjects for future study.

Bibliography

BAR CENDÓN, MÓNICA. 2000. 'Escritoras dramáticas gallegas: dos propuestas subversivas', in *Breve historia feminista de la literatura Española (en lengua catalana, gallega y vasca): Vol. VI*, ed. by Iris M. Zavala (Barcelona: Anthropos Editorial), pp. 219–36

CAMIÑO NOIA, MARÍA. 2000. 'La narrativa gallega de mujeres', in *Breve historia feminista de la literatura Española (en lengua catalana, gallega y vasca): Vol. VI*, ed. by Iris M. Zavala (Barcelona: Anthropos Editorial), pp. 237–64

GONZALEZ FERNÁNDEZ, HELENA. 2000. 'Las poetas y las poéticas desde la posguerra hasta hoy: "¡Yo también navegar!"' in *Breve historia feminista de la literatura Española (en lengua catalana, gallega y vasca): Vol. VI*, ed. by Iris M. Zavala (Barcelona: Anthropos Editorial), pp. 196–218

FORCADELA, MANUEL, and CAMIÑO NOIA, MARIA (eds.). 2011. *Cara a unha poética feminista: Homenaxe a María Xosé Queizán*, (Vigo: Xerais)

HOOPER, KIRSTY. 2011. 'Remapping Galician Narrative for the Twenty-First Century', in *Contemporary Galician Cultural Studies: Between the Local and the Global*, ed. by Kirsty

Hooper and Manuel Puga Moruxa (New York: Modern Language Association of America), pp. 272–88

MARCH, KATHLEEN N. 1986. 'Rosalía de Castro como punto de referencia ideolóxico-literario nas escritoras galegas', *Actas de Congreso Internacional de estudios sobre Rosalía de Castro e o seu tempo, Vol. 1*, (Santiago de Compostela: Consello da Cultura Galega), pp. 283–92

——— 1993. 'Amor de Tango — María Xosé Queizán', *World Literature Today*, 67: 806

MARTÍNEZ-QUIROGA, PILAR. 2015. 'City and Community in María Reimóndez's *O club de calceta*', in *Toward a Multicultural Configuration of Spain*, ed. by Anna Corbalán and Ellen Maycock (Madison: Fairleigh Dickinson University Press), pp. 43–54

MIGUÉLEZ-CARBALLEIRA, HELENA. 2007. 'Inaugurar, reanudar, renovar: A escrita de Teresa Moure no contexto da narrativa feminista contemporánea', *Anuario de Estudos Galegos*, 2006, 72–87

MOSQUERA, JAVIER. 2013. 'María Xosé Queizán Vilas Vigo, 1939: Pionera en la literatura feminista gallega', *Faro de Vigo* [online]. Available at: <http://www.farodevigo.es/gran-vigo/2013/03/10/maria-xose-queizan-vilas-vigo-1939/771325.html> [Accessed 01/06/2014]

MOURE, TERESA. 2005. *Herba Moura*, (Vigo: Xerais)

QUEIZÁN, MARÍA XOSÉ. 1965. *A orella no buraco* (Vigo: Galaxia)

——— 2011. 'Carta de María Xosé Queizán ao Consello Municipal da Muller de Vigo', *Brétemas* [online]. Available at: <http://bretemas.blogaliza.org/2011/09/15/carta-de-maria-xose-queizan-ao-consello-municipal-da-muller-de-vigo/> [Accessed 01/06/2014]

——— 2015. *Son noxento*, (Vigo: Xerais)

REIMÓNDEZ, MARÍA. 2014. *Dende o conflito*, (Vigo: Xerais)

RODRÍGUEZ RODRÍGUEZ, MARISOL. 2013. *Feminismo e innovación en la narrativa gallega de autoría femenina — Xohana Torres, María Xosé Queizán, Carmen Blanco y Teresa Moure*, (New York: Edwin Mellen)

ROSEMAN, SHARON R. 1997. 'Celebrating Silenced Words: The "Reimagining" of a Feminist Nation in Late Twentieth-Century Galicia', *Feminist Studies*, 23: 43–71

THOMPSON, JOHN PATRICK. 2008. 'A Tango of Lost Democracy and Women's Liberation: María Xosé Queizán's Feminist Vision in *Amor de Tango*', *Bulletin of Hispanic Studies*, 85: 343–59

VILAVEDRA, DOLORES. 2010. 'Una voz senlleira', *Grial*, 188: 17

WOOLF, VIRGINIA. 2004. *A Room of One's Own* (London: Penguin)

Notes to Chapter 8

1. Teresa Moure is a critically acclaimed Galician writer whose 2005 novel *Herba Moura* won the *Premio Xerais*, the *Premio da Asociación de Escritores en Lingua Galega*, the *Premio Irmandade do Libro*, the *Premio Benito Soto á mellor novela do ano* and the *Premio da Crítica*. María Reimóndez is a Galician feminist writer, translator and activist whose novel *Dende o conflito* (2014) also won the *Premio Xerais*.
2. Unless otherwise stated, all translations are my own.
3. The two books are: Camiño Noia and Manuel Forcadela's edited volume *Cara a unha poética feminista: Homenaxe a María Xosé Queizán* (2011), which consists of critical studies of her work, interviews with the author and homages; and Marisol Rodriguez's monograph *Feminismo e innovación en la narrativa gallega de autoría femenina — Xohana Torres, María Xosé Queizán, Carmen Blanco y Teresa Moure* (2013), which analyses Queizán's work as part of one of two generations of Galician feminist writers who have contributed to the changing face of Galician literature.
4. The *Xerais* publishing house is also based in Vigo.
5. This is a reference to Virginia Woolf's essay 'A Room of One's Own' (1929) in which she states that 'a woman must have money and a room of her own if she is to write fiction' (4).
6. *Nova Narrativa* was a particular style of writing favoured by Galician writers, such as Carlos

Casares, Xosé Luís Méndez Ferrín and Queizán from the 1950s to the 1970s and was influenced by the French *nouveau roman*.
7. *Xerais* was not founded until 1984 and it was therefore impossible for Queizán to have been published by them in the 1960s.
8. See, for example, Queizán's novel *A semellanza* (1988), which deals with themes of homosexuality and transsexuality.
9. 'Eu tamén navegar' was used intertextually by Chus Pato in her poetry book *Fascinio*, in which she references both Rosalía de Castro and Xohana Torres. The line reads as follows: 'extranjera en mi propia historia/en mi propio paisaje/en mi propia lengua// yo también/ OCÉANO' (quoted in González Fernández: 2000, 217). Torres also used the phrase as her inaugural speech when entering the *Real Academia Galega* in 2001. It was further used as the name of a prize awarded by the *Xunta de Galicia* in 2008 to recognize the efforts of people and organizations working to prevent violence against women in Galicia. The prize was worth 5,000 euros.
10. Interestingly, the word 'figa' in Galician is the name of an amulet that protects against witchcraft and the evil eye.
11. As will be discussed later on in this section, it is the *Consello de Mulleres de Vigo* who led the campaign to get Queizán elected as a member of the RAG in 2011.
12. The text engraved on the stone is as follows: 'Escribo para ti/As letras son vínculos de amiga, pontes/Ponte como queiras para lerme/Ponte para o íntimo encontro/Ponte a miña conciencia/E déixame a túa/Ponte debaixo da magnolia' [I write for you/The letters are bonds of friendship, sit yourself down/Sit wherever you like to read me/Sit yourself down for the intimate meeting/Put yourself in my consciousness/And let me into yours/Place yourself under the Magnolia tree].
13. A pioneer in military terms is 'one of a group of soldiers detailed to make roads, dig entrenchments etc. in advance of the main body' (OED).
14. González Fernández in 2013/14 coordinated a project to digitize *Festa da Palabra Silenciada*. She has also contributed to the feminist journal and is therefore in personal contact with Queizán.
15. The president of the RAG at this time was Queizán's ex-husband, the writer Xosé Méndez Ferrín.

INDEX

A orella no buraco (1965) 148, 149, 152
A Room with a View (1985) 123
A semellanza (1988) 151, 157 n. 8
¡Abajo los Borbones! (1868) 65
Abad, Francesc 41
Abramovic, Marina 43
Accions (1984) 37, 39, 49
Acevedo-Muñoz, Ernesto 129
Afàsia (1998) 48, 54
Agustina de Aragón (1950) 122
Alas, Leopoldo ('Clarín') 63, 69, 105, n. 11
Alatriste (2006) 130, 133
Alba de América (1951) 122
Alfonso XII 62
Aguilar, Paloma 120 n. 5
Allbritton, Dean 131
Almodóvar, Pedro 129
Alonso Perujo, Niceto 97
Altman, Rick 129
Álvarez Tardío, Manuel 120 n. 6
Amador de los Ríos, José 14, 15, 17
Amantia (1984) 149, 152
Amar en tiempos revueltos (2005–12) 128, 130, 131
Amaya, Carmen 146 n. 4
Amor de tango (1992) 151, 152
Amor gitano (1910) 137
Anduaga Engaña, Aitor 98
Anthropometries of the Blue Period (1960) 39, 40, 49
Antígona, a forza da sangue (1989) 152
Antonio, Nicolás 13
Antúnez, Marcel·lí 6, 37, 38, 39, 40, 41, 42, 43, 44, 45, 47, 48, 49, 51, 52, 54, 55, 56 n. 3
Aphrodite 1
Aprendizaje sentimental (1981) 90 n. 21
Aramaio, Aitzol 32, 33
Aranda, Vicente 122
Archibald, David 131
Arcimis, Augusto 95, 105 n. 3
Arkinstall, Christine 71 n. 2, 92, 105 n. 5 and n. 8
Arintero, Agustín 101, 102, 103
Armendáriz, Montxo 126, 131
Arnold, Matthew 31
Arregi, Ana 35 n. 7
Artaud, Antonin 42
Arteta, Aurelio 28, 29
Asensi, Julia de 6, 7, 58, 59, 60, 61, 62, 63, 64, 65, 66, 67, 68, 69

Asociación da Escritoras e Escritores en Lingua Gallega 151
Atalanta 1
Atlantic (Ocean) 5, 26, 27, 28, 30, 31, 32, 33
¡Ay, Carmela! (1990) 122

Bakhtin, Mikhail 52
Balmés, Jaume 94
Baltic Sea 32
Bar Cendón, Mónica 151, 152, 155
Barcelona 41, 42, 43, 55, 82, 88 n. 2, 92, 94, 96, 102, 105 n. 8, 138, 143
Barcelona Olympic Games (1992) 37, 88 n. 2
Basaldúa, Pedro 31
Basque Country / Basque 4, 5, 20, 25, 26, 28, 29, 31, 32, 33, 35 n. 7, n. 16, n. 19, 36 n. 20, n. 22, 131
Batchelor, David 48, 51
Bauhaus 42
Beauvoir, Simone de 149
Becerra Mayor, David 117, 120 n. 3
Beck, Jay 121, 129
Bécquer, Gustavo Adolfo 63
Belgium 31, 36 n. 22
Benito, Jordi 39, 41
Bergson, Henri 38, 47
Bibliothecas 13
Bilbao 27, 29, 30, 31, 146 n. 7
Bilbao-New York-Bilbao (2008) 5, 25, 26, 27, 28, 32, 33
Birkerts, Sven 23 n. 3
Blanc, Charles 51
Blasco Ibáñez, Vicente 63
Bloom, Harold 23 n. 3
Böhl de Faber, Cecilia (Fernán Caballero) 23 n. 4
Boix, Vicente 66
Boletín Oficial del Estado 30, 62
Bonet, Juan Manuel 109
Borrull, Mercedes 146 n. 6
Bou, Enric 24 n. 9
Bouterwek, Friedrich 13, 14, 16, 21, 23 n. 5
Boyd, Carolyn P. 105 n. 17
Boym, Svetlana 33, 35 n. 17, 126
Bragado, Manuel 154
Braidotti, Rosi 44
Bretón de los Herreros, Manuel 105 n. 11
Breu història sentimental i altres contes (1995) 90 n. 21
Breve historia feminista de la literatura española (2000) 152
Brossa, Joan 41, 56 n. 4

Brown, Joan L. 120 n. 2
Brus, Günter 41
Buckley, Ramón 77, 78, 79
Buenos Aires 28, 32
Burguera, Mónica 60
Butler, Judith 151

Calderón de la Barca, Pedro 23 n. 4
Camba, Julio 108
Camino Noia, María 152, 153, 156 n. 3
Campoamor, Clara 82
Camporesi, Valeria 146 n. 1
Canal, Jordi 71 n. 4
Cánovas, José 95, 105 n. 17
Cantares gallegos (1863) 35 n. 11
Cap Arcona 32
Cara a unha poética feminista (2011) 153, 156 n. 3
Carbajosa, Mónica 111, 114, 116, 117
Carbajosa, Pablo 111, 114, 116, 117
Carlist Wars 61, 62, 71 n. 4, 109
Carlos I 15, 58, 66
Carnero, Guillermo 23 n. 4
Carrillo, Santiago 83
Casares, Carlos 156 n. 6
Castro, Rosalía de 35 n. 11, 149, 153, 154, 157 n. 9
Catalan 4, 6, 14, 15, 17, 20, 31, 37, 38, 39, 42, 54, 56 n. 2, 88 n. 9, 94, 130, 146 n. 4
Catalonia 37, 41, 42, 55, 71 n. 4, 146 n. 10
Cejador y Frauca, Julio 14
Cela, Camilo José 108
Celan, Paul 32
Celos gitanos (1909) 137
Cercas, Javier 25, 34 n. 2
Cervantes Saavedra, Miguel de 136
Cervera 100
Chacón, Dulce 128
Chariots of Fire (1981) 123
Charnon-Deutsch, Lou 137, 140, 146 n. 10
Chromophobia (2000) 48, 55
Cichet, Guillaume 105 n. 4
Civil War (Spanish) 8, 26, 28, 29, 31, 33, 34 n. 1, 35 n. 19, 73, 75, 77, 82, 84, 107, 109, 111, 113, 116, 118, 121, 122, 123, 124, 125, 126, 127, 128, 129, 130, 131, 132, 133, 137, 138, 151
Claret, Antonio 99
Colección de los Mejores Autores Antiguos y Modernos, Nacionales y Extranjeros (1872) 62
Coixet, Isabel 129
Colmeiro, José F. 125, 128
Comediants 42
Comparative History of Literatures in the Iberian Peninsula (2010) 20
Concello Municipal da Muller de Vigo 150, 153, 154
Consello de Mulleres 150, 157 n. 11
Conte, Rafael 74, 85
Contemporary Spanish Cultural Studies (2000) 6

Cook, Pam 128
Cooter, Roger 94
Cornejo Parriego, Rosalía 7
Coronado, Carolina 63
Coruña 28
Crary, Jonathan 105 n. 1
Crónica del desamor (1979) 78, 80, 83, 88 n. 9
Crónica sentimental de la transición (1985) 90 n. 21
Cruces Roldán, Cristina 146 n. 3
Cruz Romeo, María 60, 61
Cubí, Mariano 94, 95, 105 n. 12
Cuéntame cómo pasó (2001–) 130, 131
Cuerda, José Luis 126, 131
Cunqueiro, Álvaro 108
Cybele 1
Cyborgs and Barbie Dolls (2007) 45, 52

D'Lugo, Marvin 122
d'Ors, Eugenio 108
Danvila y Collado, Manuel 66, 67
Darwin, Charles 38, 47, 106 n. 21
Davies, Ann 131
Davis, Stuart 11 n. 7, 23 n. 3
De com s'inicia l'educació sentimental de Mundeta Claret i altres contes (1998) 90 n. 21
De l'Allemagne (1813) 13
De tu ventana a la mía (2012) 123, 126, 129, 130, 131
Del Rey Reguillo, Fernando 114, 120 n. 6
Deleuze, Gilles 38, 47
Delibes, Miguel 109
Denizard Rivail, Hippolyte Léon (alias Allen Kardec) 92, 95, 96
Diana (pastoral) 18
Díez Ménguez, Isabel 58, 62, 63
DMD Europa (2007) 48
Domingo Soler, Amalia 7, 92, 93, 95, 96, 98, 99, 100, 101, 102, 105 n. 8, 106 n. 20
Domínguez, César 21, 24 n. 9
Don Carlos 61
Don Quixote (1605–15) 14
Draper, William 92, 105 n. 3
Duende y misterio del flamenco (1952) 138
Ďurišin, Dionýz 20, 22

Edelman, Nicole 105 n. 4
El año y la viña (2013) 123, 126
El bosque (2013) 126, 127, 131
El dibuixant (2005) 38, 39, 44, 47, 48, 49, 54
El doctor Centeno (1883) 97
El dolor de Euskadi (1937) 31
El Encubierto 58, 59, 62, 63, 64, 65, 66, 67, 68
El encubierto (1883) 6, 58, 59, 61, 62, 65, 67, 68
El encubierto de Valencia (1840) 65
El encubierto de Valencia. Leyenda histórica del siglo XVI (1852) 66
El espinazo del diablo (2002) 126, 129, 131

El Espiritismo refuntando los errores del catolicismo romano. Colección de artículos (1880) 92
El espíritu de la colmena (1973) 122
El Globo [newspaper] 100
El laberinto del fauno (2006) 125, 126, 127, 129, 130
El mar (2000) 126
El Mundo [newspaper] 108
El País [newspaper] 73, 74, 88 n. 4, 91 n. 25, 108, 110, 144, 146 n. 13, 152
El pintor y su modelo (date not known) 49
El portero (2000) 126
El pueblo gallego [newspaper] 150
El Satanismo; o sea, la cátedra de satanás combatida desde la cátedra del espíritu santo; refutación de los errores de la escuela espiritista (1879) 92
El secreto del puente viejo (2011–14) 131
El Teatro de Arte y Ensayo (Asociación de la Prensa de Vigo) 150
El telescopio moderno (1878) 95
El tiempo entre costuras (2013–14) 123, 125, 130, 131
El viaje de Carol (2002) 125, 126
Elizabeth (1998) 123
Els Joglars 42
Elsaesser, Thomas 131, 132
England 13, 31, 105 n. 11
Epizoo (1994) 38, 43, 44, 45, 47, 48, 52, 54
Erice, Víctor 122
Espigado Tocino, Gloria 63, 71 n. 2
ETA (Euskadi Ta Askatasuna) 29
Euler, Leonhard 98
Even-Zohar, Itamar 5, 20, 21

Falange Española 108
Falklands War 35 n. 15
Faro de Vigo [newspaper] 150
Faulkner, Sally 122, 133
Feldman, Sharon 37, 39, 41, 42, 49
Fernández, Cayetano 97
Fernández Bremón, José 105 n. 11
Fernández Herreros, Manuel 66
Fernández Rubio, Andrés 120 n. 3
Fernando VII 61
Feminismo e innovación en la narrativa gallega da autoría femenina (2013) 153, 156 n. 3
Feministas Independentes Galegas (FIGA) 150, 157 n. 10
Festa da Palabra Silenciada [journal] 149, 150, 157 n. 14
Fish, Stanley 115
Flammarion, Camille 95, 96, 97, 98, 101
Flanders 32
Fluxus 41, 56 n. 3
Follas novas (1880) 35 n. 11
Fóra de min (1994) 151
Forcadela, Manuel 153, 156 n. 3
Foxá, Agustín 8, 108, 109, 115

Franco, Francisco / General Franco 1, 8, 42, 72, 74, 77, 79, 81, 83, 84, 87, 88 n. 2 and n. 8, 89 n. 13 and n. 17, 107, 108, 109, 110, 113, 118, 137, 138, 140, 141, 146 n. 3
Franco Barreiro, Navia 152
Francoism / Francoist 29, 32, 35 n. 16, 60, 77, 79, 84, 89 n. 12, 107, 108, 109, 110, 111, 112, 113, 114, 116, 117, 118, 121, 122, 130, 132, 133, 137
Frankfurt 27
Fuente, Vicente de la 95, 96
Fura dels Baus, La 37, 38, 39, 40, 41, 42, 43, 48, 49, 54, 56 n. 1

Gabilondo, Joseba 5, 24 n. 10
Gaceta de Madrid [newspaper] 62
Galería de Arte 'Roizara' de Vigo 150
Galicia / Galician 4, 9, 14, 15, 16, 17, 20, 28, 35 n. 11, 148, 149, 150, 151, 152, 153, 154, 155, 156 n. 1, n. 3 and n. 6, 157 n. 9 and n. 10
Gallego, Ferrán 120 n. 4
Gallego, Javier 88 n. 8
Gallego, Olga 153
García Gutiérrez, Antonio 65
Garcia Lorca, Federico 109, 136
García Serrano, Rafael 108
Garcilaso 23 n. 7
Garrido, José Ángel 137
Germanías, Rebelión de las 58, 64, 66
Gernika 31
Gernika (2016) 122, 123
Giannetti, Claudia 43, 44
Gies, David T. 71 n. 7
Gil Vicente 18
Gil, Felisa 82
Gilbert and George 51
Gilroy, Paul 27, 28, 33
Giménez Caballero, Ernesto 108
Gimferrer, Pere 109, 111, 112
Giotto's Joy (1980) 51
Gómez Aparicio, Pedro 105 n. 18
Gómez de Avellaneda, Gertrudis 63
Góngora, Luis de 23 n. 7, 24 n. 8
González, Felipe 109, 110
González Cuevas, Pedro Carlos 114, 117
González de Pablo, Ángel 105 n. 13
González Fernández, Helena 152, 153, 157 n. 9 and n. 14
González-Ruano, César 108
Gorak, Jan 23 n. 3
Goytisolo, Juan 73
Gracia, Jordi 117
Graham, Helen 6, 120 n. 5
Gran Hotel (2011–13) 131
Grandes, Almudena 25
Groot, Jerome de 124, 125
Grosz, Elizabeth 6, 37, 38, 47
Grup de Treball 41, 54

Guernica (1937) 26, 29

Habana 28
Hamburg 32
Hampa. El delincuente español (1898) 142, 143
Hayles, Katherine 44, 45
Herder, Johann Gottfried 23 n. 2
Herrera Garrido, Francisca 148, 152
Higbee, Will 132
Higgins, Dick 41
Higson, Andrew 123
Hipermembrana (2007) 41, 48
Hippomenes 1
Historia de la literatura española (1804 / 1829) 14, 23 n. 5
Historia de la literatura fascista española (1986) 109
History of the Conflicts between Science and Religion (1876) 92
Hollywood 125, 128
Holocaust 26, 32, 33, 113, 120 n. 5, 128
Homage to New York (1960) 40
Hooper, Kirsty 11 n. 4, 28, 35 n. 11, 59, 149, 151
Horta, Gerard 105 n. 5

Ideologies of Hispanism (2005) 4
Ingraham, Edgar S. 68
Instituto de Bachillerato Alexandre Bóveda de Vigo 150
Intermedia (1966) 41
International Comparative Literature Association 20
Iris (2004) 126, 127, 131
Isabel II 58, 61, 62, 65, 66, 95, 99, 105 n. 16
¡Ispansi! (2010) 126

Jiménez de Enciso, Diego 71 n. 6
JoAn, l'home de carn (1992) 43
Jones, Amelia 39
Jordan, Barry 6, 40, 45, 49
Juliá, Santos 91 n. 25, 120 n. 6

Kandinsky, Wassily 51
Kent, Victoria 82
Kipling, Rudyard 105 n. 11
Klein, Yves 39, 40, 49, 56 n. 3
Klüver, Billy 40, 43, 54
Krishnan, Armin 3
Kristeva, Julia 6, 51, 52, 54
Kuhn, Thomas 94

La dama de Amboto (1857) 63
La Época 64
La España Moderna 97
La familia de León Roch (1888) 97
La gitanilla (1613) 136
La Historia de las germanías de Valencia: breve reseña del levantamiento republicano de 1869 (1870) 66
La Historia de los Conflictos entre Religión y Ciencia (1876) 105 n. 3

La hora violeta (1980) 79, 80, 82, 83
La Leona de Castilla (1951) 122
La Luz del Porvenir (1879–1900) 92
La ópera cotidiana (1989) 76
La polémica feminista en la España contemporánea, 1868–1974 (1986) 59
La Sigea (1854) 63
La Sociedad 94
La vida de los astros (1877) 95
La voz dormida (2011) 124, 126, 128, 129, 130
Labanyi, Jo 6, 34 n. 1, 76, 127, 137
Labrador, Germán 91 n. 27
Lain Entralgo, Pedro 93, 115
Landsberg, Alison 126
Las ilusiones del doctor Faustino (1879) 97
Las mujeres españolas, americanas y lusitanas pintadas por sí mismas (1881) 142
Las 13 rosas (2007) 124, 125, 126, 128, 129, 130
Lawless, Geraldine 105 n. 9
Lázaro-Reboll, Antonio 129
Leblon, Bernard 146 n. 10
Ledesma Ramos, Ramiro 110
Leerssen, Joep 23 n. 2
Leyendas 63
Leyendas y tradiciones en prosa y verso (1872) 62
Libertarias (1996) 122, 125
Linz, Juan José 120 n. 4
Lippard, Lucy 41
Llano, Samuel 146 n. 1
Llimós, Robert 41
Linares, Augusto González de 95
Lo que mueve el mundo (2012) 25, 26, 31–33
Locura de amor (1948) 122, 130
López de Ayala, Ana 105 n. 8
López Villaverde, Ángel Luis 117, 120 n. 5
Los girasoles ciegos (2006) 125, 126, 131
Los gitanos (1975) 143, 147 n. 20
Los santos inocentes (1984) 130
Los tarantos (1963) 138, 146 n. 4
Los últimos de Filipinas (1945) 121
Loudun 100
Lourdes 100, 140
Loureiro, Ángel 120 n. 6
Loxham, Abigail 124, 130
Lübeck 32

Madrid 1, 2, 28, 29, 88 n. 2, 143
Madrid de corte a checa (1938) 109, 111, 116, 117
Maeztu, Ramiro de 8, 115, 120 n. 7
Mainer, José-Carlos 111, 117
Manterola, Vicente 7, 92, 93, 96, 97, 98, 99, 100, 101, 102
Manual del Librero Hispanoamericano (1949) 71 n. 5
Mar Mediterrània (1992) 37
Marcantonio, Carla 129
March, Kathleen N. 152
Marías, Javier 73

Markuleta, Gerardo 35 n. 7
Marsh, Steven 122
Martín Gaite, Carmen 89 n. 17, 90 n. 22
Martín-Escudillo, Luis 6
Martínez Cachero, José María 113, 117
Martínez Lázaro, Emilio 126, 128
Martínez-Quiroga, Pilar 150
Martínez Ruiz, José ('Azorín') 108
Marx, Karl 33
Masuzawa, Tomoko 101
Mate, Reyes 88 n. 10
Mellor, Anne K. 60
Memoria de la Transición (1996) 91 n. 25
Mena, Juan de 23 n. 7, 24 n. 8
Méndez Ferrín, Xosé Luis 156 n. 6, 157 n. 15
Menéndez Pelayo, Marcelino 94, 95, 105 n. 3, 105 n. 7
Metamembrana (2009) 48
Mexico 31
Miguélez-Carballeira, Helena 148
Millington, Mark 6
Miralles, Fina 43
Mistral, Silvia 82
Mohedano brothers 13
Molins, Maria 131
Molta roba i poc sabó... i tan neta que la volen (1970) 90 n. 21
Monedero, Juan Carlos 76, 77
Monk, Claire 124, 129
Montserrat 140
Montemayor, Jorge de 18
Montero, Rosa 7, 74, 75, 78, 79, 80, 83, 88 n. 8, 88 n. 9, 89 n. 15, 89 n. 17, 90 n. 19
Montes, Eugenio 108
Mora, Constancia de la 82
Mora, José Joaquín 23 n. 4
Moraña, Mabel 4, 5
Morgan-Tamosunas, Rikki 6
Mosquera, Javier 150
Montseny, Federica 82
Mr Ong 101
Moure, Teresa 148, 156 n. 1
Muehl, Otto 41
Muller, Max 101
Mulvey, Laura 127
Muntadas, Antoni 41
Museo de Bellas Artes de Bilbao 29

Nafría Fernández, María Jesús 35 n. 12
Nair, Parvati 137
Napoleon 23 n. 2
Nash, Mary 60
Navajeros (1980) 142
Neuengamme 32, 35 n. 18
Neville, Edgar 138
New Hispanisms: Literature, Culture, Theory (1994) 6
New Spain, New Literatures (2010) 6
New York 27, 28, 31, 54, 92

Nieto-Galán, Agustí 93, 105 n. 9
Nietzsche, Friedrich 33
Nitsch, Herman 41
NO-DO (Noticiario y documentales) (1943–81) 8, 9, 137, 138, 139, 140, 141, 143, 144
Nofre Mateo, David 95, 105 n. 9
Nora, Pierre 26, 27, 35 n. 10

O club da calceta (2006) 150
Odysseus 83
Offen, Karen 68
Oliete-Aldea, Elena 123, 125, 128, 132
On the Margins of Social Science (1979) 94
Ondarroa 28, 29, 30, 31, 33, 36 n. 21
Oppenheim, Janet 105 n. 4 and n. 13
Orduña, Juan de 122, 130
Orígenes de la poesía castellana (1754) 13
Ortiz, Lourdes 7, 74, 75, 79, 88 n. 9, 89 n. 14, 89 n. 17, 90 n. 19
Ouka Leele 1, 2, 10 n. 1, 11 n. 3
Owen, Alex 105 n. 4

Pa negre (2012) 123, 125, 126, 131
Padrissa, Carles 56 n. 1
Palomar, Quico 56 n. 1
Padrós, Antoni 41
Panero, Leopoldo 108
Pardo Bazán, Emilia 63, 64
Paris 150
Pato, Chus 157 n. 9
Paul VI, Pope 141
Pearson, Ann E. 52
Pemán, José María 108, 110
Pérez de Ayala, Ramón 115
Pérez Galdós, Benito 97
Perros callejeros (1977) 142
Pi i Margall, Francesc 62, 63
Picasso, Pablo 26, 29, 49
Ping Body (1996) 45
Pitollet, Camille 23 n. 4
Pla, Josep 108
Plurality of the Inhabited Worlds (1862) 95
Poe, Edgar Allen 105 n. 11
Pol (2002) 48
Pollock, Jackson 39, 40, 49
Pope, Randolph 5, 7
Pozuelo Yvancos, José María 23 n. 3
Preston, Paul 120 n. 5
Prieto, Carlos 135 n. 2
Prieto, Indalecio 29, 35 n. 14
Prisciliano 149
Pubill Calaf, Pedro 146 n. 4
Puig, Teresa 56 n. 1

Queizán, María Xosé 9, 148–55, 156 n. 6, 157 n. 7, 157 n. 8, 157 n. 11, 157 n. 14, 157 n. 15

Quintana, Ángel 124, 125, 126

Rabelais and His World (1965) 52
Ramírez Heredia, Juan de Dios 142
Ramona, adiós (1980) 80
Ramos, Dolores 105 n. 5
Rappelle-toi Barbara (1987) 1, 2, 10 n. 1
Rauschenberg, Robert 40, 43
Raza Española (journal) 142
Real Academia Galega 9, 148, 153, 157 n. 9
Reimóndez, María 148, 150, 156 n. 1
Resina, Joan Ramon 3, 5, 11 n. 4, 21, 72, 79, 80, 88 n. 4, 120 n. 8
Restoration 95, 99, 101
(Re)viewing Creative, Critical and Commercial Practices in Contemporary Spanish Cinema (2014) 130
Rhythm 0 (1974) 43
Ridruejo, Dionisio 108, 109, 112
Rieber, Robert W 105 n. 14
Riera, Carme 7, 74, 75, 79, 81, 82, 88 n. 9, 89 n. 17, 90 n. 19
Rigney, Ann 76
Rinolacxia (1991) 42
Rinos, Los 37, 42
Rio de Janeiro 32
Ríos, Blanca de los 142, 146 n. 16
Ríos-Font, Wadda 115, 116
Rito y geografía del cante (1971–73) 143, 146 n. 3
Rodríguez, Isidro 147 n. 21, 147 n. 22
Rodríguez Ortega, Vicente 129
Rodríguez Puértolas, Julio 109, 110, 111
Rodríguez Rodríguez, Marisol 151, 153, 156 n. 3
Rodríguez Zapatero, José Luis 123
Roig, Montserrat 7, 74, 75, 76, 79, 80, 82, 83, 88 n. 9, 89 n. 17, 90 n. 21
Romancero gitano (1928) 136
Rome 140
Romeo and- Juliet (1597) 138
Rosa Krüger (1984) 110
Rosales, Luis 108
Roseman, Sharon R. 149
Rossetto, Mimi 139, 146 n. 7
Rothberg, Michael 6, 26, 33
Rousseau, Jean-Jacques 23 n. 2
Rovira-Beleta, Francisco 138
Royal Astronomical Society 95
Rubin, Gayle 151
Ruiz, Pedro 76, 81
Ruiz-Castell, Pedro 97, 105 n. 10 and n. 15

Salabert, Pere 45, 47, 49, 55
Salilla, Rafael 142, 143, 147 n. 18
Salmerón, Nicolás 105 n. 3
San Román, Teresa 147 n. 19
Sánchez-Biosca, Vicente 137, 138, 146 n. 12
Sánchez Mazas, Rafael 34 n. 2, 108, 109

Santander 36 n. 21
Santaolalla, Isabel 137
Santiago de Compostela 150
Sanz Villanueva, Santos 73
Sárraga, Belén de 105 n. 8
Saulier, Tony 146 n. 7
Saum-Pascual, Alex 25, 26, 35 n. 5
Saura, Carlos 122
Saz, Ismael 120 n. 4
Scanlon, Geraldine 59
Schlegel, August Wilhelm 13
Schlegel, Friedrich 13
Sebastian I of Portugal 65
Second Republic 59, 60, 71 n. 2, 81, 82, 89 n. 18, 107, 112, 113
Second World War 123, 140
Sender, Ramón J. 109
Serra, Kaldo 122
Seville 88 n. 2, 99, 143
Silencio roto (2000) 125, 126, 131
Silke 131
Silva, Emilio 85, 89 n. 12
Silva, José María da Costa 18
Sin novedad en el Alcázar (1940) 122
Sismondi, Sismonde de 13, 21
Sizemore, Tom 131
Smith, George 101, 106 n. 21
Smith, Paul Julian 6, 123, 125, 127, 130
Smith, Valerie 76
Snyder, Jonathan 2, 10 n. 2
Sobre la Libertad Religiosa (1869) 95
Sociedades Astronómicas de Camille Flammarion 98
Soldados de Salamina (2001) 34 n. 2, 120 n. 8
Sólo pude conservar una fotografía (1980) 8, 82
Sommer, Doris 77, 78
Somorrostro 138
Son noxento (2015) 155
Sotero dos Reis, Francisco 19
Spadaccini, Nicholas 6
Spanish Cultural Studies: An Introduction (1995) 6
Spectroscopisti Italiani 95
Staël, Madame de 13
Standard (1976) 43
Stelarc (Stelios Arcadiou) 44, 45
Stoller, Robert T. 151
Stone, Rob 131
The Structures of Scientific Revolution (1962) 94
Suárez, Adolfo 83, 90 n. 20
Suz/o/Suz (1985) 37, 40, 41

Tantinyà, Pere 56 n. 1
The Black Atlantic (1993) 27
Thompson, John Patrick 151
Ticknor, George 13, 15, 16, 18, 21
Tiempo de cerezas (1977) 79, 83
Tier Mon (1988) 37

Tikhomiroff, Nicolas 146 n. 7
Tinguely, Jean 40, 43, 54, 56 n. 3
Todesfuge (1948) 32
Toffoletti, Kim 44, 45, 52
Toledo 122
Tolliver, Joyce 60
Toro, Guillermo del 125, 126
Torrente Ballester, Gonzalo 108
Torres, Xohana 149, 157 n. 9
Traidor, inconfeso, mártir (1849) 65
Tranche, Rafael 137, 138, 146 n. 12
Trapiello, Andrés 8, 107, 109, 110, 111, 112, 114, 115, 116, 117
Trasa V = BPLWB (1978) 39
Tres amigas (1880) 67
Triana-Toribio, Nuria 122
Tusquets, Esther 7, 74, 75, 79, 84, 88 n. 9, 89 n. 17, 90 n. 19

Über dramatische Kunst und Literatur (1815) 13
Ultraorbism (2016) 55
Unamuno, Miguel de 35 n. 10, 115
Unión Romani 142, 146 n. 15
Uribe, Kirmen 5, 25–28, 30, 32, 33, 35 n. 7, 35 n. 9, 35 n. 13, 35 n. 19, 36 n. 21
Urraca (1982) 88 n. 9, 89 n. 14
Usos amorosos de la posguerra española (1987) 90 n. 22

Valencia 58, 64, 66
Valera, Juan 97

Vázquez Montalbán, Manuel 73, 90 n. 21
Velázquez, Luis José 13
Vidal, Belén 124, 125, 126, 129, 131
Viennese Actionists 41, 56 n. 3
Vigo 28, 148, 150, 151, 153, 154, 156 n. 4
Vilavedra, Dolores 149, 152
Villamandos, Alberto 7
Vinyes, Ricard 76, 89 n. 11
Vivanco, Luis Felipe 108

Wallis, Roy 94
Washabaugh, William 146 n. 3
Wells, H.G. 105 n. 11
Western Canon, The (1994) 23 n. 3
Wheeler, Duncan 123, 129, 130
White, Hayden 128
Winter, Alison 94
Woods Peiró, Eva 137
Woolf, Virginia 150, 156, n. 5
Wundt, Wilhelm 95, 105 n. 14

Yetano Laguna, Ana 60
You're the one (2000) 126

Zaj (music group) 41
Zambrano, Benito 126, 128
Zaragoza 99
Zarzuela 1900 (1959) 122
Zorrilla, José 63, 65

www.ingramcontent.com/pod-product-compliance
Lightning Source LLC
LaVergne TN
LVHW061252060426
835507LV00017B/2035